16$\underline{^{25}}$

Multinational Excursions

Multinational Excursions

Charles P. Kindleberger

The MIT Press
Cambridge, Massachusetts
London, England

This book was set in Baskerville by The MIT Press Computergraphics Department and printed and bound by The Murray Printing Co. in the United States of America.

Library of Congress Cataloging in Publication Data

Kindleberger, Charles Poor, 1910-
   Multinational excursions.

   Bibliography: p.
   Includes index.
   1. International business enterprises. I. Title.
HD2755.5.K56   1984   338.8′8   84–935
ISBN 0-262-11092-X

Contents

19

20

Foreword

With the slightest encouragement from a publisher, I seem to be unable to resist the temptation to gather papers emitted on a subject over the years into hard—and with luck also soft—covers. The reason is doubtless egotism. The excuse is to tidy up for my literary executor, and perhaps in addition to search for consistency and unity of thought. In any event what one finds is a certain amount of repetition. I have excised a portion of this but by no means all, since the gains in the large would frequently have been won at the cost of loss of coherence in the local passage.

The collection is assembled from the usual mishmash of outlets, articles in *Festschriften* and symposia, testimony before congressional committees, pieces appearing in ordinary journals, though some outside the confines of economics, plus a few unpublished lectures. One book review was accepted for publication in a journal that folded up before the scheduled issue. No attempt has been made to unify the scholarly apparatus of notes and references, or the lack of such. Nor have I thought it worthwhile to bring the facts up to date. The knowledgeable reader of the discussion of Volvo's investment in the United States and Volkswagen's holding back will understand that it worked out exactly the opposite, with Volvo withdrawing at the last minute and Volkswagen changing its mind—indicating how close some of the investment decisions are. Some purists will be particularly upset that discussion of oil prior to 1974 uses prices that seem medieval. The unity, to repeat, is meant to be of thought, not chronological.

Multinational Excursions

1

Multinational Companies in World Affairs

Raymond Vernon of the Harvard Business School, maker of vivid phrases and pundit on the multinational corporation, wrote one book on the subject in each of the 1960s and the 1970s. The first was entitled *Sovereignty at Bay*, the second *Storm over Multinationals*. Both titles reflect conflict. In the first the nation-state is seen as under attack from an aggressive, highly mobile set of corporations which can be restrained only with difficulty; in the second the implication is that the tide of battle has changed, and the storm rages over the corporations themselves, beset, presumably, by governments and especially by public opinion.

For the 1980s I propose to stay clear of a judgment as to how the contest is coming out but to deal with continuing conflict more generally. Such conflict abounds: between states and firms; sometimes more narrowly between parts of governments such as the tax collector and firms; between two or more governments through the corporation, as one government tries to tell subsidiaries of its national firms abroad how to behave on such issues as "trading with the enemy"; within the corporation between head office and subsidiary, or top management and its agents; between the peoples and culture of the host country and those of the home country, using "host" to signify the country where the subsidiary of a multinational corporation is located, and "home" for the country where the head office is located. Home labor may resent the export of jobs to foreign subsidiaries, and within the host country there may be antagonism between the multinational firm and the work force. If one lists various groups, divided into host and home — firms in the industry and their owners, managers, labor, consumers, voters and governments — a bewildering variety of conflict is

A lecture at the University of Utah, May 13, 1982.

possible among two or more groups. One is tempted to say not only possible but inevitable.

Conflicts are the essence of politics and interpersonal relations. In economics we assume often, perhaps too often, that buying cheap and selling dear in competitive markets is a form of cooperation with persons frequently unknown to the buyer or seller, who is dealing in effect with Adam Smith's "invisible hand." Conflict exists in economics, however, when a monopoly buyer forces prices down or a monopoly seller forces them up. It is present also in a pie when it is not growing — over the distribution of income among profits, salaries, wages, and rents — often resulting in inflation as each group seeks to shove a burden onto others. A popular book by my MIT colleague, Lester Thurow, calls the United States *The Zero-Sum Society* in which one person's gain is another's loss. Anne Krueger, then of the University of Minnesota, now at the World Bank, calls much economic activity today "rent seeking," rent being the term for payments to a factor of production that is limited in amount but much in demand, so that additional payments do not increase the supply. Those of us interested in sport are aware that there are large scarcity rents from the desire of fans to watch on television the Superbowl, World Series, Stanley Cup, and the like, not to mention the game of the week. The limited (?) number of such attractive spectacles, plus scarce television channels, at least for the moment, produces enormous rents that are fought over by networks, TV stations, advertisers, sports-club owners, and most recently, with great success, by the athletes themselves. Most economists I know have more than a touch of Henry George about them — he wanted a "single tax" on land to divert the rent from a scarce resource provided by Nature from private gain to public use — and we should like, for example, to see government auction off scarce broadcasting channels, as lately it has done with offshore oil-drilling rights. Few, however, have much expectation of such an outcome.

Conflict over rents is intense at the level of the multinational corporation, but the range of conflict goes wider. To the neoclassical economist the multinational corporation may start with a scarce resource, or a new technology yielding a product or process innovation that it has patented and owns alone. Initially rents are substantial, but the corporation usually fails to hold them for long. The rent may be taken over by the host government, as in higher royalties and taxes on companies operating oil or mineral rights, or the initial monopoly advantage from the innovation in product or process may be dissipated by diffusion of the technology and entry of competitors who drive down the price of the output and the rent. In this last case the rent may be said to be captured by consumers, as an addition to "consumers' surplus," a term that measures the difference between what the consumer would be willing to pay for a good and the lower price he actually pays in a competitive market. High profits are a signal that more of the good is desired by consumers. So long as there are competition and free entry, such high profits are an essential part of the market mechanism and prove to be transitory.

Let me retrace a step or two to underline that the theory of foreign direct investment, involving the ownership and control of business in one country by a business in another, starts out with the concept of rents. Stephen Hymer who initially developed the theory in 1960 insisted that to operate abroad, a firm must have a clear and distinct advantage over other potentially competitive businesses in the host country. Operating at a distance from its headquarters where decisions are made constitutes an important disadvantage. Distance inhibits effective communication. If the cultures of the home and host countries differ—as they must do to at least some degree—there is another disadvantage, as the foreign corporation will put its foot wrong from time to time when the native competitor will not. To overcome the disadvantages of working in a strange environment at a distance from its control center, the investing firm must have a strong initial advantage on which it seeks to appropriate the rent. In this effort it finds itself in conflict with others.

Some part of the rent may be siphoned off by employees of the corporation, who are in at least some sense in conflict with the owners. Corporate finance is now addressing this question as "the agency problem," as it recognizes that employees have different economic interests than corporate owners. The agency problem consists in the costs of monitoring their activities to keep top management and salaried staff working for the corporation and not for their personal interests, and bonding those with access to the corporation's assets. Another expensive device to win fidelity to the stockholders' interest is to give management the right to buy stock at below-market prices (so-called stock options), but this is typically not available to local employees of the multinational corporation, since the firm seldom issues extra stock applicable to a subsidiary in a given host country. The agency problem is not new of course. Berle and Means discovered the conflict between management and stockholders back in the 1930s, and the problem has been further addressed by James Burnham in *The Managerial Revolution*. More recently J. Kenneth Galbraith has written about the technocratic structure that manages the corporation, not always in the interest of the stockholders.

Even these discoveries are far from new. Nepotism was sensible in primitive societies when maintenance of high ethical standards was frequently limited to the narrow circle of the family, and outsiders had little sense of wrong in stealing from an unrelated master. In the eighteenth and nineteenth centuries, fixed pricing in retail stores came into practice to replace the bazaar practice of bargaining that persists in some underdevloped parts of the world today, when retail establishments grew in size beyond that which could be managed by a single family, and outsiders could not be counted on, in dealing with the public, to bargain in the interest of the proprietor, especially when the customer might be a member of the employee's family, or a friend. The problem was enormous in those early exemplars of multinationalism, the chartered companies of the seventeenth and eighteenth centuries, like the Royal African, the Levant, and especially the British East India Company, where the company's civil servants in India all ran personal businesses on the side, the company's directors siphoned off profits by selling supplies to the company at high prices from their personal private firms, ship captains took on freight for their own account, and especially the Clives and Hastings received "presents" from the local rulers, whom they helped to choose. The agency problem has been greatly moderated since the eighteenth century and the East India Company. It has not been solved.

The Chicago school of economics which helped formulate the problem in these terms appears less concerned with the ethical than with the economic aspect of the conflict of interests. Economic man maximizes. This means, if he is risk-neutral, that in contemplating any action in self-interest which is against the law, he calculates the benefit of the transgression and compares it with the probability of getting caught times the penalty if caught. The decision is then made on the basis of a cost-benefit comparison. Or society may choose to invest resources in internalizing a high moral standard of behavior for its members, another cost-benefit problem but with public costs and private benefits in reducing the monitoring and bonding costs needed to be paid by principals to keep agents in line, or to limit the damage when they go astray. Ethical standards may grow up without conscious implantation, but there is considerable likelihood that these standards will differ in at least some respects from one sociopolitical entity or country to another, confronting the corporation that straddles national boundaries with a problem of conflict.

The agency problem probably differs somewhat within the multinational corporation, depending on whether the agents or employees— the salaried management that runs the subsidiary—are members of the home or host society. If home, they have a problem of choosing between the advice of Polonius "To thy own self"—read country or culture—"be true," on the one hand, and "When in Rome do as the Romans do," on the other. An American representing an American international accounting firm in Milan once told me that the Italian corporate income tax system is fair. Everyone knows that the tax authorities will double the declared statement of income and of tax, so that each native corporate taxpayer halves its statement of profits and what it deems is the appropriate tax. But American managers have great difficulty in deliberately understating what the letter of the law says to be the tax due. This was said to have been one of the reasons that the Ford Motor Company ultimately decided against buying Ferrari. On the other hand, American managers have less compunction than their native counterparts in taking development subsidies to start up a plant, say in a development region abroad, and then closing it down when the subsidies run out and it proves unprofitable, something that is not in violation of the letter of the law but that the Italian authorities promoting the development of the south—and Italian businessmen—regard as unethical. The biggest issue today is over the fine line that must be drawn among commissions, finder's fees, presents, and bribes in different cultures. The issue hardly presents itself for countries where differences in the traditions of home—say the United States—and host countries—take Australia, Canada, Great Britain, or New Zealand—are relatively narrow. In others, where the head office hires local managers, there may be the sort of cultural clash that is evident in the uproar over recent U.S. legislation on bribery. The Securities and Exchange Commission requires firms only to disclose bribes for the sake of communicating fully to stockholders, but American definitions of what constitutes a bribe—in the Congress any present worth more than $5, or was that the lofty private rule of the late Senator Paul H. Douglas?—do not always converge to those in other countries.

I want to leave the question of the clash of cultures, but before doing so, cannot escape the mention of two problems very much in the news: apartheid in the Union of South Africa, and the Nestlé company's promotion of bottle-feeding of babies in less developed countries where, in particular, water supplies are often contaminated, mothers' views on sterilization may be rudimentary or nonexistent, and breast-feeding is believed by many to be safer as well as more nourishing than formula milk.

On apartheid, I have long adopted a schizoid attitude that irritates purists on one or the other side of the issue. The views on race of the dominant Afrikaner party in the Union of South Africa are repugnant and even abhorrent to most Americans—although perhaps few of us remember the extent to which they mirror attitudes in the Deep South of this country half a century ago and bear in mind the enormous difficulty with which those attitudes have now been largely changed. As a political and ethical animal, I want to put people with such views in Coventry, have nothing to do with them, and cut them off from normal social, sporting, and commercial intercourse. This is the attitude that has led many church groups, and some investing bodies, most recently including Harvard University, to refuse to buy the securities of U.S. corporations that have subsidiaries in the Union, and in fact to dispose of those they own. Some would embargo trade as well, although the dependence of our country on South African supplies of chrome, platinum, vanadium, and manganese gives commercial authorities unhappiness when they contemplate such a course.

The political economist in me, however, recognizes that discrimination against blacks and coloreds in the Union will break down faster the more the rest of the world trades with and invests in South Africa. The big advances of black people in reducing adverse discrimination in this country occurred during the inflations of World Wars I and II, when labor was in very short supply and employers had strong economic incentives to break the color line. On the other hand, discrimination increased during the Great Depression of the 1930s when the last-hired blacks were the first fired. If this experience is applicable by analogy to South Africa, as I think it is, more trade and investment will ease the problem of apartheid, and less will make it worse. The formula has a certain element of "Killing the cat by stuffing it with cream." For multinational corporations to set up investment in South Africa to put pressure on employers, both multinational and native, to break the color lines first in hiring and then in housing, is, I suspect, a counsel of perfection. It is true that Polaroid blunted the opposition of their black employees in the Cambridge area to investment in South Africa by sending a delegation of them to that country to interview Polaroid black and colored employees on the issue. The idea of an embargo or a pullout was greeted by these employees as highly dysfunctional. As between the extreme positions of the embargoists and the Machievellian economic tactic of full steam ahead, I suppose the most practical policy that addresses our ethical condemnation without making native Africans pay for our emotional catharsis is the General Motors tightrope worked out by the Rev. Leon Sullivan, which calls for continuous operation, obeying the law at the edge of it nearest equal rights, and applying continuous pressure to redress the imbalance.

Those who want to crunch Nestlé instead of eating Nestlé Crunch (i.e., embargoing the products of the largest food company in the world because it applied methods appropriate to the developed world in less developed countries) have been successful in getting the company to modify its practices. In particular, Nestlé is undertaking to advertise the importance of proper handling of their formula milk powder— providing what we call today the software that teaches people how to use a given product, whether hardware or materials—and to stop some subtle practices of providing free samples to doctors and hospitals which have had the effect—and probably the intention—of getting mothers to embark early on bottle-feeding. The embargo has thus been a great success. Before its organizers switch to another company and another problem, however, rather like the March of Dimes which found it impossible to shut down after polio had been defeated, it may be useful to give a moment's thought to whether the experience should be generalized. One of the highest rules of ethics is the categorical imperative of Immanuel Kant, which calls on us to take only those actions which can be generalized, that is, to refrain from undertaking those actions that can succeed only so long as only a few people do so. Do we want economic vigilantes running about the world deciding whether given products are suitable in given milieux and enforcing their decisions by embargo when they prove negative, or is that a matter for local governments? Many such governments, to be sure, are inadequately staffed both in numbers and in education and experience, and on this account are frequently overwhelmed by the myriad tasks they have to discharge. It may be granted that the success of the Nestlé embargo is likely to be highly salutary in leading other multinationals to reflect whether they are taking undue advantage of the ignorance of customers. Nonetheless, I have a sneaking nostalgia for the invisible hand of Dr. Adam Smith, operating in anonymous markets in which I do not know and need not know the character and intentions of the people from whom I buy or to whom I sell. Perhaps the size and prominence of the multinational corporation makes a return to that qualified Paradise impossible. And surely any egregious violation of human rights is of concern to men and women of goodwill worldwide.

But to turn at last to economic conflicts! A favorite device proposed to reduce the turbulence in multinational direct investment is the joint venture. In this sort of arrangement a foreign corporation takes a local partner, perhaps on a fifty-fifty basis, and the local partner instructs the outsider how to behave in the particular sociopolitico-cultural-economic framework. One hears less of this proposal these days. When it was continuously put forward in the 1960s, one student and advocate of the practice, Professor Wolfgang Friedman of the Columbia Law School, wrote at least two books on the subject. The salient fact to emerge from these studies, as I saw it, was that most attempted joint ventures failed. Although both foreign and local investors are presumably interested in maximizing income, they frequently operate with different time horizons and different interests in space. The local owners tend to want dividends sooner, are generally less able and/or willing to plow back profits or to sustain initial losses, and in particular concern themselves with the profits of the particular subsidiary rather than those of the multinational corporation as a whole. Joint ventures have thus proved to be a device for exacerbating conflicts of interest at the business level, rather than reducing them between business and the local society, and in most cases after a time one partner buys the other out. In some Japanese companies, for example, the American partner was prepared to wait several years for profits and to put in more money meanwhile; the Japanese partner was not. Or when profits are earned, the local partner may want to have them distributed immediately, whereas the foreign investor, operating at a lower implicit rate of interest, prefers to reinvest dividends and defer payouts for the future. The most troublesome cases are those where the multinational corporation has two subsidiaries in different countries, A with a local partner and B without, and chooses to divert sales from A to B so as to take over 100 percent of the profit instead of only a portion.

Where governments tax corporate profits, every company has a silent partner with which it is obliged to share, and in the case of the multinational corporation with local partners there are four interests at stake: multinational corporation, local partner, home tax collector, host tax collector. One of the first outstanding multinational tax cases arose when an Australian tax commissioner woke up a number of years ago to the fact that two oil refiner-marketers in that country using imported crude oil had very different profit performances. Company A was 100 percent owned by an American oil giant; Company B was 50 percent foreign owned with the other half in local hands. The 100 percent owned company had no profits in Australia and paid no Australian corporate income tax; the joint venture did have profits and did pay taxes. Investigation showed that the 100 percent owned company was paying a higher price for its imported oil. This was a period now seemingly lost in the mists of antiquity when Middle East oil was sold at a discount from posted prices of under $3 a barrel. The joint venture was furnished petroleum at the discounted price and made profits which kept the local partner happy. With no partner the 100 percent owned subsidiary could divert profit to the oil-producing arm of the multinational organization where it could apply the U.S. depletion allowances and thus reduce the total income tax of the corporation worldwide. Later discoveries that U.S. pharmaceutical companies were overcharging their Colombian subsidiaries for the materials used in pill making, to divert profits from Colombia into a Panamanian tax haven, compounded the problem of different interests among the tax departments of the United States, the Colombian government, presumably Panama where taxes were not zero, as well as home office and subsidiary.

Conflict over taxes between corporation and government, and between government and government, has been reduced by widespread attention to the possibilities of arbitrary transfer prices on transactions between parts of a multinational corporation, as opposed to the legal but often national standard that such prices should conform to those that would be set in arm's-length transactions. United States corporations, in particular, have been persuaded to adopt an austere standard by the threat of the Internal Revenue Service that it would determine the income to be taxed where it found evidence of tax avoidance or evasion by arbitrary pricing. Tax havens have been shrunk in number and size by provisions of the revenue code which refuse tax deferral on profits earned in jurisdictions where less than 30 percent of manufacturing processes are carried on. The recent accusation of an employee against Citicorp that it had indulged in wash exchange dealings at fictitious prices to transfer profits to a tax haven in the Bahamas dealt with an alleged attempt to evade British and French but not U.S. taxes.

There is still a long way to go, however, in resolving conflicts among taxing governments, head offices, and subsidiaries. Most have to do with how income and expenses are defined, and how to allocate costs, for the purpose of determining the location of profits subject to tax in a given jurisdiction. Assuming that the tax rates are the same in host and home country, differing definitions of income can result in a sum of income to be taxed in home and host which is more than the total income as seen by the corporation, resulting in some degree of double taxation, or less, leading to tax avoidance. The Internal Revenue Service in the United States has lately become more demanding that some portion of joint costs of running a multinational company—for example, the expense of maintaining the headquarters and the salaries of top management, or the cost of research and development undertaken in the United States—be allocated to foreign operations, not those in this country, thus increasing U.S. taxable income. Host governments on the other hand are reluctant to see a deduction from the net income of the subsidiary for the maintenance of laboratories thousands of miles away and for glass cathedrals in the canyons of New York City. Work on appropriate definitions of income by country is going forward in bilateral tax agreements. Perhaps by the end of the decade the world will arrive at the analytically sloppy, but highly practical, method used for allocating U.S. national corporate income by states and for determining state tax obligations where these are levied. Given the theoretical impossibility of allocating joint costs, a state is assigned a share in the corporate net income earned nationally by the application of a percentage representing the average share of the state in the corporation's national assets, gross sales, and employees.

Apart from taxes, multinational corporations can find themselves squeezed from several sides by governments in the application of other laws, such as antitrust, financial disclosure and the like, and in foreign policy. This last includes the widely discussed trading with the enemy issue, in which countries may have different views on the wisdom of embargoing trade with a given country—for example, the Soviet Union, the Peoples' Republic of China, or Cuba. A number of countries have resented it when, say, the United States wants to extend the range of its foreign policy jurisdiction by directing the head office of a corporation or bank to order its subsidiaries abroad to behave in a certain way. When the U.S. government asks General Motors, for example, to direct its Argentine subsidiary not to export trucks to Cuba, the Argentine government perceives an intrusion by the United States into its jurisdiction and a suborning of its authority. The issue is an old one and turns on the question whether a wholly owned foreign subsidiary of an American corporation should be regarded as American, and required to conform to American policies, or must be entirely subject to the laws of the state in which it is legally incorporated. In domestic law, as I understand it, American courts typically "pierce the corporate veil," to look to the true ownership of assets, and not to the formal arrangements. In Britain the practice is not to pierce. But in foreign policy both countries make exceptions when it meets their immediate interests. The most recent intrusion by the United States of course relates to the blocking of Iranian assets in American banks outside the United States at the time of the taking of the Embassy hostages in 1980. In this case an obviously extralegal action was taken by the United States, allowed by the banks concerned and tolerated by the countries where the various branches were located. The banks cooperated partly because there was no opposing pressure from Britain,

Switzerland, Luxembourg, and so forth, and partly because they had countervailing claims on Iran which they wanted to be in position to collect. The foreign governments consented because they approved the purpose of the action and did not want to take action of their own. Nonetheless, the precedent of accepting an assertion of extra-territorial power is seen by lawyers as disturbing.

Thus far we have dealt with conflicts within the corporation, between host and home country owners of a joint venture and between cultures and governments affecting different portions of a corporate entity. We have still to break down separate countries into component classes (or factors of production) and show how the interests of these classes or factors may be competitive or complementary. It would be tedious to lay out a taxonomy of all the possible permutations and combinations. I discuss two: the relations between foreign management and the local business elite, and those between labor groups in two or more countries.

Let me quickly dispose of the relationships of business elites. They can go either way. Domestic business leaders may resent the intrusion of competitors who bid up wages, interest rates, the prices of factory sites and the like, and sell competitive goods more cheaply. They may, as in General Motors in Australia some years ago, be put to work as suppliers to the foreign entity and achieve large gains in productivity by being both instructed in techniques and held up to higher standards of performance. Or, as is widely claimed for less developed countries, the foreigners may combine with the reactionary political forces of the country (e.g., IT&T in Chile), complementing one political group and coming into open conflict with others. I suspect that ideological cases of this last sort, though prominent when they occur and are discovered, are not as widespread as is the common impression. Most corporations choose to maintain a low profile and a thoroughly pragmatic position. And so increasingly do some countries. Charles Goodsell's book *American Corporations and Peruvian Politics* indicates that Peru, after having adopted a highly negative and ideological position on American corporations—nationalizing some, driving others out—has moved to a much more pragmatic position of seeking to solve disputes and work out positive solutions in which Peru gets the benefits of new capital, technology, government revenue, and national income, and the foreign corporations make profits.

The position of labor is more problematic. On the basis of J. Kenneth Galbraith's analysis of the American economy, with corporations rising from local to regional to national stature and in the process inducing the rise in countervailing power of national government, on the one hand, and national unions, on the other, one should be able to forecast a rise of world government—following the loss of sovereignty posed by Vernon through the necessity to harmonize taxes, policies, and the like—and the development of world labor unions. The beginnings of this last have been evident in the International Organization of Chemical Workers in Geneva, Switzerland, organized some years ago by the Canadian Charles Levenson. Automobile workers have been trying for some time to organize so that if Ford, for example, is struck in one country it cannot shift its orders easily to a subsidiary in another. Prospects for international unions are not bright, however. Workers in the separate subsidiaries of a given multinational corporation have conflicting, not converging interests. The capacity of the multinational firm costlessly to shift production from one country to another is doubtless exaggerated, but equally or more so is the power of international unions to counteract such shifting as may take place. About 1910 the Third Socialist International was thought to have had sufficient solidarity across national boundaries to prevent war. As it turned out, the workers proved to be more nationalist than attached to class on an international basis. Such is the likely position if and when a multinational corporation confronts trade union ranks and files in a series of countries.

Thesis and antithesis should be followed by synthesis. If the multinational corporation appeared to be on top in the 1960s, and if in the 1970s it was attacked on all sides and for all sorts of reasons—accused of weakening balances of payments in both home and host country, causing unemployment, worker alienation, malnutrition, the widening gap in incomes worldwide, the oil crisis, and the like—the 1980s offer an opportunity for resolving the set of conflicts on a continuing basis. Conflict is inevitable, since interests frequently diverge and hands on both sides are visible. Moreover there is a fundamental conflict between the economics and the politics of the case. In economics, it frequently occurs that there are economies of scale, and large is efficient; in social relations and political, small, as a rule, is cozy. The optimal economic area, to use a bit of economic jargon, for most goods and services is the world; the optimum sociopolitical area must be small enough so that every individual can have a sense of participation. Belgium is too small to be an efficient economic unit, too large, in the light of the antagonistic history of the Walloons and the Flamands, to be an ideal political unit. The confrontation between the economics and the sociology and politics of the multinational corporation is something the world will learn to live with. The quieter 1980s than the 60s or 70s suggest that peoples are learning to do so.

A number of observers want to resolve the conflict inherent in the multifaceted divergences of interests referred to by writing codes, constitutions, agreements, and the like, setting forth the rights and duties of host and home countries, and of corporations. In some cases, as in the UN Commission on the Transnational Corporation, responding to the Populist sentiments of the UN Assembly, the emphasis will be on the rights of host countries and the duties of corporations; in other cases such as the drafts of the International Chamber of Commerce, the emphasis shifts to the rights of corporations and the duties of host countries.

On the whole these exercises in constitution writing are a vain oblation. It may be possible to paper the cracks with forms of words, but where there is at basis no meeting of minds, the exercise is one in futility. Better than detailed codes of conduct would be a loose framework for dealing with cases, one at a time, within the broadest set of principles, while actual work consists in resolving particular cases pragmatically with an eye to working out reasonable compromises. Common law, not constitutions, is the requirement for the years ahead. The world must learn to live with some minimum of conflict in the field of international direct investment as an inevitable accompaniment of the gains for all parties from combining foreign capital and technology with domestic labor and natural resources. With luck, the passions associated with such conflict will subside, leaving to the various parties the task of working out supportable solutions, not graven on tablets of stone.

2

Size of Firm and Size of Nation

Introduction: The Notion of Optimum Size

This chapter deals with the optimum size of firm in a world of nations of various size and the optimum size of the nation in a world of firms of various size. It is assumed that it is neither possible nor desirable, at this juncture in history, to have the world one nation, with a single set of laws governing business activity, or for all firms to be of world size, selling in all regional markets. It is evident, however, that firms are getting bigger and that countries are subject to two pressures: one for integration with other countries, at least in economic matters, and one for separation of parts with different values, largely cultural, religious, and language. It is not obvious, however, that there is any optimum economic size for the nation or the firm, nor that the various functions discharged by the firm and the national should all be conducted on the same scale.

There are other optima that could be discussed than size of firm or the area within which it operates. One could deal, for example, with the optimum range of products for the firm. It is taken as axiomatic in this chapter, however, that firms specialize by commodities and achieve scale economies in production, marketing, distribution, research, and the like, rather than apply highly developed management techniques to a wide range of commodities, in so-called conglomerate firms. On the basis of casual empiricism this specialization in a single line, or in closely related lines such as oil and petrochemicals, produces greater efficiency than the attempt to apply standard techniques of management to widely different production and distribution problems.

Previously published in John H. Dunning, ed., *Economic Analysis and the Multi-national Enterprise* (London: George Allen & Unwin, 1974), pp. 342–362.

The notion of optimum size has come into economics most recently from the literature on currency areas. Mundell introduced it in the *American Economic Review* a decade ago, making the point that a currency should cover an area within which factors of production are mobile but beyond which they do not normally move in quantity. Immobility removes a mechanism of economic adjustment; currency revaluation or depreciation provides a replacement.[1] The optimum currency area, at least for large countries like Canada, may be a region smaller than the nation. In the ensuing discussion McKinnon argued that an optimum currency area should be a closed unit that trades mainly within its collective borders (rather than with the outside world) so that changes in the value of its currency feeding back on the prices of foreign-trade goods would not be so noticeable as to be disturbing to consuming groups.[2] On this showing the optimum currency area would tend to be larger than a region of immobile factors, and frequently larger than a country. Countries that trade heavily with one another should join together in an optimum currency area. Finally, in private conversation, Claudio Segré has noted that the optimum currency area would be one that has control of an arsenal of macroeconomic weapons, such as monetary and fiscal policy. Such an area would typically be identical with the nation-state, although it might, if integration went beyond trade and factor movements to encompass monetary and fiscal policy, include wider units of integrated states.

So much is well known to economists. But the notion of an optimum area evidently has wider connotations for other social sciences. The optimum political area differs for each political function and with changes in circumstances, such as level of income, technology, tastes. The optimum education area in France has been thought to be the nation; that in the United States has been the village, town, or city, with some functions regulated or provided by the state or nation. In some fields there is need for successive overlapping regional coverage, for example, local police who know the residents of an area, state police who mainly regulate highway traffic between cities, and national police who match the mobility of criminals in nationwide operations. A fourth level of "Interpol" develops as crime moves up to the international level.

In cultural matters social cohesion and vitality seem to be advanced by smaller units. The late unification of Germany and Italy delayed economic development in both countries but promoted vigorous provincial life in art, music, and letters. There are economies of scale to agglomeration in a New York, Paris, or London, but these are likely to have a deadening effect on the rest of the country. Berlin failed to dominate Frankfurt, Munich, Cologne, and Hamburg in the way that London did Liverpool, Manchester, and York, or Paris did Marseilles, Lyon, and Toulouse. Milan, Turin, Venice, Bologna, and Florence testify to the fact that the optimum cultural area tends to be smaller than the optimum area of economic growth.

The Optimum Production and Financial Area of the Firm

The optimum production area of a firm, that is, the size of the market it will try to serve from a given production source, depends on a host of considerations which will differ depending on the nature of the outputs, inputs, and their production functions, the costs of transport for outputs and inputs, and on the size of markets as determined by numbers, incomes, and tastes, on the one hand, and state interference, on the other. Moreover the organization of the firm will play a role. Economies of scale in production, marketing, finance, and the like, may be offset in varying degrees by diseconomies of scale in centralized administration. Our interest in the precepts derived from location theory or from business administration is limited. It is rather in how the optimum production area and the optimum area of other processes within the firm are affected by differences in the sizes of cultural and political units.

It is self-evident, even without location theory, that commodities based on natural resources that are unevenly distributed over the earth's surface will be produced at the earliest stage where they are located in greatest abundance consonant with accessibility. If processes are strongly weight losing, or bound to specific inputs such as large amounts of power, further processing will be drawn to the particular input supply. Where on the other hand, assembly adds bulk, processes may be footloose, and costs of production at separate stage—or special considerations like taste—will dominate. A remarkable feature of the postwar period is that declining transport costs and increased efficiency in production have made footloose commodities out of such previously strongly supply-oriented products as steel and veal. In steel, Japan and Italy import both iron ore and coal and produce so much more cheaply than the older regions that Japan, for one, can practically sell steel to Pittsburgh. In veal, Italy imports young calves by airplane from the United States and fattens them on imported feed grains and oil cake to the taste specifications of the Italian market.

Supply and market pulls may be affected by the intervention of the political authorities. Export taxes on primary materials may attract processing to supplies, and import duties on finished products will pull the final stages of production to the market. It is an interesting exercise to contemplate how much of international direct investment is based on the principles of location theory, plus the oligopolistic competition on which the theory of direct investment rests, and how much is owing to state intervention. The Eastman Kodak company, for example, is said to maintain that the economies of scale in production and processing of photographic film are so great, and the costs of transport so small in relation to value added by manufacture, that if there were no tariffs, it would manufacture its film for world use and process all color film in the single location of Rochester, New York. In a market-oriented industry like automobiles, Volkswagen had manufacturing plants in a number of high-tariff areas, such as Australia and Brazil, but none in the United States, its largest market which was supplied from Germany because of only moderate tariffs and high labor costs in the United States and inexpensive modes of ocean transport. A number of manufacturers, like Volvo, cover the world from a single point. In a world of zero tariffs direct investment would continue in supply-oriented industries where vertical integration is needed to reap the economies of coordination in production, transport, processing, and distribution of bulky commodities, difficult and expensive to store, and in the distribution facilities of differentiated products or those that required specialized servicing.[3] Doubtless in many manufactured commodities the economies from market orientation in major markets would outweigh differences in manufacturing cost, reduce the optimum production area, and pull investment away from the innovating manufacturing area.[4]

The optimum production area is a function not only of the existence of a tariff but of its potentiality. It has been widely noted that the formation of the European Economic Community provided foreign investors an opportunity to rationalize production within the six countries, and has offered another such opportunity since the six became nine. Apart from the International Business Machines company, however, there is little evidence that the opportunity was widely seized. French irritation with Sperry Rand and General Motors (Frigidaire) which closed down plants that became noncompetitive was duly observed, and the rule of thumb found expression: "To sell in France, produce in France."[5] Tariffs are thus not the only facet of national policy that affect the optimal production area. Another of course is vulnerability to nationalization. In petroleum the host country wants refining facilities located within its borders, but the international oil company wants to separate production and refining to allow no sovereign jurisdiction to have a free hand in obtaining a complete unit.

The consequence is that all countries that produce oil or have pipelines passing through them are host to oil refineries, most of them too small to be efficient.

Assume for reasons of location theory, of tariff barriers, or of other actual or potential exercise of political sovereignty, a manufacturer of a consumer's good has production facilities of some sort spread all over the world. What is the optimum area for a wide range of other functions that the firm performs beyond production, in personnel, capital budgeting, new product planning, research and development, marketing, finance, and the like? In business administration the question is put as to which of these functions are properly centralized in the head office and which left to the production, marketing, or service units abroad, with a middle range of regional areas—operated by a regional headquarters, for example—that coordinates or even makes decisions concerning the given function in several countries. For example, European marketing in some companies is divided between a German division, typically headquartered in German-speaking Switzerland, covering Germany, Austria, Scandinavia, the Netherlands, and perhaps the Flemish portion of Belgium; a Latin division in Paris or Rome for France, Italy, French-Switzerland, Spain, and Portugal; and a British Commonwealth group, extending overseas from Europe, operating out of London. The basis for separation is partly language, partly culture. Cultural differences or state interference may change the optimum scale. In research and development, for example, a firm may be required to undertake research and development in a given market, or may think it wise to do so even in the absence of a formal requirement. Or it may even be economical to take advantage of factor prices in the science world, giving up economies of scale for cheaper inputs. A Unilever executive at a lecture at the Harvard Business School asserted that his company performed its highly theoretical and abstract research in India because of the abundance and modest salaries of Indian theoretical physicists.

The widest optimum area is typically in finance. For many companies finance is run from the home headquarters, with the optimum financial area the world. Where there are many subsidiaries, there may be diseconomies of scale to dictate the intervention of a layer of regional staffs, perhaps one in London and one in Tokyo or Hong Kong for Europe and the Far East, respectively.[6] In a world of fixed exchange rates without foreign-exchange controls, finance is one of the easiest functions on which to economize, using surplus cash in one area to make up for deficiencies in others and reducing the need for capital through the insurance principle. Where exchange rates fluctuate or there are foreign-exchange controls, or both, finance becomes too important to be left to the separate subsidiaries, except where these possess a high degree of sophistication.

There is a tendency in Europe to think of firms as too small and operating within too small an area. Governmental pressure has been applied to encourage firms to merge, to plow back profits, acquire other firms through takeovers, and the like, to beef up firm size. That firms may be above optimum size and produce over too wide an area—leaving aside the optimum size of the separate areas in which they produce—is evident in the failures in multinational enterprise in recent years. Gallaher in Australia, Scovill in France, Maytag in Germany, Raytheon in Italy, General Tire in the Netherlands, Roberts-Arundel in the United Kingdom, and St. Gobain in the United States, to name but a sample. Apart from empirical evidence, however, there is an a priori case that in a world of defensive investment, firms will spread themselves too widely. Defensive investment, it will be remembered, is undertaken not for positive profits but to avoid losses, prospective or hypothetical. A firm feels the need to be represented in all markets lest its competitors gain an advantage over it by making large profits in one. In such cases the firm will be too large, making less than normal profits or even losses in markets where it is acting defensively. In the longer run it must serve these markets from other sources, if at all, and shrink the size of its productive span.

International Banking and Optimum Areas

Just as the financial function is likely to operate in the widest economic sphere within the firm, so banks may cast a wider spatial net than the normal industrial firm. Much will depend on whether a bank is interested only in positive profits or feels obliged, as a form of defensive investment, to be represented in all important markets where its domestic customers may have occasion to look for banking assistance. This is defensive investment where the bank earns less than a normal profit in a particular market but ascribes to the operation part of the return to operations in other lucrative markets which it might lose to a competitor if it were not on hand. Specialized banks like Barclays DSO in Africa and the Bank of London and South America (Bolsa) serve particular clienteles. Worldwide banks moreover operate with considerable profits in some markets, even while they react defensively in others. The subject has not been sufficiently studied to enable one to say much of a positive nature. On the whole foreign banks lack the access to demand deposits which provide the cheap raw material for loans and in fact have to buy the funds they lend out by paying interests, and thus miss out on the seignorage enjoyed by local banks.[7] This handicap can be overcome in some markets by aggressive competition in the provision of services ignored by local banks: installment finance, factoring, and lately, through the one-bank holding company, computer services, management advice, and the like. Where local banking is monopolistic in character, as is alleged, for example, in Germany, foreign banks, if permitted entry, can earn positive profits higher than at home, though perhaps less than those enjoyed by local banks with demand deposits. The monopoly feature of the market makes the case depart from the standard theory that to operate abroad, the firm must have an advantage that enables it to earn more abroad than at home and more abroad than the local enterprise.

Major accounting firms similarly maintain offices worldwide where they may be able to render service to domestic clients whom they would be unhappy losing to a rival firm of accountants or auditors. This is defensive investment to the extent that such firms maximize in the long run rather than the short. An accounting firm hates to lose a client, which it considers equivalent to the loss of an annuity, and will take virtually infinite pains to avoid that unhappy event.

Both location theory and economies of scale in developed money and capital markets add to the tendencies for international firms to centralize their financial operations and for international banks to be represented in major financial centers. The costs of transfer of money in space are lower than for commodities or services, thus making concentration at a few points practical. Economies of scale in financial centers derive from the fact that the broader the market, and the greater the volume, the smaller the margin between bid and asked prices for loans or existing securities, and therefore the cheaper the service to lender and borrower, buyer or seller. With greater liquidity the lender or buyer of a security acquires a different type of asset on which he is prepared to accept a lower return. In long-term capital markets it is possible to sell new securities simultaneously in a number of locations by means of widely spread syndicates connected by telephone, telex, telegraph, and so forth. Such markets need not be concentrated. But the secondary market, the quality of which is critical for the liquidity of an issue, requires concentration in space, as the purchase and especially the sale of one or a few bonds will not bear the expense of searching out separated markets for the best bargain among separated sellers or buyers.

One money market also tends to dominate, currently the Eurodollar market in London unless the devaluation of the dollar and Britain's joining the European Economic Community produce a change. Note that the financial center of a company need not be identical with its regional headquarters for decisions on production and marketing. The point is clear when one recalls that General Motors has its production-marketing headquarters in Detroit and its financial headquarters in New York. The international firm finds its European general head-quarters increasingly attracted to Brussels, the seat of the Commission of the EEC. Where the financial center of the Common Market will ultimately be located is unclear at this writing.[8] If no clearly dominant financial center emerges quickly, the head regional offices of the large international banks, largely American, may be drawn to the head regional offices of the companies they have gone abroad to serve, rather than to an existing financial center.

That American banks are more European than the banks of separate countries of Europe—apart perhaps from such specialized institutions as the European Investment Bank—rests on the fact that they have roots in no country in Europe to which they owe special allegiance or within which their horizon has been traditionally confined. The indigenous banks in Europe operate primarily within a single country, with limited numbers of foreign branches—except for the British overseas banks—and lack the habit of work that would make them continuously scan opportunities outside their own borders. When the Commerzbank of Germany, the Crédit Lyonnais of France, and the Banca di Romo of Italy form a consortium for European loans, it is mainly window dressing, with no bank able to commit the group without consultation and many loans or investments, intended to be general, in which one or two of the group holds back. Whether this will change, and truly European banking will develop as the Common Market moves to monetary unification is an open question on which it is difficult to formulate an opinion with confidence. Although the major banks in each country started out in a single city and expanded to national coverage by establishing branches throughout the country, frequently moving their head office from a provincial center to the national financial center, it does not seem likely that the same process will be followed as integration proceeds to successively higher stages. The U.S. banks may remain the only true European banks for some considerable period.

The Optimum Area in Technology

The optimum area poses a particularly critical question in the field of technology. Once the limit of efficiency in a product has been reached, it is optimal because of economies of scale in production, consumption, and maintenance to adopt the same technical standard all over the world. Prior to that stage, however, there is much to be said for preserving independent, competitive technologies, so as to permit exploration of a variety of possibilities and to avoid settling prematurely on a design that will ultimately prove inefficient. The difficulties are either that one standard will be adopted widely early, and command the field through economies of scale, or that differing standards will be adopted in separate economic regions and become so ingrained that the investment necessary to shift to a common standard, if there should be a means of choosing it, becomes so large as to be prohibitive.

Examples of both tendencies are easily provided. The British standard railroad gauge of 4 ft 7.5 in was widely adopted in Europe early, although the 5-ft-wide gauge provided a more stable roadbed for trains at the speeds later achieved. Some countries like Russia with a wide gauge and Australia with different standards in each state lacked the benefits of standardization at the international or national level, respectively. American-German color television got established before the Franco-Russian standard of allegedly finer grain could be perfected and marketed. The 78 rpm gramophone successfully held the field for years before the 33 and the 45 rpm versions were simultaneously launched to drive it from the market. British trains drove on the left, so the British automobiles did. France, Italy, and Switzerland patterned their trains after Britain but their road traffic after the United States which first mass-produced the automobile. Austria, Czechoslovakia, and Sweden, which once drove on the left, changed convulsively, the first two after foreign conquest, the last after lengthy deliberation and weighing of the costs and benefits. The most pervasive example of all, however, is the British shift of its duodecimal coinage and system of weights and measures to the decimal and metric systems, the first under the influence of computer technology, the second as a step toward efficiency in interchangeability and integration in the Common Market.

The multinational enterprise plays a role in this process in imposing the standards of the developed, frequently rich country on the rest of the world. This may occur at a premature stage, and thus cut off a line of independent experimentation and practice which might ultimately lead to improved designs and standards. In electricity, AEG with the help of the Edison Company in the United States came along just in time with its strong current to defeat the Siemens weak current transmission system. With smaller companies involved, the outcome would have been probably not change to the better standard, or a block to progress at the weaker, but failure to standardize, as in London and New York, with various types of current (AC and DC) and various voltages, expecially 110 and 220, not to mention in London a bewildering variety of fittings. Standards are sometimes set by government, as part of the contribution to infrastructure, and sometimes by a dominant firm. International agreement, as on the pitch of the screw thread agreed in World War II between the United States and Britain, is limited primarily to the military field. But the presence of giant companies in international trade and investment may make it difficult for new and improved standards to be adopted, except insofar as they originate with and are promoted by the giant firms themselves. In discussion, for example, Professor Stephen Hymer has suggested that if Canada had had an independent company in the field of electrical appliances rather than subsidiaries of the leading American firms, such a company might have undertaken an independent research effort and achieved independent results in new processes or products, the latter possibly more suitable to Canadian needs than the products developed in the United States. Such a view probably exaggerates the barriers to new entry for individuals with new ideas, who often start small companies in the backyards of the giant companies (i.e., in the United States). It may understate as well the international integration of the intellectual market for science and technology which prevents research from being completely independent anywhere in the world. Existing standards are continuously being challenged by the introduction of new processes and products, although the difficulties of overcoming the head start of established standardized products must be recognized.

The dilemma exists independent of the size of the firm. Some unpublished research of G. Cole at Oxford shows that the Bristol bus company preferred to have its buses of the same make and model to simplify the problems of maintaining inventories of spare parts, training mechanics in maintenance, and the like. With technical improvements occurring discontinuously, but depreciation and the need for replacement taking place in a steady flow, the achievement of the (internal) economy from standardization of equipment was virtually impossible. Similarly during war, military services are continuously faced with the choice of whether to fix on a given design and get larger and cheaper production or keep back from long production runs while they work on improving design still further. Important to the choice is the fact that the earlier the design is frozen and a standard adopted, the more difficult it will be later to replace it with better equipment, when and if developed.

On the other hand, multinational firms tend to introduce modern machinery in most cases in less developed countries, finding that the gain from standardization of equipment within the company outweighs the loss from a technology unsuited to local factor proportions and factor prices. Size of course affects the gains from standardization, but the dilemma begins at a very limited scale.

If we abstract from localization factors and concentrate on assembly-line processes, the optimum size of firm from the viewpoint of the world economy may turn on whether at a given point in time technical change is rapid at the beginning of the introduction of a product or a process or slows down near the end of the product or process cycle. At early stages the larger firm—and by definition the international firm is larger than the national one—is likely to speed up standardization to achieve efficiency in production, though it may slow down technical change. If big firms innovate more than small firms, however, as Schumpeter believed, there is another consideration to be added to the choice.

The Multinational Firm and the Sovereignty of the Nation-State

Size of Enterprise and Size of State

Before considering the impact of the large multinational firm on the optimal size of country, it is necessary to say a few words by way of digression about the comparison, almost universally made, between the respective size of companies and states.[9] General Motors sales, for example, are said to be larger than the national income of the Netherlands, and the Standard Oil Company of New Jersey's profit for a given year larger than the national income of, say, Costa Rica.

Most of these comparisons are illegitimate. Sales of course are a gross figure, including value added and purchased inputs, whereas national income is a net figure, representing value added only. One could properly compare value added by a company and the national income of a country, though the comparison would be less striking, or gross up the national income of the country in question to include inputs bought both abroad and within the country by one firm from another—if the figures for the latter were available as they would not be outside of manufactures.

One could make other comparisons such as the value added by General Motors, its dealers and suppliers, and their suppliers, and the national income of a country or the number of employees of General

Motors, its dealers, suppliers and their suppliers, and the labor force of a country—not the population unless one added into the first figure the employees' dependants. Possibly the comparison between the employees of General Motors alone and the labor force of, say, the Netherlands is relevant, or the annual profit of a large firm and the tax receipts of a government. But why are these comparisons wanted?

There is no doubt that GM and Esso (now Exxon) are big companies compared with other companies and that the Netherlands is relatively small in economic terms as countries go. The comparison between them in the usual case produces a statement comparable to "this apple is bigger than this watch," of dubious interest and importance. Most people make the comparison to furnish some idea of the relative power of General Motors and the Netherlands, and this may well be incomparable.

Both GM and the Netherlands have the power of the purse. That of GM is measured less well by sales, because it has to pay its suppliers, or even value added, since it has to pay its workers, dealers, and executives, than by profit—although the annually expected dividend may be regarded as an expense—and by its power to borrow in money and capital markets. The Netherlands' power of the purse could be represented by tax receipts, though normal taxation for normal running expenditure is akin to the monies GM must use for purchased inputs. Perhaps the best measure would be the Dutch governmental power to raise taxes for new expenditure, plus its capacity to borrow. One test that might be said to be fair would be the relative amounts the two bodies could borrow and the rates of interest they would have to pay perhaps after adjustment for tax discrimination and investor discrimination based on the eligibility of government securities for certain trustee purposes for which GM debt is ineligible. The argument becomes complex and uninteresting, however.

But the Netherlands has several powers General Motors lacks: the power to tax, the power to issue money which may be regarded as the power to tax via inflation, and in more general terms police power. Galbraith to the contrary notwithstanding, the corporation does not have the power to compel the individual to act against will in ways it chooses. The state does. The state is sovereign; General Motors is not.

The Multinational and Smaller States
The sovereignty of the state, surely the small state but the large state as well, has been eroded by the international corporation, among other influences in a world of easy mobility and communication.[10] This is

true in the areas of taxation, monetary policy, labor policy, regulation of shipping, and the like.

In taxation, though corporations complain of double taxation, the fiscal authorities tend to believe that the international corporation uses differences in rates of taxation and definitions of income to distort its operations or transfers income, possibly through the adjustment of prices used in intracorporation dealings, so as to avoid or evade taxation. The result is pressure to harmonize levels of taxation, definitions of income, including investment credits and the like, to reduce incentives for companies to move in ways that are uneconomic.

The pressure on small-to-medium states to harmonize taxes, definitions of income, and perhaps one day governmental benefits is not felt by the very small countries—Panama, the Bahamas, the Seychelles, Liechtenstein, Luxembourg, and a number of Swiss cantons which have little to offer in the way of real economic advantages and thus compete to attract a portion, often minimal, of a firm's operations by offering it very low tax rates. The appeal of tax havens has been very much reduced by the Revenue Act of 1962 in the United States which subjects to U.S. taxation, without the credit for foreign income taxes paid, income earned in countries with limited production facilities and in the Swiss-German double-taxation agreement of 1971 which prevents tax avoidance by German companies through Swiss dummies. It seems likely that the pressure of the larger jurisdictions will bring the practice to a halt in a few years and that, like Delaware, the smaller jurisdictions will lose their power to entice legal and accounting operations.

Harmonization reduces the sovereignty of states by making them conform to a general standard. The smaller the country, the less its capacity to produce change in the standard. Such capacity is likely to be divided asymmetrically. In the field of monetary policy, for example, the United States used to set the level of world interest rates, except for countries cut off from world money and capital markets by fluctuating exchange rates or effective exchange control, and other countries are bound to follow except for small differences. It seems likely that a similar asymmetry of power to affect the set of harmonized corporate regulations exists, pending the development of effective international institutions. The system is of course looser than for short-term interest rates. A change in taxes, definitions of income, investment credit, and a fortiori public expenditure favorable or unfavorable to corporations in one country is likely to be followed elsewhere only very slowly. Nevertheless, as corporate mobility increases, the limited conformity is achieved more rapidly.

High mobility has enabled shipping companies to operate virtually independent of national regulation, except where they are paid to do so by mail contracts, construction subsidies, and the like. British shippers can ignore Plimsoll loading regulations, American tankers the labor regulations laid down by the Maritime Commission, by the device of flags of convenience. Norman notes that the shipping companies in Norway are virtually independent of government influence.[11] Other production processes are of course less mobile than shipping in the short run, and government can exercise its sovereignty and police power over international corporations to the extent that they have fixed assets within its borders and are organized under the laws of the state with a preponderance of domestic officers and shareholders. It is unclear whether the location of the assets or the nationality of the corporate parent and its shareholders has the larger effect on the behavior of a corporation in a given set of circumstances. If a company like Aramco owned in the United States but with its most important producing asset in Saudi Arabia were being pressed in opposite directions by the two governments involved, the outcome would probably depend on the particular circumstances. But the force of circumstances, especially in the developed world but to some extent among developing countries as well, tends to produce uniformity of treatment.

It is fair to remind ourselves, however, that the multinational enterprise does not take much sovereignty away from the small state, since it is unlikely to have much in the first place. Dupriez notes that small states like Belgium not only cannot have an independent monetary policy, they cannot permit their prices and costs to get out of line with those of their neighbors, so quickly is the balance of payment likely to respond.[12] Drèze has noted that Belgium produces and exports only standardized products because its market is so small that it can achieve efficient scale of production only in products already adopted by others.[13] (This generalization must be qualified, however, for products of high style in which a particular country develops a quality that gains acceptance abroad: Danish furniture, Swedish china and glass, Swiss watches, Italian knitted goods and shoes, French wines, Czech jewelery and glass between the wars, etc. In these products the efficient unit of production can be small if marketing is undertaken cooperatively, as in the case of Swiss watches, or the products may be bought by large international corporations, in this case the department stores and department-stores chains in major cities in the larger countries which are always on the lookout for style leadership.) The Belgian attempt to maintain a foreign-exchange control that differentiated between the trade currency and the finance currency was a failure from the start; arbitrage between the two markets was virtually perfect and prevented the rates from diverging. The international corporation may subtract something from the economic independence of the small state, but there is little enough to begin with.

The optimal size of state will vary depending on the variable concerned. In economic terms the state should be large to achieve economies of scale, insofar as these are possible in given economic circumstances—production functions, location theory, and the like. If cultural identity and cohesion are sought, it should perhaps be smaller than Belgium with its antagonism between Walloons and Flamands. Within the political field there is, first, the variable to be, say, maximized—whether stability, order, independence, power in world affairs, efficiency in internal administration, and the like, all of which doubtless give different answers; and second, the serious question of hysteresis which makes political institutions adapt only very slowly to changes in parameters. It has been observed before, but it may be useful to repeat, that farmers are universally overrepresented in political legislatures because of Engel's law and the lag of political behind economic change. Economic power shifts from landholding to commerce to industry and perhaps currently to the service class, or technostructure, but political power accompanies it only with great reluctance and after a long lag (a fact not noted by Marx). The county in the United States, a political institution adapted from England and which fulfilled certain functions in eighteenth-century America survives, when its raison d'être has disappeared. The difficulty of redrawing urban jurisdictions as people escape to the periphery is well known. Tradition, the accretion of interest in old institutions, and reluctance to induce political change for fear it may get out of hand in chain reaction tend to perpetuate political arrangements that are far from optimal.[14]

Where the political variable is power, larger may be better. Where it is independence, the status quo or self-determination which makes smaller units out of larger may win out. The two motives are often in conflict, as in the French attitude toward the Common Market. Independence as a political goal is also opposed to the loss of sovereignty represented by the interpenetration of efficient-sized corporations. The optimum economic organization of America north of the Rio Grande, for example, would run north and south, instead of east and west, with separate nations for the East Coast and the Maritimes (with perhaps Quebec thrown in); a separate West Coast, covering Alaska, the Yukon, British Columbia, Washington, Oregon and California; and perhaps a single country for the rest in between. A political organization that emphasized power would include Canada as part of the United

States. However, with independence large in the objective function, Canada insists on independence from the United States, and French Canada is increasingly interested in separation from English Canada, which the latter resists on the basis of power. The Gray Report cannot be faulted for its insistence on a Canadian identity, if that is what Canadians choose, but only for its belief that this goal is identical with, or at least consistent with, a policy of optimal intervention in direct investment which maximizes Canadian real income at the same time.[15] Most economists are prepared to recognize that optimal tariffs are based on a sometimes heroic assumption of no retaliation. A simple shift of United States policy from discrimination in favor of Canada to nondiscrimination in such matters as the interest-equalization tax, Federal Reserve lending regulations, and the automotive agreement would be costly to Canada in terms of income and growth.

The Multinational Firm and the Larger State
If the multinational enterprise does not take much power from the very small state, which has little, does it do so from those larger? Is it appropriate for the larger state to do something about it, and if so, how? Is it self-evident that as the optimum size of the corporation and corporate functions increase, the effective state must grow in size or in centralized power?

The answer to these questions cannot be given with any confidence in the present state of our knowledge of international relations. The multinational corporation is by no means the only force on the economic side making for a larger optimum size of the state; the same pressure arises from the increases in mobility of capital and labor and the reduction in transport and communication costs relative to the prices of goods and other services. On a Marxian model of economic determinism, increased mobility requires increased state size or a yielding up of the sovereign powers of the small or medium state to larger units. But economic determinism is not universally agreed. Even if it were, it is not clear whether it would be adequate to cope with the increased mobility by voluntary associations of states, as in diplomatic arrangements whether bilateral or multilateral, though formal intergovernmental agreements, like the General Agreement on Tariffs and Trade, through economic unions of the sort represented by the European Economic Community and the Andes Pact or through political union. Harmonization to a greater or lesser degree seems inevitable. The economist would prefer to leave the analysis of the nature of such harmonization to the political scientist, though one is unlikely to find the latter ready to make much of a positive contribution.

The cultural arguments for a smaller optimum size of state will be addressed in the next and final section. The conclusion there is that they are unlikely to prevail. Political considerations point in no particular direction. Whether they overwhelm the economic pressures for a larger state or are dominant will vary from case to case. It is significant that Denmark joined the Common Market but that Norway did not. In these circumstances prediction is impossible. The economic pressure is there. The state isolates itself from the pressure at its economic peril, unless it is enormously adroit as Japan has been. The choice is between losing sovereignty to the economic pressures or yielding it to larger aggregates. Which will strike political units as the preferred short-run option is impossible to forecast. In the long run, however, political agglomeration to harmonize policies and to contain economic mobility seems inevitable.

Conclusions

It seems likely then that the optimum economic area is larger than the nation-state, the optimum cultural area smaller, and the optimum political area, based on the objective of independence and subject to the hysteresis mentioned, identical with it. To the extent that corporations function beyond the confines of the state, they may serve the state's power purposes, as claimed by Gaullists, or the state may serve corporate interests, as Marxists think, but there is at least a presumption that their scope assists in the achievement of optimum economic size and wars against cultural and political goals. The rise of the neomercantilist attack on the international corporation by Gaullists, Marxists, and especially political scientists reflects the view that the nation-state is threatened by the growing optimum economic size of nations and corporations. The preservation of the power of the state, a good in itself, may require restriction in the international corporations originating in other countries, if not the increase in the number of such corporations whose officers and seat are domestic and which can therefore serve as instruments of power.[16]

The most interesting contraposition of these points of view has been suggested by Hymer and Rowthorn (1970), who argue that it would be better to have companies integrated across industrial lines within a given state than organized within industries across national lines.[17] The view implies judgment as between economic welfare and political independence for the state, though not necessarily for its citizens, and rests on a subjective basis. It may well be that for a given level of economic welfare and freedom for its citizens, more political independence is better than the same or less and that for a given amount of political independence and freedom, more economic welfare is better than the same or less. If economic welfare is to be traded off against political independence, however, one needs an implicit series of prices to reach an equilibrium solution. It is improbable that all observers would agree on what an ideal series of trade-offs would be, much less on how in the real world one substitutes for the other in given circumstances. The problem of how much economic welfare to give up for how much nationalism is very much on the Canadian agenda today, without, however, a contemplation of integration of industries in the national setting.

Perhaps the example of Eastern Europe, the Soviet Union, and Comecon is too complicated by other considerations, but I find that the failures in national planning within states and the absence of international pricing which would make possible efficient specialization between Socialist countries make the economic cost of the Hymer solution very high, even without counting what appears to be a very high implicit price in loss of political, social, and economic freedom for the individual. It is not without interest that individual voices are beginning to be raised in Eastern Europe for the establishment of convertible currencies and international corporations.[18]

In any event cultural independence and cohesion are probably doomed. The most serious charge one can level against the international corporation is that it produces a homogenized world culture, of wall-to-wall carpeting, tasteless meals, Americanized English, traffic jams, and gasoline fumes.[19] The clash between social and economic values recalls the strictures against the industrial revolution of Karl Polanyi in *The Great Transformation* (1947) and his outrage that economic values should have dominated over social. Like Friedrich Engels, and current observers like Edward Thompson and Eric Hobsbawm, Polanyi exaggerated the delights of rural life in a Malthusian world.[20] More significant, however, where politics have made a choice in favor of preserving old values—the French peasant, the small retail shop, the guild system of artisan production—it has generally been economically unsuccessful and politically disastrous. There can be no doubt of the tragedy that befalls people displaced from performing accustomed tasks in accustomed ways. It is exceeded, however, by the tragedy implicit in the political efforts to prevent economic change, or to return, as Fascists, Nazis, and Poujadists have sought, to an idyllic life that never existed.

There are utopian solutions. At the extreme affluence a la Galbraith eliminates scarcity and the need for economies of scale, efficiency, or international interdependence, and the brotherhood and sisterhood of man and woman eliminates the need for order, government, and the state. Affluence eliminates the need for economics; true participation with instantaneous decision making eliminates the need for political science, and perhaps sociology. Some observers predict both by the end of the century.[21]

A personal view, again for what it may be worth, is that scarcity and the need for order are with us for the foreseeable future. This implies that the resolution of the conflict between the optimum economic area and the optimum political area should be sought not by reducing the economic dimension to the narrow political one of the nation-state but rather by building international political institutions capable of regulating the international corporation in the interest of Pareto optimality. In the short run this means more international organization; over the longer term it may mean world government. But I see no virtue in the implicit position of most political scientists that the nation-state as it exists today is sacrosanct and eternal and that other world forces should be bent to its preservation. If the scale of political efficiency changes, why should not the nation-state follow the county not into oblivion but into the museum of antiquarian interest with the city-state?

The need to exceed the optimum cultural area saddens me. The moves to separate Bangladesh from India, French Canada from Canada, are understandable, possibly successful in the short run but futile. A pity for our descendants who will find the world much more alike. Some of the new less developed countries, it should be noted, will be much better off.

Notes

1. See Mundell (1961).

2. See McKinnon (1963).

3. Despite the fact that Volkswagen has no production facilities in the United States, it has of course a considerable investment in distribution facilities, including stocks of spare parts.

4. In his 1960 thesis Stephen Hymer recorded the view that when any market reached a volume of 50,000 tires a year, it was worthwhile for a tire company to invest there in productive facilities. This no longer appears to be the case, and the efficient-sized plant is said to produce 25,000 tires a day. A new plant in Turkey, for example, starts with a capacity of 750,000 tires a year. In some industries, on the other hand, the size of efficient plant is reduced by innovation, rather than increased. In 1964 it was said in Luxembourg that the efficient steel plant had been reduced in size from 7 or 8 m tons a year to 2 or 3 m.

5. See Johnstone (1965).

6. Anyone who doubts the reality of diseconomies of scale should contemplate the wartime practice of armies since the time of Napoleon of adding a new headquarters whenever the number of subordinate units exceeds three. When a fourth division is added to a corps, for example, a second corps headquarters is produced to make two corps of two divisions each. The same applies to army groups, armies, corps within armies, regiments in divisions, and so forth. Only the corporal who commands twelve soldiers in the American army is thought capable of managing more than three units.

7. See Koszul (1970).

8. The first open question is whether the financial integration of the Common Market will replace that of the North Atlantic "community," now based in the Eurodollar market with its primary location in London. If a European currency and a European money and capital market do develop separately from the dollar, the evident candidate for leadership in the system is London. The author has reservations, however. London dominated the Eurodollar market because of the presence there of large American bank branches. To furnish the center for a European money and capital market, London would have to resume international lending. The author believes that it is not sufficient to offer brokerage services; the market is made where there are financial institutions prepared to buy when demand is insufficient and to sell when it is excessive. British savings, channeled through pension funds and insurance companies, are normally invested in domestic government and local authority issues and not abroad. There is of course investment in British companies which themselves undertake direct investment abroad, but this is outside the capital market proper. On this showing, Amsterdam and Frankfurt are more likely candidates. It is even possible if a new currency were established, rather than an existing currency adopted by the market as a whole, that the political pull of Brussels would bring financial institutions there.

If a European currency is unable to develop in competition with the dollar, it seems unlikely that the financial center would move back from London to New York, even if United States restrictions were removed. The convenience of a world money and capital market located in the European time zone, and largely free of government regulation, is too compelling, even though for really large sums of money—over $125 m—New York is a much more efficient market.

9. Seers (1963), however, carefully avoids the vulgar comparisons.

10. See the title of Raymond Vernon's book (1971a), on the multinational enterprise.

11. See Norman (1971), p. 36.

12. See Dupriez (1966), pp. 281 ff.

13. See Drèze (1960).

14. There is a substantial literature that traces the final unwillingness of the German bourgeoisie to agree to constitutional reform after the revolution of 1848 to the view that, terrified by the Lumpenproletariat, the bourgeoisie was unwilling to restrict the monarchy, separate justice and administration, provide for a wider franchise to dilute the aristocratic dominance of parliamentary institutions—all in its own interest—for fear it would open the floodgates of change. Historians also claim that Italian business steered away from reform of the governmental bureaucracy in Italy after World War II for fear that they could not limit reform.

15. See Government of Canada (1972).

16. Note that the operations of the Deutsche Bank in Italy were undertaken for political motives—to help Italy engage in a tariff war with France—and were regarded subsequently as having had major political benefits; see Helfferich (1956), p. 127.

17. See Hymer and Rowthorn (1970).

18. See Vajda (1969), pp. 128 ff.

19. Note, however, the declaration of Margaret Mead in favor of a world culture, as she received the Kalinga prize from UNESCO, *Journal de Genève*, 24 February 1972.

20. See, for example, Braun (1965), chapter 4.

21. See Galtung (1970).

References

Braun, R. 1965. *Soziale und kulturelle Wandlung in einem ländlichen Industriegebiet im 19. und 20. Jahrhundert.* Stuttgart: Eugen Rentsch Verlag.

Drèze, J. 1960. Quelques réflexions sereines sur l'adaptation de l'industrie belge au Marché Commun. *Comptes rendus de Travaux de la Société d'Economie Politique de Belgique,* No. 275.

Dupriez, Léon H. 1966. In *Diffusion du progrès et convergence des prix, études internationales.* Paris: B. Nauwelaerts.

Galtung, J. 1970. The Future of Human Society. *Futures* 2(2):132–142.

Government of Canada. 1972. *Foreign Investment in Canada* (The Gray Report). Ottawa: The Queen's Printer.

Helfferich, K. 1956. *Georg von Siemens.* Krefeld: Richard Serpe.

Hymer, Stephen, and Rowthorn, R. 1970. The Multinational Corporation and International Oligopoly: The Non-American Challenge. In C. P. Kindleberger, ed., *The International Corporation.* Cambridge: The MIT Press.

Johnstone, A. W. 1965. *U.S. Direct Investment in France.* Cambridge: The MIT Press.

Koszul, J.-P. 1970. American Banks in Europe. In C. P. Kindleberger, ed., *The International Corporation.* Cambridge: The MIT Press.

McKinnon, Ronald I. 1963. Optimum Currency Areas. *American Economic Review* 53 (4):717–725.

Mundell, Robert A. 1961. Optimum Currency Areas. *American Economic Review* 51 (4):657–665.

Norman, Victor D. 1971. *Norwegian Shipping in the National Economy.* Bergen: Institute for Shipping Research.

Polanyi, Karl. 1947. *The Great Transformation.* Philadelphia: Blakiston.

Seers, Dudley. 1963. Big Companies and Little Countries. *Kyklos* 26 (4):599–607.

Vajda, I. 1969. The Problem of East-West Trade. In P. A. Samuelson, ed., *International Economic Relations.* London: Macmillan.

3

The Clash of Economics and Sociology and Politics in the Internationalization of Business

As in all other professions, economists are mostly inclined to mind their own knitting, but they occasionally lift their heads and peer about them to see what is going on in the outside world—in this discussion the world of other social sciences. Both activities have their uses. We need to cultivate our own garden because there are a number of unanswered questions about international business—though I have stopped to rest on several occasions in the belief that we know most or all of what we should know. But especially we must look up and around at politics and sociology because of a gap in communication. Economists for the most part believe the multinational corporation is extending efficiency, bringing technology, management, and capital from areas where it is abundant to those where it is scarce, and advancing the world toward Pareto optimality which is efficient in the sense that no one can be made better off without making someone else worse off. At the same time politics is decrying the multinational corporation as a menace to national sovereignty, while sociology suggests it makes for dependence, exploitation, anomie, and worse.

Norway is a good country in which to raise these issues. Yours was one of the first countries to take action against foreign business when in 1905 the Norwegian Parliament enacted legislation making it difficult for foreigners to own natural resources in the country. On previous occasions I have mocked this view as an example of misplaced concreteness, the view that natural resources are different from other capital assets, when to an economist they are the same to the extent

A lecture to a conference at the Norwegian School of Business, Bergen, Norway, November 1973. Published in Bedrifter i Okende Internasjonal Konkurranse, *Hostkonferansen 1973*, pp. 21-26.

that they produce the same net income and that depreciation allowances, on the one hand, and depletion allowances, on the other, can be used to maintain the value of the asset, if not in its original form, at least in earning power. The reason for your government's action, however, was political, and a response to Britain's Boer war. You were concerned lest British investors acquiring residence in the country would furnish an excuse to the British government to intrude to protect its citizens, along the lines of Jamison's raid.[1] You were thus in early on the political discussion of international business. Moreover one of your compatriots, a distinguished sociologist, Johan Galtung, is quite negative on multinational business from a social point of view. In his view, as I understand it, and I may do him less than justice, all dependence is exploitation. Even interdependence is exploitation, though such a view raises philosophical questions such as what the word can mean. Husband and wife can best live together, he believes by taking the same job, each working at it half the working day and doing housework the other half. Or city and country can estimate their mutual dependence, the city producing food through hydroponics and similar advanced methods, the country producing manufactures through machines managed by computers. With affluence there is no need for dependence, no scarcity and no economics.[2] (I have the feeling that Professor Galtung dismisses political science equally by sleight of hand—with full participation in decision making, there is no need for order, and hence no politics; with economics and political science thus eliminated, sociology reigns supreme. I doubtless caricature.) This then is a good place to discuss the clash between the economics of international business and its politics and sociology.

I had thought that the economics were fairly well worked out. Let me summarize succinctly: Hymer made clear that international business belongs to the theory of industrial organizations, not to international trade or to capital movements. Business goes abroad to exploit an advantage, to earn a higher rent than it could by selling its management, technology, capacity to assemble capital, and the like, through competitive factor markets. Often the investment is defensive: to prevent losses on other business; to penetrate a rival's territory so as to signal the rival to take it easy in competition in one's own; or to extend one's network for fear that if one did not, a rival might steal a march (i.e., a client), an order, or a market.

It should be noted that though direct investment comes from monopolistic competition, it often breaks up local monopoly and thereby improves efficiency. The national corporation in the United States is accepted as having raised wages and lowered interest rates in the south to a degree beyond that achieved by factor movements—labor moving north and capital south—or by goods movements functioning via the factor-price-equalization theorem. Similarly, the international corporation has started to add its weight to trade and factor movements in the direction of factor-price-equalization, though there is evidently a long way to go.

From an economist's point of view the argument for international business is the argument for efficiency; the arguments against are all second best or noneconomic. At a high level of abstraction all second-best and noneconomic arguments come down to the same thing: the market does not work well. The market may not work well in public goods, such as national defense, open space, and the like, or because of external economies and diseconomies, such as learning or pollution, or because of monopoly, imperfections of knowledge, and a host of other reasons. When the market does not work well, it is wrong to be doctrinaire in insisting on its use. If the Italian capital market is riddled with inefficiency, it may be a mistake to sell off firms in difficulty to foreigners merely because there are no capitalists at home to lend to them or buy them—which accounts for the state financial enterprises or IRI, GEPY, EMI, and the like. Economists call these "second-best" arguments because the best policy, most believe, is to repair the market mechanism and let it function. Improve knowledge in the capital market, and the infant industry or temporarily illiquid firm can borrow the necessary finance. Put subsidies on activities with positive external effects and taxes on those that are negative. There will still be public goods, which must be dealt with outside organized markets for goods and factors, handled by budgets instead of markets. With private goods, however, the first-best line of action is to adjust private to social values and let the market perform.

The public-good exception may provide a basis for circumscribing the operations of the international corporation, when a country is strongly nationalistic or puts a high value on social cohesion. Nationalism can be regarded as a public good; if the Pantagonians choose to remain pure in their Pantagonianism, they may wish, as a matter of public policy, to keep out foreigners, to limit the proportion of industry or agriculture, land or property, which they permit foreigners to own. In so doing, it is likely that they will have to accept a somewhat lower national income and level of living, but if the choice is made consciously, the economist who takes tastes as given and is interested primarily in satisfying such tastes in the most efficient manner is in no position to object. Opponents of foreign investment often claim that limiting the right of foreigners to invest in a country adds to national income. This is possible in static terms if the country itself is a monopsonist in the investment field and can get such investment as it permits cheaper, and there may be certain groups in the country who would be better off if foreign investment were limited, since it competes with them and lowers their incomes. We can regard these as second-best arguments, under which total welfare would be improved by advancing competition and redistributing income through transfers, or we can cling to Pareto optimality as the badge of efficiency and eliminate all distributional arguments—both internationally—the optimum tariff or the optimum restriction on capital flows, and internally the Stolper-Samuelson factor redistribution from altering endowments through factor movements.

If direct investment enhances Pareto optimality under first-best conditions, and in the absence of public goods, is there a presumption that one ought to embrace a policy of laissez faire for foreign investments embodying equity ownership and control? One advantage that professors have is that they can find out questions to which they don't know the answer by asking them of students on examinations. I put to students of international economics on a "general examination" (i.e., not restricted to any one course or body of learning), the following:

1. Is there a presumption of laissez faire in international trade in goods and services?

2. Is there a presumption of laissez faire in the movement of portfolio capital?

3. Is there a presumption of laissez faire in the movement of direct investment?

4. Is there a presumption of laissez faire in international migration?

The last question could readily have been divided into skilled and unskilled categories to refine it still further. A place might be found for tourists, known to be committed to go away, or even for visiting lecturers who come only for a weekend.

It could have been useful to have had the question fed to the students by a dispensing device, one part at a time, requiring them to turn in the answers to the early parts before they were aware of the existence of its further branches. Without that refinement, however, most students were inclined at one end to accept the presumptive case for laissez faire in goods and services but to resist such a case for labor at the other. It was recognized tht second-best and non-economic considerations legitimately qualify the case for free trade, but even with this it was believed that there was a presumption that economic first-best considerations would dominate. At the other extreme few believed in laissez faire for migration, especially of unskilled labor.

The economic argument against migration of unskilled labor has to make a distinction between static and dynamic conditions. Under static conditions free migration increases welfare in a Pareto-optimal sense by equalizing wages worldwide. Dynamically, for a movement of labor from a country that has not accomplished its Malthusian revolution and where the emigrants are replaced by Malthusian survivors there is an ambiguous outcome. It can be argued that world welfare is reduced, since income per capita declines. It can also be argued that welfare is raised because world income increases and that added population at the old level of living adds to welfare. But few economists argue for free migration of, say, the hordes from, say, India or China to Europe and the United States, and the reasons are not so much dynamically economic as social and political.

Between free trade and free migration there was disagreement over the movement of capital through securities traded on exchanges and through direct investment. A case can be made against portfolio investment to the effect that the conditions for first-best capital allocation—the existence of a single market with harmonized conditions—do not exist, and much capital movement will respond not to real scarcities but to differences in tax laws, fear of confiscation, availability of complementary factors, and the like. For the most part, however, the students took a much more favorable attitude to portfolio than to direct investment or free migration. The reasons, I claim, are largely political and social rather than economic.

On earlier occasions I have asserted that man in his elemental state is a peasant with a love of his own turf; a mercantilist who favors exports over imports; a Populist who distrusts banks, especially foreign banks; a monopolist, who abhors competition; a xenophobe, who feels threatened by strangers and foreigners, and above all, a child who wants to have his cake and eat it too, in this case to have the benefits of foreign investments but not the costs. In international economics we are inclined to patronize these views as juvenile and regard our task in education as extirpating some or all of them, particularly intuitive mercantilism and love of monopoly. I would argue, however, that most people, even those taught at length in international economics, retain their antipathy to intrusion by foreigners. International politics is perhaps designed to teach internationalism rather than nationalism, though many teachers of international politics seem to choose their historical heros from the ranks of the nationalists—Metternich, Bismarck, de Gaulle. I ascribe much of the mounting distaste for international intercourse as one moves from goods to portfolio capital, to direct investment to migrants, to implicit xenophobia or nationalism. Intuitively, and until we have had it trained out of us, we resent the ownership and control of resources in our midst by persons who are not of our tribe. We may not know or consort with similar capitalists who are nationals of our country, but except for those of us who are Marxists, we take a milder view of their activity and are readier to regard them as benevolent. Shipping goods is not intrusive or threatening, nor shipping money against securities. Taking over the management of industry, even if that industry is created by them, or owning the natural resources which God intended us to have is otherwise. So is immigration, unless as in the United States until World War I and Israel today there is a strong tradition of freedom from oppression in another country and asylum for the oppressed.

It is of some interest to recall that trade was once intrusive. One means around this was silent trade, in which the parties involved would bargain without talk. The Moors would bring their salt to the riverbank and withdraw. The Ashanti would inspect it and its amount, bring up a certain amount of gold, and retire. The Moors would return. If they were content with the implicit gold/salt price, they would adjust the price by retiring some salt. As C. S. Bovill tells it in *The Golden Trade of the Moors*, on one occasion the implicit price worked out at one pound of gold for a pound of salt needed to cure the Ashanti meat — terms of trade that producers of salt no doubt look back on with nostalgia. Trade need not involve social intercourse.

Nor need direct investment be highly intrusive in the sense of requiring much cultural interaction. It is of some interest that investment in foreign enclaves is today regarded as exploitive. The Europeans mining guano in Peru brought their own management, equipment, and imported labor in coolie gangs from China because of the difficulty of (or so not to have to undertake) organizing the work of the Indian and mestizo peasant, unacquainted with the culture of unremitting toil. The picture painted by Jay Levin in *The Export Economies* contrasts with modern foreign investment in Peru's fishing fleets, as depicted by Michael Roemer, in *Fishing for Development*, where foreign as well as native investors produced positive linkages in economic development, training Peruvians in modern skills, stimulating the establishment of new industries, and the like. The latter produced more development; the former better preserved the separation between the cultures, while obtaining some economic benefits for Peru through taxation and royalties.

It has been argued that it is not the quantity of intercultural contact that is offensive in direct investment but the quality. In *The Great Transformation*, Karl Polanyi opposes the calculation of benefit through the market not because of exploitation but because of the cultural catastrophe that occurs when two cultures mingle. The weaker one is degraded. What is significant is not economic exploitation, as often assumed, but disintegration of the cultural environment of the victim and the loss of self-respect and standards.[3] He suggests, for example, that India benefited economically from British rule and investment but was socially "disorganized and thus prey to misery and degradation."

Quantity and quality are doubtless related. A Switzerland which can absorb Italians up to one-quarter of the labor force will balk at one-third, a number believed to threaten its national integrity, and a Canada which accepts 25 percent of its manufacturing in foreign ownership resists when the proportion passes beyond 50. The argument, however, is political and social, not economic.

It is more social than political in the national-defense sense of the latter. Many Canadians claim to be concerned at the extent of foreign investment from the United States on the ground that it makes them dependent. This raises the Galtung concern that dependence is exploitation. We should perhaps stop long enough to note the ambiguities in the notion of exploitation, since it must always be interpreted in relative terms compared to some alternative, and not to some wished-for but the most likely alternative or some objective standard. If an American company in Patagonia hires its native labor force at a dollar an hour, this is not exploitation because the wage rate in the United States is three dollars an hour. If one dollar is slightly above the going rate in Patagonia, I would argue that the likely alternative is, say, ninety cents, and it is wrong to call it exploitive. If the American company is a monopsonist, and the only employer, the rate may be properly compared not with the likely alternative, which might be no wage at all but the rate that would be reached in a competitive market. Exploitation is an entirely appropriate concept under monopoly/monopsony conditions where a firm holds back on sales to raise prices, or on hiring labor to reduce wages. Here the alternative is the competitive price or wage, which must of course be reached by intellectual experiment. It is highly ambiguous in bilateral monopoly or game-theoretic cases, where it is impossible to find an alternative standard.

I find particularly confusing the suggestion of Professor Galtung that dependence is exploitation. Canada depends on the United States for a considerable volume of manufactured goods supplied partly by import and partly by U.S. firms in Canada; the United States depends on Canada for pulp and paper, minerals and metals, asbestos, electric power, supplemental oil. Trade involves mutual dependence and thus mutual exploitation. Canadian direct investments in the United States cover liquor, beer, nickel, farm machinery, banks, a far shorter list than that which runs in the opposite direction but not without strengths. Of great interest is that the ingenious suggestion that Canada trade its holdings of securities on the New York Stock Exchange for the ownership of American firms in Canada produced no positive reaction whatsoever among Canadian investors. They greatly preferred to retain portfolios of IBM, Xerox, Polaroid, not to mention General Motors, and perhaps even some lemons, like Penn Central, rather than to invest only in raw material exporting industries or import-competing manufacturing. Mutual investment, including the exchange of portfolio securities for direct investment, increases interdependence but provides welfare to investors who have an opportunity to diversify and to hold a proportion of growth stocks along with the normal run of the country's industries. It may not appeal to those with strong left-wing views to claim a benefit in welfare for, say, the Norwegian investor if foreign direct investment in the country permits diversification of Norwegian investor portfolios. There is, nonetheless, a positive gain in welfare for investors from diversification, to set alongside the normal distributional effects of foreign investment, and this will increase welfare under the rules of Pareto optimality, unless the diversification positively reduces the welfare of others.

In chapter 2 I claim that the optimum economic area is larger than the optimum cultural area, and this is where the trouble lies. It is assumed that the purpose of economic activity is to increase real incomes. To this end the wider the market and the greater the degree of specialization, the better—in the general case. Some markets are necessarily local—those for ordinary medical services—but for many diseases patients are flown round the world. Such are the economies of scale in the Eastman Kodak company whose transport costs are so low that they could provide film and undertake color developing and printing in their Rochester factory for the whole world. Economies of scale are fewer and transport costs higher in most other industries, but a high optimum scale of production is a major factor assisting the internationalization of business as industry seeks lower costs.

Society thrives on integration and cohesion, and for these purposes the optimum scale is much smaller. It seems to me cultural values make Belgium, for example, too large as a society, but it is universally agreed to be too small economically. It is true that some classes of society in constant and full communication across national lines achieve a measure of cohesion: middle-class youth grows long hair, wears blue jeans, listens to rock music, smokes pot, and so on, over a wide area of the globe. But though xenophobia is relaxed for certain groups vis-à-vis their peers abroad, at least temporarily, it remains a general force to be reckoned with.

Optimum political size will vary depending on the objective function. For glory, bigger is better, so long as one does not unduly dilute languages, the quality of patriotism, administrative efficiency, and the like. If the target, however, is merely getting along without trouble, size above or below a certain optimum may mean involvement: above as an active participant; below as the object of another country's aggression.

On this showing the antithesis between economics and, say, sociology is unavoidable. The interesting question becomes which force is the stronger. To a Marxist the economic forces must dominate because of the capitalist system. The Christian Socialist Polanyi thought it possible to retain efficient production but to dispense with the market, though he offered no clear program. The student of international business who observes the costs of transport and communication continuously declining must wonder whether sovereignty is not at bay and cultural independence threatened.

The clash between international business and cultural and political independence is fought along a fluctuating border. Howard Perlmutter has suggested that companies develop with time and exposure to the world market from ethnocentric to polycentric to geocentric. The same point may be put, in a less mouthfilling way, by suggesting that there is a line of evolution from

1. national firms with foreign operations, and

2. multinational corporations, to

3. international corporations.

The first feels fully at home only within the borders of the country where it started. The second has become more aware of cultural differences and problems and tries to be a good citizen of each country where it has operations. This third, in a sense the highest stage, tends to disregard nationality questions and to optimize in the sense of maximizing profit over some time horizon everywhere in the world.

The differences among these stages of evolution in international business can be illustrated for a variety of the functions of the firm, and the scheme immediately reveals that there is no need for a corporation to advance in steady progress across the entire spectrum with closed ranks. Let me illustrate by taking a single function, the attitude toward exchange risk, and suggest that this attitude changes as the corporation evolves. A domestic corporation with foreign operations is perfectly at home in its home currency but is concerned with risks in foreign exchange. Ordinarily risk averse, for example, it will borrow abroad for investment abroad, rather than bring funds from its home country, if that is possible. Later it may go long or short of foreign exchange. In a technical sense when it is long of foreign exchange, it is short of its currency, but it tends to think of foreign exchange risk as associated with foreign currencies.

At the next stage of development, with subsidiaries in perhaps six to ten countries, the multinational corporation, trying to be a good citizen everywhere, is unwilling to take a short position in foreign exchange anywhere, since that is unfriendly to the host or home country. Not being willing to go short, it cannot go long. It may vary the timing of the remittance of dividends, as a factor of foreign-exchange speculation, though a mild one, but in general it is risk averse out of a sense not of fear but of loyalty to its new hosts.

The international corporation, in this arbitrary classification, has evolved beyond unwillingness to take risks and is more sophisticated. It will go short or long of any currency, provided it does it in not too conspicuous fashion so as to earn the disapproval of national financial authorities (we assume there are no foreign exchange regulations; if these exist, they will be adhered to). It is no more safe in the home than in a foreign currency, except to the extent that its equity is denominated in the home currency, which is a partial offset to net assets denominated in fixed money terms.

This same evolution of behavior can be outlined in tabular form for a series of other functions, as set forth in table 3.1.

This profile is of course highly stylized and of dubious applicability in particular cases. It is relevant for our purposes, I think, because it shows that the clash between international business and social values is not a simple matter of intrusion. This is the case in the first stage, where a firm goes abroad to do the thing it learned to do at home because it can exploit its advantage there to greater effect and in unsophisticated ways. In the "multinational" stage of development it is much less noticeable, for the firm attempts to be a good citizen of each country in which it operates. As an "international" corporation, there is likely to be an increase in the intrusive aspect, for the firm ignores the advantage of any particular country in the interest of minimizing cost and maximizing profit.

The intermediate stage at which the "multinational corporation" acts as a good citizen is one worth noticing, since it may do so at the expense of its economic function of moving toward Pareto optimality and factor-price equalization. The effort to safeguard the national interest of the host country may be efficient, if it is a reaction to undue chauvinism of the national corporation with foreign interests. On the other hand, if it is an alternative to the allocation of investment and effort based on purely economic considerations—in a world of competitive and well-functioning markets—it is inefficient. It may help if I illustrate.

Assume that an American company with copper mines both in Canada and the United States has to cut back production because of shrinking markets. The Canadians fear that a "national corporation with foreign operations" will cut back its Canadian mines further than its United States, even though they are more efficient, because its American workers vote in the jurisdiction in which it is most deeply involved and will give it a hard time via their elected representatives until it does its utmost to protect their jobs. "A commodity is known by the senators it keeps," as the saying goes. Canadian workers don't vote in U.S. elections, and a national corporation with foreign operations will often ignore the interests of foreign workers, even in the face a of strong tradition of never discharging workers into unemployment, as in France in the widely publicized and perhaps misunderstood case of General Motors (Frigidaire) at Gennevilliers and Remington-Rand at Caluire near Lyon.

On the other hand, suppose foreign investors safeguard Canadian interests fully. They may sustain employment at the same percentage of capacity in the two countries, regardless of efficiency. Equalizing marginal cost is the efficient long-run solution, which presumably the international corporation follows. It is the one called for by economists, but it is not warmly welcomed by other social scientists.

Some years ago I had occasion to review the now standard work on foreign investment in Canada by A. E. Safarian, and to comment on the fact that the limited information on profits of U.S. firms in Canada suggested that they were not very high. (Parenthetically I may say that this was at a time when the Hymer theory of direct investment requiring higher profits abroad than at home had not been qualified, as it must be today, for the class of defensive investment in which the real return is not reflected in the return on the specific investment, since it may well include a reduction in the possibility of loss on other operations. This extension of the theory destroys the prima facie case that efficient foreign investment has a rate of return higher than the

Table 3.1
Evolving behavior of corporations with direct investment by function and attitudes

	National corporation with foreign operations	Multinational corporation	International corporation
Foreign exchange risk	Long or short of foreign exchange; feels safe in home currency	Unwilling to go short of foreign exchange of host countries	Adjusts exchange position to perceived risk after allowance for costs, all currencies
Profits	Requires higher profits abroad than at home	Accepts profits in countries where located	Seeks to equalize profit net of risk in all countries by real-locating investment
Reinvestment of profits and depreciation	Undertaken reinvestment of profits in promising ventures	Reinvests profits in all countries regardless of outlook and maintains investment through reinvested depreciation	Willing to divert depreciation allowances and profits from unpromising to promising
Research and development	All at home	Some in each country	Concentrates where cheapest and most effective
Personnel hiring	Top management all from home country	Top management mostly local	No interest in nationality of top personnel
New products	Developed at home for home market and produced abroad when profitable	Developed in each market for that market	Developed anywhere for any world market
Response to local custom	Ignores; wants no truck with foreigners	Highly conscious of and adheres faithfully	Takes into account and calculates whether efficient, inefficient
Attitude toward joint ventures	Abhors	Willing to enter freely	Reluctant to enter because of built-in conflict of interest

Articulation of production	National, or connected with U.S. requirements	Determined separately each country	Worldwide based on efficiency possibly modified by threat of nationalization
Concern for national balance of payments	Concern for that of host	Worries about balance-of-payments impact in host and home countries	Ignores balance of payments

rate in the home country, and higher too than that in the host country.) I suggested that this might be due to the fact that United States investment in Canada was taking Canadian needs and desires into account to an undue extent and that, in acting in Canadian ways, they were failing to serve the interests of efficient production. The remark produced an angry response, somewhat off the point, from a left-wing critic in the *Canadian Forum*, but the argument is still valid, I think, on the assumption that defensive investment in Canada is not extensive. The original Canadian "guidelines" for foreign investors brilliantly illustrated the economic ambiguity in asking firms to act competitively but to work to buy Canadian inputs instead of importing, to hire Canadian managers instead of bringing staff from the home office, and to export from the Canadian operation. What if foreign inputs are cheaper than Canadian; home personnel more efficient per Canadian dollar of expenditure than Canadian executives; and Canadian-sourced output, protected by tariffs, higher priced than some other source?

Pressures to make the firm act as a citizen thus are helpful when the firm is a home-country nationalist, harmful when the firm has a cosmopolitan viewpoint. The quintessence is seen in joint ventures where the firm has different partners in each of a number of countries. If it is assumed that the international corporation's equity varies from 100 to 1 percent in a series of countries, maximizing its total profit will give quite different results in terms of efficiency than maximizing the total of firm profit and domestic investors alike, which is the Pareto-optimal solution, and both may well run into serious objection from a number of countries concerned as inconsistent with the national interest.

It is odd in a way to worry as much as we do about the foreigner ignoring the interest of the local population, since the initial view seems to have been that the intruder was going to be bilked by the native, or even by his own countrymen, to such an extent that foreign representation was trusted to no one outside the family. This is familiar to all of us in banking. The five Rothschild brothers could set up interrelated firms in Vienna, Frankfurt, Paris, London, and Amsterdam, and the eight Seligmann brothers went from New York, New Orleans, San Francisco to spread over Frankfurt, London, Paris, Vienna. But even in early direct investment in manufacturing one relied on family: the earliest American manufacturing investment I have discovered is the Haviland plant in Limoges, founded in 1842, so early in fact that most of the world, and especially the French, regard the enterprise as of French origin. (The original American producer did settle in Limoges to be sure and brought his family up as French.)

Werner Siemens who founded Siemens und Halske in 1847 set up offices in London and St. Petersburg, in 1850, both manned by brothers. Today it is insisted that the management be brothers of inhabitants of the host country. Tomorrow, under the international corporation, the nationality will make little difference, and the staff can be chosen on merit from anywhere in the world.

In the clash between economics and the other social sciences over Pareto optimality as against social cohesion, and let us say political nationalism, the "multinational solution" in which the corporation seeks to be a good citizen everywhere may be a good temporary solution, a saddle point in the trade-off between economic benefits and social costs but a second-best economic solution because the first-best economic outcome is socially intolerable. I suspect in the long run, however, that we are moving unevenly to the cosmopolitan solution. Cheaper communication and transport, more interaction, increased contact, are making countries less and less able to sustain the useful myths of national superiority, God-given missions, and the like, and making it easier to tolerate intrusion. I suspected that the Middle West would respond negatively to British Petroleum's purchase of the Standard Oil Company of Ohio some years ago, and so did *The Economist* which accused the Department of Justice of obstructing the takeover on nationalistic grounds. A limited informal poll taking on the occasion of a visit to Cincinnati convinced me that Ohioans were interested but in no way apprehensive about a foreign takeover; later it became evident that the Department of Justice's question was based squarely on the grounds claimed: when an arrangement was worked out to sell enough gasoline stations to prevent BP from having more than 40 percent of the outlets in a given corner of Ohio, the antitrust division withdrew its objection, and the deal went through swimmingly. I have heard word that there are New Yorkers who shudder at the prospect of Brown and Williamson, the British tobacco company, acquiring the well-known Gimbel's department store in that city, but I have never met one. The filters that society has felt obliged to maintain—as in silent trade—are less and less needed. It is true that there are some people of whom it is said, as it was of a well-known unsuccessful candidate for president of the United States, that it was impossible to dislike him until one got to know him, but with whole nations it is rather *au contraire*. It is possible to overdo it. Canada is prepared for a large amount of economic integration, a certain amount of cultural integration—insofar as it cannot resist the impact of U.S. media—but is a long distance from readiness to accept political integration. I suspect that Norway which has once rejected integration with Europe, or a certain part of it, will one day yield on that score, will be prepared to give up a certain amount of political sovereignty, but will cling to its cultural identity. As a tourist who has visited your country on previous occasions twice for a fairly extended period, I hope so.

For let it be said, cultural integration is not very attractive. Homogenized hotels, standardized living quarters, modern architecture (in place of stave churches), identical cuisines, instead of the Norwegian breakfast with fish and pickles which I so much admire, reduce the savor of life. Economic integration promises more, but if it is more of the same, uniform and drab all over the world, it is not clear to this consumer that more is better. The tension between economics and sociology and politics is thus probably built into the system. I fear that the economics will in the long run win. The more's the pity.

Notes

1. Edvard Bull, *Sozialgeschichte der norwegische Demokratie* (Stuttgart: Ernst Kiett Verlag, 1969), p. 51.
2. Johan Galtung, The Future of Human Society, *Futures, The Journal of Forecasting and Planning* 2 (June 1970):137, 141.
3. Karl Polanyi, *The Great Transformation* (New York: Farrar and Rinehart, 1944), p. 157.

4

Restrictions on Direct Investment in Host Countries

Economic history and a number of specialized fields of economics, such as agriculture, are filled with debate between those who claim that man is economically irrational in many respects (or possibly consciously maximizing a noneconomic variable) and those who believe that economic sense can be made of actual choices, if only on a Darwinian basis. This chapter explores restrictions on direct investment by host countries to see whether these can be rationalized in economic terms. That such restrictions abound is taken as needing no demonstration. Various countries maintain prohibitions against whole classes of investment—in natural resources, transport, communication, banking, retail distribution, newspapers, and so forth—and within allowed fields, most countries require ad hoc application to the foreign-exchange or fair-trading authorities who may decline a given proposal on one ground or another. The question is whether such prohibitions and rejections are in the true economic interest of the host country, or whether they are noneconomic responses reflecting the peasant, mercantilist, Populist, nationalist, xenophobic instincts that most people start life with or the irrationality that indulges in the fallacy of misplaced concreteness (or wants to have its cake and eat it too).

The contribution of direct investment is capital, technology, management, access to markets and other similar advantages needed to make direct investment possible. These are sought after by the host country. What is resisted is foreign ownership and especially control, or decision making. We exclude two possible bases of restriction unconnected with foreign control: (1) the monopsonistic argument that

Previously published in Jagdish N. Bhagwati and Richard S. Eckaus, eds., *Developing and Planning: Essays in Honor of Paul N. Rosenstein-Rodan* (London: George Allen & Unwin, 1972), pp. 201–209.

a country might limit capital inflows in order to obtain capital more cheaply and (2) the income-distribution argument that would limit (or accelerate) capital inflows in an effort to prevent a reduction in the return to capital in the host country (or a rise in the marginal product of labor). The first is often given as a reason for restricting capital outflow in an effort to prevent the fall in the average return on foreign investment. It is an optimum-investment argument, comparable to the optimum tariff, and can be inverted to restrict inflows as well as outflows. The second is analogous to the Stolper-Samuelson theorem about tariffs and income distribution. We exclude these arguments for restriction on the grounds that the optimum tariff is unrealistic in policy terms: tariffs do improve the terms of trade but historically are imposed for different purposes, typically for protectionism or to change income distribution. Moreover, though restrictions on foreign invest- ment could be imposed for reasons of income distribution, there is no evidence that they are being so used. Most restriction sought by disaggregated interests is industry specific, not factor oriented. Pressure for restriction on direct-investment outflows has been expected on the part of, say, labor in the United States. It arises only in limited groups, like the United Automobile Workers.

Reference to the optimum tariff and the Stolper-Samuelson theorem suggests the line of argument: restriction on inflows of direct investment can be justified on the same grounds as a tariff for national defense, infant industry, and second best, plus one more argument not found in tariffs, antimonopoly.

The national-defense argument goes back at least to Adam Smith, to "Defense is greater than opulence." It is used to exclude domestic dependence on foreign military supplies or on foreign sources for critical survival items such as food and fuel. In every case, however, the economic cost of greater self-sufficiency must be calculated and the cost of alternative sources of supply that can be turned to in timely fashion in the event that a foreign economical supply is interrupted. Self-sufficiency is a matter of degree, and some degrees are so expensive that they are abandoned. Thus most less developed countries and many developed ones import sizable proportions of their military sup- plies, and Britain depends on imported oil coming through two deep- draft ports highly vulnerable to nuclear attack, because dependence on local coal and North Sea gas for its fuel requirements would be too expensive.

The national-defense argument in direct investment goes beyond weapons, food, and fuel in several dimensions. In the first place the production of food, fuel, and weapons inside the geographical boundaries but under the business control of foreign nationals poses a defense problem of uncertain dimensions. The foreign owners might destroy a plant needed for defense or sabotage its output. It is hardly very likely. Bausch and Lomb and General Analine and Film, German owned and operating in the United States, were taken over very early from foreign control. By the same token the International Telephone and Telegraph Company minority interest in the Focke-Wulf airplane company in Germany presumably had no impact on German military capabilities.

An extension of the national-defense argument leads into transport and communications, industries that are excluded from foreign ownership in the United States and Canada on the ground of their vital importance in the maintenance of the national existence. Still further extended to prohibit cabotage, the use of foreign vessels in transporting freight from one U.S. port to another or permitting foreign aircraft going to more than one airport of the United States to carry passengers between them smacks of protection, not national defense. National defense, like patriotism, may be the last refuge of a scoundrel who is seeking selfish protection but willing to wrap the flag around his interests; this is true both in tariffs and in prohibitions against foreign direct investment in particular fields.

A wider extension of the national-defense argument leads to national independence, including cultural independence and pure nationalism. Albert Breton has called nationalism a collective consumption good which the electorate may choose to buy and which should presumably be included in national income on some opportunity-cost basis.[1] The Canadian Watkins report on the structure of Canadian industry emphasized "national independence" as a goal of policy, which is mentioned in four of five paragraphs listing separate goals.[2] This raises the question of how much foreign ownership and control of separate industries, broad sectors, or beyond a percentage or range of the total economy (or the more dynamic portions of it) compromise independence. Brecher and Reisman asserted that foreign ownership of a Canadian firm would make no difference to its behavior because if both foreign and Canadian owners maximized in the same fashion, they would behave identically.[3] This statement was unacceptable insofar as it implied that the Canadian firm was a local one and the American firm international. Operating in a different spatial horizon (and possibly within a different temporal one) and facing different pressures overall, both firms might maximize and behave differently. But assuming that the Canadian and American firms were of equal size and extent, would their behavior differ in Canada or the United States because of nationality? The answer is probably yes. In such matters as trade with Cuba and mainland China, antitrust, or remittance of profits to the United States for balance-of-payments reasons, the U.S. government could direct the behavior of the American subsidiary in Canada through the U.S. head office, but not the Canadian head office in Canada through its subsidiary in the United States. If the Canadian people objected to this intrusion of U.S. policy into the Canadian body politic, they could prohibit or limit direct investment at a cost in investment, technology, and management for domestic industry from the United States. Or they might find cheaper and easier ways of accomplishing the same end: insisting that foreign subsidiaries in Canada follow Canadian rather than U.S. policy in these matters or negotiating directly with the United States on the extraterritorial extension of U.S. policies via corporate subsidiaries.

Opinions will surely differ as to the importance of the extension of the policy of one country to the policy of another via foreign subsidiaries, the extent to which foreign control of national firms compromises national independence, and how much national independence is worth. The economist has nothing to contribute to these issues beyond urging that various degrees of national defense, national independence, cultural independence, or simply nationalism should be costed in terms of the economic growth and efficiency they would sacrifice and that alternative means of achieving the same ends be similarly priced. If a country wants to pay for something and has found the cheapest way to get it, the economist has nothing more to say, since, on the basis of revealed preference, the national defense bought is worth the amount of opulence the society will give for it.

A number of countries worry about foreign ownership of key industries, especially banking and communication, "the commanding heights of the economy." There may be something to the point about newspapers, radio, television, telephone, telegraph, where unfriendly foreign ownership may distort information, intercept significant government and private messages or, in extremis, yield the control over communication to outsiders at critical times. It seems unlikely. Prohibition of foreign ownership of banking facilities seems based more on populist fears, or protection from foreign competition, than on reasonable measures for national protection.

The infant-industry argument for tariffs also goes back as far as Adam Smith. Today economists regard the tariff solution as a poor one and prefer a combination of taxes and subsidies that aims directly at the distortion between social and market value that limits the efficiency of market choices. Adding direct investment to the analysis raises the question of whether by infant industry we mean the existence of the industry within the national boundaries or the existence of the industry run by citizens of the host country. A tariff by itself may encourage foreign interests to come and start the industry. If what is sought is industrialization by domestic rather than foreign factors, the infant-industry tariff should be accompanied by an infant-industry prohibition of direct investment.

Again of course it is important to be clear about the benefit, the cost, alternative ways of achieving the same objective, and the use of the argument by those who are basically protectionists not entitled to claim the privileges of infants. With respect to the benefit, the question of foreign control arises again. Does it make a difference whether the industry located within the borders is foreign or domestically controlled? If foreign entry into retail trade is prohibited, for example, is this because of the industry's fear of competition or because there is a serious training effect to be gained by schooling in the commercial arts native citizens, long excluded perhaps by Chinese domination of trade? Where the population is homogeneous, the infant-industry argument may be valid for a tariff, but the investment prohibition may degenerate into an instinctual xenophobic attack on foreign control.

As far as costs are concerned, the interest on the lost income of the community while the infant is growing to manhood must not be neglected. The relative costs to be compared are the present discounted values of the income to the country of foreign investment in the industry and of domestic industry, each presumably with a different time profile. If the prohibition of foreign industry and reliance on domestic industry involves a long wait and substantial outlays until the capital is amassed, the difference in costs includes interest on the additional costs and the income foregone in the near term.

The infant-industry argument presents itself especially in connection with natural resources. These mineral deposits, let us say, are our resources, God-given, and in the domain over which our sovereignty has been traditional. These arguments are the instinctive reaction of the peasant, or the fallacy of misplaced concreteness which implies that natural resources are different from other capital assets. If the present discounted value of the deposits is worth more to the country through sale to a foreign interest, or through a concession valued at the present value of the stream of future taxes than would be the case if it were exploited by domestic interests, it is better to sell or concede the deposits to the foreigner. The value of domestic use includes all external effects of training which are incremental to those from foreign exploitation. But the slower time profile of returns from domestic use imposes a substantial cost, if a proper shadow rate of interest is used in the calculation, which is seriously limiting to the applicability of the infant-industry defense of prohibitions, valid though it be.

From time to time foreign investment has been prohibited in non-essential industry (e.g., coffee bars, soft drinks), simple products (e.g., ink), or for balance-of-payments reasons. These can be justified only on the basis of the second-best reasoning. There must be failure of the market to reflect social values, and a better way to correct the discrepancy must be unavailable.

In nonessential industries the typical pattern is to prohibit foreign investment in, say, coffee bars but to permit domestic resources to be used in competitive enterprises. This is surely mistaken. If consumer sovereignty is rejected as failing to follow social priorities, and inter-ference with the market is called for as a second-best policy, prohibition of foreign investment in coffee bars should be accompanied by similar prohibitions for domestic investors. Better would be excise taxes which produce the socially correct market prices.

The notion that foreign investment should be excluded from the production of simple goods, such as textiles and ink, or simple activities such as retail trade, and limited to complex, modern industries is normally another example of the fallacy of misplaced concreteness. A second-best argument can sometimes be made for it on the ground that foreign investors use capital-intensive factor proportions whereas the shadow price of labor is very low and domestic labor-intensive methods are needed to give employment. Where foreign investors would use the same technology as domestic entrepreneurs, their will-ingness to invest in retailing, textiles, or ink suggests that profits are unduly high in these fields. To prohibit external investment is to preserve domestic monopoly.

A last example of a second-best argument may be drawn from the balance of payments. Here foreign investment is sometimes prohibited on the ground that it is "expensive," or it may be restricted to export- or import-saving industry to ensure that transfer of profits to the foreign owner will not put undue burdens on the balance of payments. An Indian statement suggested that in considering applications for foreign investment, the authorities would balance the contribution of the enterprise to productivity against its burden on the balance of payments. This last statement is virtually meaningless (apart from monopoly considerations). The more productive an enterprise, the higher will be its burden on the balance of payments. A balance between the two suggests two intersecting curves. When the functions are highly correlated, the two must be balanced against an external standard.

The statement that foreign investment is expensive presumably means it is profitable, and this, again apart from monopoly aspects, means efficient. With free entry, high profits are transitional, calling attention to what the society wants or can produce more cheaply than it has been doing. There may be a second-best argument for prohibiting foreign entry where domestic monopoly would be created. A better course of action on the face of it, however, is to encourage entry by lower tariffs, action against retail price maintenance, or government competitive enterprise.

The second-best argument that the economy cannot remit profits on foreign investment and had therefore best prohibit investment in the domestic as contrasted with the foreign-trade sector is lamentably true in some circumstances. It reflects a failure of the economy to capture enough of the productivity of the investment to meet service (rarely), or failure to expand exports or reduce imports in lines other than that of the investment sufficiently to effect transfer. This may be the result of an inflationary expansion of purchasing power, associated with the investment, which obviates the necessity for its purchasers to contract expenditure or increase output and income in other directions. A microeconomic solution (prohibiting investment) for a macroeconomic problem (the balance of payments) is always inefficient. There can be little doubt, however, that balance-of-payments problems of many developing countries which have gone a long distance in expanding exports to the point of inelastic demands, or contracting imports to the point where imports of consumers' goods are at low levels and only imports of capital equipment, raw materials, and foodstuffs are left to cut on any scale, are obdurate.

Finally, monopoly. It is increasingly recognized, with Hymer, that direct investment belongs more to the theory of industrial organization than to that of international capital movements. The direct investor operates at a disadvantage in a foreign market, using foreign factors of production, and at a long distance from his decision center. To overcome these disadvantages, he must have a substantial advantage of some kind. (In a limited number of cases direct investment takes the form of policing of each other's markets by oligopolistic competitors, or defensive investment by erstwhile monopolists who are just about to be pushed out of a market.) The advantage may lie in technology, management, access to markets, the huge amounts of capital needed for entry into the industry, and so on. If the direct investor can take over a competitor, perhaps the only competitor in a national market, he can establish a monopoly which may prove costly for the economy.

But the monopoly features of direct investment are complex. Many of its features reflect bilateral monopoly, that is, a monopoly firm, bargaining with a monopoly government. The outcome of such bargaining, as is well known, is indeterminate. A given investment may introduce a monopoly advantage but destroy an old monopoly; a large foreign firm may compete with and put out of business small but noncompetitive enterprises that have settled into a rut of low volume and high markups. Or sustained high profits in the oil industry may be in process of decline because of widespread entry when governments of the oil-producing states move in to try to take over and maintain the monopoly.

Monopoly is thus no basis for rule-of-thumb exclusion of foreign investment. As a rule the competitive effects of direct investment in breaking down old monopoly are likely to be more significant than the spread of monopoly, and the cry of exclusion is not on the side of the angels who favor competition. Nor is the rule of thumb allowing new production but not takeovers a sure guarantee of preventing the spread of monopoly and ensuring competition, though the addition of another firm in the industry is prima facie a move toward more workable competition. The added new firm may join with the domestic cartel, or the old firm, taken over by new management with new technology, may become a vigorous competitor.

The monopoly argument requires that decisions about direct investment be made on a case-by-case basis, going against the grain of those who want government by law and not by men. If Company A merges with Company Alpha abroad, competition may be reduced, whereas if Company B is the partner, competition may be increased. Decision must be made on the basis of the facts, and in particular on the potential gain or loss from increased entry and competition in crowded, inefficient, and high-markup industry now as compared with limited numbers of deliberate rather than enthusiastic competitors later.

But prohibition is in any case a second-best remedy. Tax and subsidy are presumptively superior in any case. Where there are balance-of-payments problems, the remedies are macroeconomic. Where competition is stodgy, a more effective approach than discouraging foreign entry of firms may be to enlarge competition by reducing tariffs and encouraging imports, and possibly to render monopolistic practices illegal.

Bodies politic want to have their cake and eat it too. So do governments. In the bilateral bargain between company and host country, the latter frequently signs up for extended periods of tariff protection for a new entrant and then complains when the company makes large profits. Or Australia is tolerant of retail price maintenance and then irritated when foreign investors find the resultant monopoly profits attractive. Monopoly for us and competition for them is a beguiling fantasy, but it is not the way of the world.

In summary, there are valid arguments for restriction on direct investment: national defense, including cultural independence, anti-monopoly, infant-industry and second-best reasoning more generally. Each must be applied in particular situations with extraordinary care, taking into account the particular circumstances, the costs as well as benefits of the action, and the alternative costs and benefits of other approaches. When so weighed, it will probably be found that there is a presumption in favor of laissez faire, perhaps even a stronger presumption than in tariffs where the "effective rate of a tariff" discussion makes clear that tariff reductions in particular cases may lead to increased rates of protection.

Notes

1. Albert Breton, The Economics of Nationalism, *Journal of Political Economy* 72 (August 1964):376–386.

2. Task Force on the Structure of Canadian Industry, *Foreign Ownership and the Structure of Canadian Industry* (Ottawa: Queen's Printer, January 1968).

3. I. Brecher and S. S. Reisman, *Canadian-American Economic Relations* (Ottawa: Queen's Printer, 1957), ch. 8.

5

Direct Investment in Less Developed Countries: Historical Wrongs and Present Values

Introduction

In an effort to narrow and simplify the scope of this chapter, we shall deal only with relations between host countries and foreign firms specializing in primary products for export. This leaves out consideration of the home country and the problems of investment in import-competing manufactures. The former could readily be added by extension of the technique; the latter by its modification, some suggestions toward which are indicated along the way at particular points.

The chapter offers no real discussion of historical wrongs. For the most part they are assumed to exist, most probably objectively, but certainly in the perception of the officials and public of the host country. The facts in many cases will be cloudy or difficult to interpret. In the International Petroleum case in Peru, for example, the country and the company differ about the title to land which Peru deeded in 1826, after independence, to one of its citizens, and whether this title legitimately included mineral rights; about the lease which IPC obtained from the British owner in 1914; and about the legitimacy of the international arbitration to which Peru agreed, after some British arm-twisting, in 1922. The facts are complex and debatable; the emotions to which they give rise are not. And there are numerous cases of outright "exploitation." Díaz-Alejandro contrasts the carpetbaggers who invaded Cuba (and especially the Isle of Pines) after 1898 to buy up sugar land, with the moratorium on new foreign investment in

Previously published in Luis Eugenio Di Marco, ed., *International Economics and Development: Essays in Honor of Raul Prebisch* (New York: Academic Press, 1972), pp. 387–402.

Germany after World War II, imposed until after monetary reform and the beginnings of reconstruction.[1]

Where an original bargain is lopsided owing to ignorance on the side of the citizens or government of the host country, the moral history is even more debatable. Is it wrong to take advantage of advanced technology or wider access to information so long as there is no misrepresentation, no wrongful obtaining of insider information, no bribery, corruption, gunboats, or strong-arm tactics? Is the advanced foreigner under any obligation to share his knowledge and technology with owners of natural resources prior to fixing the terms of a concession? In many instances, of course, there is no knowledge of oil or ore deposits but only a suspicion of their existence; such investment is risky. But suppose the foreigner had a monopoly of the technology, so that there was no other way to obtain it other than by making a deal with him, and suppose the proposition was risky *ex ante* but paid off big *ex post*. Is that exploitation? Is it possible to have situations that were not exploitative *ex ante* but are properly regarded so *ex post*?

In economics, bygones are bygones. The past is forgotten when it produces no income. Historical wrongs, however, may well have payoffs. They produce streams of income for political figures or political parties and may easily produce a payoff for a country in xenophobic cohesion. Social and political cohesion which is tolerant of similar units on the same or higher and lower levels is likely to be considered superior to that based on antipathy. But the latter may be better than none. Social and political cohesion based on isolationism or xenophobia may be a consumption good, which can substitute for real income in the welfare function of a country, or it may even be a producer's good, which spurs a people on to greater productive efforts or more saving, and incentive for the effort needed for development.[2] It may keep the masses quiet while unequal income distribution stimulates capital formation and growth. Compare the Mexican formula for development as expressed by a cynic: "Revolutionary slogans and high profits."

The present values of the title are of course present discounted values. A foreign firm will undertake investment when the present discounted value (PDV) of the stream of income envisaged exceeds that of costs, which are largely but by no means solely current, both calculated at some appropriate discount rate. But a given foreign investment has a present discounted value for the host country, as well as for the firm undertaking it. It would be possible to calculate PDVs for various political and social elements in the host country on a disaggregated basis. Moreover there will be alternative present discounted values of a given investment for a host country, depending on different regulations or different rates of tax. In particular there will be a different value for the investment depending on whether it is operated by the foreign firm under nondiscriminatory national treatment or nationalized, which under international law, presumably, calls for compensation. The question in all these cases is what to include in the stream of income and what in the stream of costs—this is the subject of this chapter.

The discussion is not mathematical, although it makes use of three simple equations merely to organize the discussion of the costs and benefits to different players in the nonzero-sum game of direct investment in less developed countries, and to the same player with different strategies. The models are extremely simple and would probably have to be modified for different primary products, such as tin in Bolivia or Malaysia, oil in Venezuela or Indonesia, bananas in Central America, or tea in India or Sri Lanka. Changes would be especially required, as already noted, if the models were to be applied to import-competing manufactures.

The Variables

New investment is undertaken or not undertaken on the basis of a simple formula for capitalizing a stream of income. In perpetuity, where the income is constant, it is expressed as

$$C = \frac{I}{r},\tag{1}$$

where C is the capitalized value of the investment, I is the annual income on it in perpetuity, and r is the normal rate of profit expressed in percent per year.[3] If C, the value of the asset, exceeds C', the value of the stream of costs, by some normal proportion the investment will be undertaken; if not, then it will not be. In what follows, I is disaggregated into various elements which are viewed from three vantage points: that of the foreign investor, f; that of the home country, h, but under two different circumstances, one when the investment is operated by a foreign investor, h_f, and one when it is nationalized, h_{nat}.

The three formulations permit three comparisons: first, the value of a given investment to the foreign investor and to the home country; second, the value of the investment to the host country in foreign ownership and after nationalization; and third, the value of the investment to the foreign investor and to the host country when the latter operates it itself. These three comparisons address the resulting issues in the literature: the distribution of the gains from foreign investment;[4] the appeal of confiscation of foreign investment by the developing country;[5] and the theory of direct investment.

Three Identities

The present discounted values may be approximated by three identities, as follows:

$$C_f = \frac{(S_f - w_f L - r_f K - T_h - G_f)z}{D_f}, \tag{2}$$

$$C_{h_f} = \frac{T_h + (w_f - w_h)L - G_h + EE_{G_f} + EE_f + N_f}{D_h}, \tag{3}$$

$$C_{h_{nat}} = \frac{S_h - w_h L - r_h K - pRDM - G_h - A + EE_h + N_h}{D_h}, \tag{4}$$

where

- C is the present discounted value of an investment,
- S is annual sales,
- L is labor required by the project,
- T is annual taxes paid by the project over time,
- K is capital stock,
- G is the annual cost of services provided by government or government investments,
- RDM is foreign technology and management,
- EE is external economies,
- A is annual compensation payments over a long period,
- N is satisfaction from national ownership (h) or dissatisfaction because of foreign ownership (f), normalized as annual return on a public good or evil,
- D is the discount rate in percent per annum,
- p is the price of foreign technology and management per year,
- w is the annual wage rate,
- r is the rate of return on capital in percent per annum,
- z is an element of political risk, where $1 > z > 0$, and 1 represents no risk and 0 represents a certainty of loss owing to political factors.

Marketing

First compare S_f and S_h, the sales of output of a particular investment in foreign hands, and after nationalization. Under well-functioning international markets and perfect competition, $S_f = S_h$. The nature of the ownership would be a matter of indifference to sales. But this is by no means the only outcome. Many observers in less developed countries, such as Prebisch, and most Marxist and strongly left observers, believe that S_h under nationalization would exceed S_f, because of the overcoming of monopsony. Julien, for example, or Magdoff claim that United States firms pay low prices but get large amounts of needed raw materials at high profits.[6] Presumably when S is decomposed in PQ, Q may be high, but P is unduly low. With different ownership Q might remain the same or decline slightly, while P would rise by more than Q declined to raise total S. Or the typical Canadian fear is that an American company that owns a high-cost mine in the United States and a low-cost one in Canada, might cut back in depression according not to economic but political consideration—how much more unpleasant it would find unemployment in Montana than in British Columbia, for example. Under these circumstances $S_h > S_f$ and, other things equal, a shift to Canadian ownership would improve Canadian and world welfare.

This is by no means the only possibility, however. The theory of direct investment postulates that the foreign investor must have an advantage over the domestic investor in order to overcome the disadvantages of operating in a foreign culture and at a distance from its decision center. One of the possible advantages, especially relevant in bulky primary products like oil and iron ore that are costly to ship and store, is that a vertically integrated company can sometimes coordinate different stages of production more efficiently than a system of disaggregated markets. Production, shipment, processing, and distribution must be articulated with some precision, if it is expensive to have excess supplies or gaps in supply at separate stages. This may require an overall directing brain which the disaggregated market, with separate decision making at each stage, does not provide. Long-term contracts are a partial substitute for this vertical integration but raise awkward questions of dependence at times of renegotiation and renewal.

There is an element of monopsony here, to be sure. Highly efficient units at a given stage may be unwilling to operate independently for fear of being cut off from sources of supply or potential marketing outlets by an oligopolistic industrial structure. Once vertical integration enters an industry with only a small advantage, it tends to spread with little or no economic justification. But the economic efficiency of coordinated operations in different stages of production, where there are economies to be gained from such coordination, must mean that there are many cases where $S_f > S_h$. This seems to be the explanation of why Japanese ownership in Australian iron mines is appropriate, why Hirschman may be wrong in recommending blanket divestment of foreign investment in Latin America, and it supports Adelman's position that the large international oil companies will still find a place when and if they have been pushed out of producing areas and when the consuming and producing countries have failed any longer to hold up the price of world oil.[7]

The foreign company's advantage over local enterprise may lie in marketing even without the economies of coordination just outlined. These economies are probably not important in copper, but both in Zambia and Chile arrangements for government acquisition of 51 percent ownership of producing mines provide for management and sales by the foreign firm. In the case of Sociedad Minera El Teniente, *SA*, the Chilean government owns 51 percent and the Kennecott Copper Corporation (through the Braden Copper Company) 49 percent, but Kennecott has a contract with the board of directors — a majority appointed by the Chilean government — to manage the operations of the mine and "an Advisory Sales Contract that calls for our advising the board on market conditions, pricing and related matters."[8] Where the marketing company has a special advantage, it must be presumed that the marketing fee includes a rent on its scarcity. But in complex bargaining situations of this sort, where there is no competitive standard, it would be difficult to measure such rent.

There is no clear indication whether S_f is equal to, exceeds, or falls short of S_h. Anything can happen — circumstances alter cases. There is every reason to examine the circumstances of a particular case and arrive at a judgment as to the extent of real economies of marketing and of monopsony power, both those that can be evaded and those that cannot.

Labor Costs

In the enclave case, where the foreign company brings in workers from the home country (or even one hundred years ago in the guano industry in Peru from China), L must be subdivided into L_h and L_f, and possibly L_f into L_{home} and $L_{contract}$.[9] Disregarding these cases, however, we may focus on the rent which local labor, L, may earn under foreign investment. This is $(w_f - w_h)L$ in equation (3) and is positive though not always sizable. This increases domestic purchasing power, and thus has local benefits. It may also have the costs of creating a dual economy and disincentives for ordinary labor to work at occupations outside the foreign investment sector, as opposed to waiting for a job in that sector.

If the shadow price of domestic labor is zero, the total $w_f L$ is a gain for the less developed country in equation (3), but the dual-economy complications are more serious. If labor unions organize and push up the discriminatory wage paid by foreign investors, the external economies in training from the foreign investment may be reduced as more home country labor is brought in, or more foreign capital, to substitute for domestic labor.

Capital Costs

Typically, one can expect $r_f < r_h$. This is another element of monopoly. One theory of direct investment asserts that plowed-back profits are the cheapeast form of savings and need to earn only slightly more than the government bond rate in the home country to make it worthwhile for the corporation to expand rather than to pay out earnings to its stockholders. Where continued expansion in its home market is likely to cut prices and profits, a company may go abroad and expand in a noncompeting area. Under this theory a firm need not earn more abroad than at home to undertake foreign investments, or more abroad than its local competitors, so long as it earns more than the long-term government bond rate at home and is able to avoid depressing home profits. To the extent the theory applied at all, it is more relevant to direct investment in manufacturing than to primary production.

Even if we reject the cost-of-capital theory of direct investment, however, it is likely that $r_f < r_h$. This is the original basis for thinking that direct investment belongs to the theory of capital movements rather than, in the present view, to oligopoly theory. With separated capital markets (and no other distinct advantage in technology, management, and the like) direct investment would flow, like portfolio capital, from capital-rich to capital-poor countries. Only with capital markets perfectly joined and perfectly competitive, with $r_h = r_f$ for all kinds of borrowers, does the cost of capital become irrelevant to direct investment. The basis for thinking $r_f < r_h$ is either that capital markets are imperfectly joined or that they are not perfectly competitive, so that larger and better-known firms have an advantage over smaller and less well-known borrowers. In this latter circumstance the foreign firm may have an advantage in borrowing at a cheaper rate than the host country enterprise, even in the host country capital market. It seems that McKinnon and Shaw are exploring the infant-industry aspects of capital markets in less developed countries to test the hypothesis that learning by doing is strong in them and that there is merit in discriminating against the borrowing by foreign firms on the ground that this inhibits the step-by-step development of a flourishing capital market, which is vital to development.

A fortiori the foreign firm has an advantange over the enterprise of the less developed country when it comes to borrowing in the capital market of the developed country, especially when the borrowing record of the less developed country is complicated by past defaults or rolling over of debts.

Technology and Management

There is no counterpart for $pRDM$ in equation (2) that expresses the present value of the investment to the foreign firm. This is because it is assumed that the costs of research and development and management, including market management, are sunk and that incremental costs of extending these services to a particular foreign investment are negligible. This will not always be true of course, particularly in instances where it is necessary to modify the technology appropriate to developed countries before it can be used in less developed situations. In addition in the long run the company may feel it necessary to spread its overhead evenly over all operations. Research and development could be regarded as an investment on which the company had to earn a return in every use. In this case it could be included with K on which the company wanted a return of r_f or with equity on which it required D_f. The question whether foreign subsidiaries are charged management fees or whether these are lumped with profits and taxed may turn on such questions as whether a given subsidiary is a joint venture or 100 percent owned. It may be necessary in some cases therefore to allow for a $pRDM_f$ which is distinct from $pRDM_h$.

Whether $pRDM_f$ is zero or positive, however, it is likely to be lower than $pRDM_h$. In less developed countries local entrepreneurs who need technology or management services, including marketing, may be expected to pay for them at competitive and not monopoly prices, that is, when they can get the RDM services at all. Many firms in developed countries choose to invest abroad rather than to license, because they keep their proprietary interest in the technology inviolate by not renting it out and because the market for technology does not squeeze out the last bit of rent available, as direct investment may do. Much technology is available on license of course, and there is a borderline where the decision to license or not is a close one. Moreover new technology can be produced to order by specialized research firms, though results cannot be guaranteed and the services are said to be expensive. A local firm in a less developed country may find it sufficient to hire management consulting services rather than employ foreign enterprise full time. Nonetheless, there is likely to be a higher cost, or less service, in research, development, and management when a firm is owned locally than when it is foreign.

Government Expenditure

G_h is provided by the host country; G_f is the annual cost of economic overhead capital of the sort usually provided by government to which the foreign investor may be required to contribute, in a few cases of large companies investing in fairly primitive economies. Aramco's construction of ports and railroads in Saudi Arabia would be one example; likewise, the United Fruit Company's initial investment in Central American railroads. For the host country this G_f may pay external economies (EE), but in most cases G_f serves primarily the interests of the foreign investor. Where it is a railroad such as that from Ras Tanura to Mecca, built by Aramco for the Saudi Arabian government with little or no benefit to the company, it is evidently in lieu of taxes and could be consolidated with T_h.

G_h is government expenditure which the host government must undertake to make the foreign investment viable. It is assumed to have no external economies or to be net of external economies. It is unlikely to be a net benefit rather than a cost, although it might be that unanticipated external economies made the *ex post* result positive rather than negative. In any case it is assumed to be no different before or after nationalization.

Taxes

Taxes raise a particular problem of the time profile because of the shift of bargaining power from a time before a foreign investment is installed until after it is fully developed. Before a concession is granted, the weight of bargaining power is largely on the side of the company. Countries grant tax concessions to compete for potential investments, although they are urged by such economists as Bhagwati, Díaz-

Alejandro, and Rosenstein-Rodan to form cartels and limit the erosion of contract terms. Once the investment has been made, however, the balance shifts. The increase in levels of taxation is most clearly seen in petroleum, where small royalties per barrel gave way to income tax schemes, taxing corporate profits at levels that mounted from 25 to 50 percent and finally as high as 75 percent, followed by calculating income on the basis of posted rather than actual prices and of hypothetical rather than realized income. The Organization of Petroleum Exporting Countries (OPEC) insists on the legitimacy of contract renegotiation, not unknown in Anglo-Saxon practice when the circumstances prevailing at the time of the original contract have drastically changed. Such renegotiation, when no objective circumstance has changed other than bargaining power, raises subtle questions of legality to which an economist has nothing to contribute.

Taxes on oil companies in the Middle East have risen from $1 billion in 1960 to $6 billion in 1969. We do not have data available on other primary products such as tin in Malaysia and Indonesia, iron ore in Africa, Latin America, and most recently Australia, or copper in Africa and Chile. It is evident, however, that the variability of profits with export prices is an important qualification to Raúl Prebisch's controversial view that the long-run terms of trade tend to turn against primary producers. Such terms of trade on merchandise account fail to measure adequately the distribution of welfare between the industrial-investing country and the primary-producing host. For this purpose we need what have been called variously the terms of trade on returned value[10] or the terms of trade on current account with the rate of profit earned by the investor, which had been declining, shown as an offset to the decline of export commodity prices.[11]

Note that the capacity of less developed countries to tax is fairly well developed when they confront a few large raw-material producers but less so in import-competing lines. In the former case they are not inhibited by the requirement of national treatment and can tax directly and indirectly through other means such as multiple exchange rates, up to the limits of the companies' reserve price at which they will pull out. It is important not to go too far. The rate of tax and the definition of what is income are both largely in the control of the host country. In import-competing industry, however, it is not so clear. There is growing evidence that some (a few? many?) foreign investors require their subsidiaries to buy equipment, components, and raw materials from an international subsidiary and charge higher than competitive prices. The purpose is to transfer profits from one jurisdiction to another, often a Panamanian- or Bahamas-based tax haven, in order to minimize taxes. The opportunities for this sort of manipulation are evidently less in raw-material production, where the bulk of the value added, apart from profit, is locally produced, than in import-competing manufacture. The remedy lies not in forbidding foreign investment so much as reducing tariffs on the final product and increasing the sophistication of tax officials so that they will be in a better position to define the income on which the taxes are levied.

Taxes are the main benefit to the less developed country from foreign investment in primary production. The rent to domestic labor and external economies, though interesting in particular cases, is typically less significant than the level of taxation. Here the host country wants high taxes on old investments where its bargaining power is strong and low taxes on the new investments it hopes to entice. Case-by-case tax determination or a discriminating monopoly is the optimum strategy for such a less developed country but is generally excluded by the nature of competition and the legal principle on nondiscrimination. Cartels to prevent competitive tax concessions, already referred to, are hardly proof against the real divergence of interests of rival countries seeking a single investment. But the national payoff to better training in tax law and fiscal economics is probably high.

External Economies and Diseconomies

EE are external economies and diseconomies. They fall into three categories: EE_{G_f}, the benefits to the local economy from economic and social overhead investment undertaken by the foreign investment firm, which may be taken to be positive; EE_f and EE_h, which are the external economies, positive and negative, from the foreign investment itself and from its nationalization. The external economies may include Hirschman-type linkages which stimulate the growth process and training effects, including those in technology and management which reduce dependence on foreign investment, change the bargaining position, and enable the host country over time to command an increasing share of the rent. It is assumed that all external economies accrue to the host country and none to the foreign firm, although this may not be true where the investor's advantage lies in his capacity to achieve economies of scale by articulating production in several markets. This last is more likely to be the case in import-competing manufacture— as, for example, the articulation of Ford production in Britain, Belgium, and Germany—than in raw-material production. The enhanced benefit to the producer from vertical integration over competitive markets at separate stages of raw-material production has already been treated in the difference between S_f and S_h.

EE_h may well be negative if the country's credit standing is affected by its action in nationalizing particular foreign-owned property. The Peruvian government, for example, has taken two full-page advertisements in the *New York Times* in an attempt to persuade investors that the trouble with the International Petroleum Company and the nationalization of certain Grace agricultural properties did not alter its policy of welcoming foreign investment.[12] These advertisements emphasize the continued investment programs of IT&T and the South Andean Copper Company, although the first involves some disinvestment, and there is evidence elsewhere in the press that the second represents a reluctant decision to keep on investing for fear of losing the substantial assets already accumulated. Any loss owing to the invoking of the Hickenlooper amendment or similar retaliation would be included under EE_h. EE_h differs from EE_f in two respects therefore. Although certain economies such as linkages are identical whether the investment is foreign or domestic operated, some training and management economies may be smaller with domestic operation, and some diseconomies may ensue from nationalization.

EE_h has a somewhat asymmetrical quality. A reputation attractive to foreign investors is difficult to build and easy to lose. An individual investor may be exasperating in the way he transgresses local law, extracts exorbitant profits, and the like, but he enjoys the protection against penalty that the local government wants to maintain a "good climate for foreign investment." With growing sophistication in the investment process on the side of investors and governments, however, it will ultimately be possible to deal with separate cases on their merits without concern for these externalities.

Amortization

Where foreign investments are bought up locally, as in Chile, Ecuador, Bolivia, and Peru in Latin America and Tanzania and Zambia in Africa, there may or may not be compensation. The doctrine asserted by the United States in the Mexican Eagle case is that compensation should be "prompt, adequate, and effective," which means the capital value of the assets, payable immediately in convertible foreign exchange. In any event this doctrine, which requires a payment to the owners equal to D_f, has been watered down. Payment is usually made on an annual basis, often in kind in the product of the investment.

The formula for discounting a perpetual stream of incomes does not properly apply to a flow of compensation payments for a stipulated period. Where the period is a long one, and the discount rate is high, however, the difference is negligible. Yet in many cases host country and firm abandon all pretense of using present discounted values for estimating payments due but rather adopt the fiction that a dollar tomorrow is the same as a dollar today. The practice is widespread in international debt negotiations of moving this year's debt service, which, say, Ghana or Indonesia cannot pay, forward to follow the last scheduled payment without regarding the debtor as in default. The present value of the payment may decline by as much as 90 or 95 percent in these cases, depending on the rate of discount applied. Creditors' consortia adopt this fiction, in defiance of the economic doctrine that bygones are bygones, because they are fearful that default and readjustment of principal may be infectious. By the same token firms are bought out by eminent domain and paid the nominal value of asset ceded, but over time and without interest, and their governments accede in the arrangement from an inability to do better. But the economist should recognize that in these cases, though

$$\sum A = \text{PDV}(S_f - w_f L - r_f K - T_h - G_f),$$

that

$$\text{PDV}(A) < \sum A.$$

Risk

Ex post, of course,

$$\text{PDV}(A) = \text{PDV}\,[(S_f - w_t L - r_f K - T_h - G_h)z),$$

where z is the risk of nationalization. But z must be calculated *ex ante* before a company can judge whether to undertake a given investment. Operationally, the *ex post* value is of limited importance.

Note that it would be possible to include z with D_f, the foreign rate of discount. It is better to separate it out, however, so as to indicate that a given firm has one rate of discount for all investments but different risks attaching to those in separate countries.

Nationalism

N, the satisfaction which a country gets from national ownership, N_h, or the dissatisfaction that it feels from foreign control over its resources,

N_f, takes us again to the contribution of Breton in "The Economics of Nationalism." Presumably, N_f is negative and N_h positive; that is, there is shame or unease from having domestic real assets owned and controlled from abroad, for reasons of group solidarity and xenophobia, and pride and satisfaction from domestic control. The values of N_f and N_h, expressed as negative or positive flows of income per year, depend on (1) the extent of foreign ownership, with N_f being larger the larger the proportion of total enterprise controlled from abroad; (2) the degree of development, with both N_f and N_h being larger for less developed and smaller for developed countries per unit of foreign or domestic control, however measured; and (3) the history of past investment, with N_h being larger the longer and more lurid the record of historic wrongdoing by foreign investors.

N_h may be positive for a country as a whole but negative for certain local groups of politicians and businessmen who work with foreign investors. Thus Frantz Fanon in *The Wretched of the Earth* believes it insufficient to nationalize foreign investment—it must be socialized as well.[13] On the other hand, the positive value of N_h may be small for the country as a whole and do little to reduce the situation of inequality, in which $C_{hf} > C_{h\text{nat}} - N_h$, but N_h is of great importance to particular politicians and even business competitors. Thus N_f and N_h, aggregated and disaggregated, are important political variables in many less developed countries and developed countries as well. The economist is perhaps in no position to measure them numerically, enabling them to be used to calculate C_{hf} and $C_{h\text{nat}}$ in equations (3) and (4), except by revealed preference.

Discount Rates

D, the rate at which streams of income are discounted to capitalize them, differs from r, the rate of interest on bonds, by virtue of business risks. z applies to political risks. Whether risks of foreign exchange control belong in D or z is a matter of indifference. As noted, z could be included in D but is not. The borderline is hazy.

In a riskless world, $z = 1$ and $r = D$. But in a classic world with a given state of the arts, economic men, modest government, no externalities, and competition, so that $S_t = S_h$, $w_f = W_h$, $r_f = r_h$, if there was still risk, D_f would probably be lower than D_h because of better capacity of some businessmen in some countries to manage business risk. This bears on the theory that direct investment arises from differences in the capacity of businessmen of different countries rather than any other advantage. In this classic world, $C_{f\text{nat}}$ would be less than C_f, and foreign investment would be desirable from the standpoint of world welfare.

D_h does not enter into the comparison between equations (3) and (4), since it is the same in both cases and so should play no part in any decision to nationalize a foreign investment. The difficulty is likely to arise when the host country is disaggregated and certain groups apply a high rate of discount to the negative items in equation (4), that is, to the need to pay for foreign capital, research, and management, and to the losses from discouraging future investments. In these cases political and business leaders presumably apply one rate of discount to the positive items S_h and N_h and a different and higher discount to the offsets. Under these conditions nationalization of foreign investment is irresistible.

Conclusion

A comparison between C_f and C_{hf} of equations (2) and (3) addresses the question of the division of benefits between the investing and the host country. This was the issue raised by Prebisch and Singer more than 20 years ago. The distributional question has a number of asymmetries where a gain or loss for one is not necessarily a loss or a gain for the other, for several reasons: z, perceived risk, which is less than 1 for the investing country but does not raise the return to the host; external economies for the host country, with no cost to the investor; N_f, which poses a political cost for the host but with no evident benefit for the home country; and even an equally divided stream of benefits would be discounted at different rates.[14]

It has already been suggested that C_f and C_h have both been growing, but C_{hf} at a faster rate than C_f in oil, and probably other areas such as iron ore, bauxite, and copper, as well. More data are needed.

A comparison between C_{hf} and C_{hnat} of equations (3) and (4) poses Bronfenbrenner's problem of the appeal of nationalization. It is assumed that in most cases the difference between all items but the last in the numerator on the right-hand side will be larger in equation (3) than in equation (4), and positive, so that apart from N_f and N_h, C_{hf} would be larger than C_{hnat}. This is especially the case if the external diseconomy from confiscation ($EE_h < 0$) is substantial, but is almost certainly the case otherwise. The critical issue is a political one. As noted, N_f is negative and N_h positive. They are not necessarily equal; they doubtless differ from country to country in absolute value, and they may have different time profiles. It is likely that in a country that feels strongly politically about foreign investment—perhaps by reason of historic wrongs—the pain of foreigner ownership ($N_f < 0$) is likely to remain high over a long time, albeit rising to periodic heights from time to time when the foreign corporations come into the news, whereas after nationalization, N_h, which is positive, will have a high value for only a short time and will thereafter decline. This may account for the willingness of some countries, such as Ghana, with a new government, to restore foreign ownership and management after nationalization.

A comparison between the value of a given project in foreign and in domestic ownership of equations (2) and (4) can be used without any hint of nationalization to illustrate the theory of foreign direct investment. Leave A, EE_h, and N_h out of equation (4)—A because it is zero, EE_h and N_h since they may be presumed small. Normally S_f will exceed S_h, and $r_f K$ will be less than $r_h K$. $pRDM$ moreover is a negative item in equation (4) not found in equation (2). The old advantage for C_h is cheaper labor.

With development, to be sure, S_h will approach S_f and even surpass it, as it contains substantial monopsony elements; $r_h K$ will approach $r_f K$ as the country's credit standing improves; and $pRDM$ will decline toward zero as doing leads to learning. The equations leave out the disadvantage at which the foreign investor works by virtue of the strangeness of the culture and the distance from the decision center. But if the time profile of returns in equation (4) changes through time, the discounting formula must be altered. The weight that future higher returns contribute to the present discounted value of the investment in national ownership then depends heavily on D_h. When it matures, the infant industry must pay for its care in childhood.

Notes

1. C. F. Díaz-Alejandro, "Direct Foreign Investment in Latin America," in *The International Corporation*, ed. C. P. Kindleberger (Cambridge: The MIT Press, 1970), p. 321.

2. A. Breton, "The Economics of Nationalism," *J. Political Econ.* 72 (1964):376–386.

3. We disregard the complications introduced by an irregular time profile of earnings, which of course is the normal expectation.

4. For the Prebisch contribution, see Economic Commission for Latin America (5, 6). See also Singer (16).

5. M. Bronfenbrenner, "The Appeal of Confiscation in Economic Development," *Econ. Develop. Cultural Change* 3 (1955):201–218.

6. C. Julien, *L'Empire americain* (Paris: Grasset, 1968), and H. Magdoff, *The Age of Imperialism: The Economics of U.S. Foreign Policy* (New York: Modern Reader Paperbacks, 1969), p. 207.

7. A. O. Hirschman, "How to Divest in Latin America, and Why," *Essays in International Finance*, No. 76 (Princeton: Princeton University Press, November 1969), and M. A.

Adelman, *The Multinational Corporation in World Petroleum*, ed. C. P. Kindleberger (Cambridge: The MIT Press, 1970).

8. See Michaelson (14). See also the similar arrangements between Zambia and the Roan Selection Trust, set out in the Statement by the Chairman, Sir Ronald L. Prain, accompanying the Roan Selection Trust Ltd. Annual Report for 1969.

9. J. Levin, *The Export Economy* (Cambridge: Harvard University Press, 1960).

10. M. Mamalakis and C. W. Reynolds, *Essays on the Chilean Economy* (Homewood, Ill.: Irwin, 1965).

11. C. P. Kindleberger, *The Terms of Trade: A European Case Study* (New York: Technology Press and Wiley, 1956), pp. 18ff.

12. *New York Times*, September 28, 1969, and November 16, 1969.

13. F. Fanon, *The Wretched of the Earth* (New York: Grove Press, 1965).

14. This presumes that there is no offsetting pride in foreign direct investments in the home country akin to the pride that countries derived from colonies. Some critics who believe in neocolonialism and imperialism may dispute this.

References

1. Adelman, M. A. The Multinational Corporation in World Petroleum. *The International Corporation*. C. P. Kindleberger, ed. Cambridge: The MIT Press, 1970, pp. 227–241.

2. Breton, A. "The Economics of Nationalism." *J. Political Econ.* 72 (1964):376–386.

3. Bronfenbrenner, M. The Appeal of Confiscation in Economic Development. *Econ. Develop. Cultural Change* 3 (1955): 201–218.

4. Díaz-Alejandro, C. F. Direct Foreign Investment in Latin America. *The International Corporation*. C. P. Kindleberger, ed. Cambridge: The MIT Press, 1970, p. 321.

5. Economic Commission for Latin America. *The Economic Development of Latin America and Its Principal Problems*. New York: United Nations, n.d.

6. Economic Commission for Latin America. *Economic Survey of Latin America, 1949*. New York: United Nations, 1951.

7. Fanon, F. *The Wretched of the Earth*. New York: Grove Press, 1965.

8. Hirschman, A. O. How to Divest in Latin America, and Why. *Essays in International Finance*, No. 76. Princeton: Princeton University Press, 1969.

9. Julien, C. *L'Empire americain*. Paris: Grasset, 1968.

10. Kindleberger, C. P. *The Terms of Trade: A European Case Study*. New York: Technology Press and Wiley, 1956, pp. 18ff.

11. Levin, J. *The Export Economy*. Cambridge: Harvard University Press, 1960.

12. Magdoff, H. *The Age of Imperialism: The Economics of U.S. Foreign Policy*. New York: Modern Reader Paperbacks, 1969, p. 207.

13. Mamalakis, M., and Reynolds, C. W. *Essays on the Chilean Economy*. Homewood, Ill.: Irwin, 1965.

14. Michaelson, C. D. Joint Mining Ventures Abroad: New Concepts for a New Era. The 1969 D. C. Jackling Award Lecture, American Institute of Mining, Metallurgical and Petroleum Engineers, Washington, D.C., February 19, 1969.

15. *New York Times*, September 28, 1969, and November 16, 1969.

16. Singer, H. W. The Distribution of Gains between Investing and Borrowing Countries. *Amer. Econ. Rev.* 40 (1950): 473–485. Reprinted in American Economics Association. *Readings in International Economics*. Homewood, Ill.: Irwin, 1967.

6

The Multinational Corporation in a World of Militant Developing Countries

In a penetrating study entitled *American Corporations and Peruvian Politics,* Charles T. Goodsell describes the Velasco-led government of Peru which came to power through a coup in 1968 as revolutionary: "Its principal values were uncompromising nationalism and economic populism; by systematic changes throughout the society and economy, the aim was to reduce social and economic inequalities, foster economic growth, and terminate dependence on the United States." "Uncompromising nationalism and economic populism" and the aim "to terminate dependence on the United States" or the developed world seem to me to characterize the environment in which the multinational corporation has had to operate vis-à-vis developing countries in the last decade or so.

Whether it is possible to reduce social and economic inequalities, to foster economic growth, and to terminate dependence on the United States, all at the same time, poses a question of fundamental importance for developing countries. Opinion on the role of private investment in economic development of underdeveloped countries ranges widely from the views of Presidents Eisenhower and Nixon that private investment ought to be relied on exclusively to furnish outside assistance, to those of the school that finds all investment and even foreign aid abhorrent and subversive of development. An Indian economist at Oxford University, Sanjaya Lall, has furnished a classification of opinion, with three classes that favor direct investment and three that oppose.

Previously published in George W. Ball, ed., *Global Companies, the Political Economy of World Business* (Englewood Cliffs, N.J.: Prentice-Hall, for the American Assembly, Columbia University, 1975), pp. 70–84.

Spectrum of Views on Foreign Direct Investment

In favor of foreign investment are (1) the business school or how-to-do-it approach; (2) the traditional economic, which emphasizes the contributions made by capital and technology; and (3) the neotraditional, which recommends investment but some international surveillance to provide countervailing power. Opposed are (4) the nationalist school, which finds many harmful aspects in private investment, believes its profits to be excessive, and wants to regulate it stringently on a national, case-by-case basis to capture its benefits without the evils; (5) the *dependencia* school with little coherent program but fear of foreign investment; and (6) the Marxists with a clear-cut doctrine of opposition.

Lall names names. The business school approach includes Robbins and Stobaugh; the traditional economic, Vernon (though he works partly in a business school) and me. Vernon and I are also partly in the neotraditional camp. Opposed to foreign investment are Streeten and Lall in the national school; Sunkel and Hymer among the *dependencia* group; and Magdoff, Sweezy, Frank, Weisskopf among the Marxists. If fear of dependence is akin to populism, as I believe, the antis, excluding the doctrinaire Marxists, emphasize nationalism and populism.

Economics and Politics of Direct Investment

There is a temptation to think of economics as favoring direct investment and politics as opposed. This is not accurate. We shall encounter later instances where economic and political analyses are in conflict, but there is a political side to the traditional economic view of our issue and an economic aspect to the nationalist. On the first score the antithesis may run between the international and national view. The traditional economic view would suggest that resources be invested worldwide where they can earn the highest return, to maximize world output in a Pareto-optimal sense. By Pareto optimal is meant a state of resource allocation in which no reallocation can make anyone better off without making someone else worse off. It is an efficiency criterion but not necessarily the most equitable distribution of income and welfare in the world. To the extent that the resulting income distribution was unacceptable, it should be altered through progressive (or possibly regressive) contributions to international programs and foreign aid: use the price and market system to allocate resources; budgets including transfers to deal with income distribution. The nationalist school, on the contrary, believes that international compensatory transfers to accomplish income redistribution are illusory, that the task of a national government is to maximize national income even at the expense of the cosmopolis. A certain amount of restriction on trade, investment, technology transfers, and the like, is acceptable despite distortion of resource allocation, if it adds to national income along lines technically known as the optimum tariff. In some cases they may be prepared to sacrifice some national income for other governmental objectives—economic objectives like higher employment or sociopolitical goals such as national cohesion. Mostly, however, they contemplate that the developing countries can be more independent and better off at the same time.

The clash between economics and politics is nowhere better illustrated than in the different forecasts made concerning the price of oil. My colleague, M. A. Adelman, who is a deep student of the economics of the world petroleum industry and who believes that cost determines price in the long run, thought the world price of oil was likely to fall from its 1973 posted level of $2.60 in the Persian Gulf more nearly to $2.10 for buyers. The Organization of Petroleum Exporting Countries (OPEC) was trying to raise the price, but Adelman thought the long-run marginal cost of perhaps 35 cents a barrel exercised a strong downward pull. He may still be right.

Meanwhile, however, another economist, Walter Levy, took the opposing view that OPEC, which inherited the position of the world cartel of the interwar period that had broken down through competition, would succeed in preserving its unity against chiseling at the margin. Neither of them, it is probably fair to say, had any idea that the Yom Kippur war would produce an oil embargo for purely political reasons with such devastating economic effects in demonstrating to OPEC the short-run inelasticity of demand. A small shut-in in production, plus a scramble for inventory, resulted in a 350 percent price increase. By the same token, however, it is likely that once the tension of the Mideast struggle is faded in memory, inching up of output by one country and another, along with small permanent reductions in demand, will make the price structure more and more difficult for OPEC to hold. Sheikh Yamani of Saudi Arabia evidently had this possibility in mind when he suggested positive price reductions in 1974. We will then be back to the 1973 position, when it was possible for the economist to predict on the basis of long-run cost that the price was too high, despite the brilliant device of an excise tax disguised as an income tax, and another to maintain that militancy of producing countries would dominate politically the economic factor of cost.

It is ironic, but not without poetic justice, that the countries that so long complained about monopoly profits on the part of international companies should now seek not to break up the monopolies so much as to take them over. The position is of course symmetrical. At the time when developed countries controlled the monopolies, there were few voices among them that inveighed against monopolies in foreign trade. Opposed to the Sherman and Clayton Acts for home consumption was the Webb-Pomerene Act which encouraged collusion in restraint of trade against foreigners.

Quasi Rents in Efficiency and Income Distribution

Much of the difficulty derives from the existence of rents and the struggle to possess them. In a world of perfect competition and no scarce resources, there are no rents. Price equals marginal cost equals marginal utility in consumption. Large consumer surpluses may exist, and some producer surpluses, if some resources are better for the production of given outputs than others. These latter rents are desirable in the economic system, though they create a political problem of unequal income distribution. Recent interpretation of the enclosures in England runs to the effect that whatever their effect on income distribution, they were desirable in the interest of efficiency. Without private ownership more efficient resources will be overused. Labor will crowd on to the best land until it drives the average return down to the wage level; for efficiency the marginal return of the last increment of labor should equal the wage. Without rent, there is overcrowding, underemployment, and opportunities to increase real output by charging rent and diverting labor into other occupations. The position can be illustrated by a problem in today's world. In the oceans, where it is impossible to charge rent, the better fishing grounds are overfished. Too many whales, for example, are killed through lack of rent. If the seas could be owned and rented, excessive resources devoted to fishing would be shifted into other occupations and world real income would be raised.

For efficient use of all natural resources, therefore, we need to charge rents on the best resources and to equalize marginal returns on other factors on these and no-rent mines, oil wells, and land. But in this, as in the enclosures, there is an economico-political problem as to who collects the rents. The Marxist view of the enclosures as primitive accumulation is that predatory members of society used force to push peasants off the land. There is some truth in this view, but much land was enclosed through voluntary negotiations, later ratified by Parliament. Similarly in the international economy access to the best natural resources was sometimes arrived at on a voluntary basis and sometimes had large elements of compulsion and force. The history of imperialism in such areas as the Belgian Congo or South Africa has been a struggle for rents. Laws worked out, not without trauma, in developed societies, were applied with the help of colonial rule to the world beyond Europe. Where the natives were not eliminated, they were typically pushed aside. Even political independence, for example, from Spain in South America, did little to alter arrangements already made with respect to rents or rules governing their future allocation. Developed countries felt that rents in resources in the developing world should go to their discoverers or to those who developed the technology for using them effectively. Native populations when they awoke at last to the existence of such rents, and especially after World War II when political independence spread widely in the Third World, insisted that these rents belonged to the new nation.

Each group based its contention on a different counterfactual argument, that is, a different scenario, if the term be permitted, as to what would have happened if the foreign company or multinational corporation had not developed the resource. To the multinational corporation, the alternative was no development; to the newly independent country, the alternative was equivalent development, perhaps somewhat delayed, with local citizens producing the capital, technology, management, and marketing, and reaping the rents.

This last is a nationalist view, and it underlies the preoccupation from 1958[1] to 1974[2] with resolutions proclaiming the permanent sovereignty of nation-states over the natural resources within their borders. It is perhaps ironic that the United Nations, established in the interests of internationalism, should be the vehicle of these strong expressions of nationalism.

With entry possible, and not too wide differences in the productivity of incremental resources, one would have expected competition to disperse most of the rent as consumers' surplus. This process has met resistance, however, from several sources: from owners of older resources, now rendered inefficient. Texas oil producers, and Ruhr, Durham, and Pas-de-Calais coal interests want to hold energy prices high to preserve and extend old rents. Moreover governments in consuming countries wanted revenue as well as to protect their fuel producers. The result has been that despite new entry—the international oil companies rising from a handful in 1928 to 5, 7, and then 40 by 1968—the price remained relatively high, and the rents on Saudi and Kuwaiti production intact. But competition was spreading:

discoveries occurred in Libya, Nigeria, Indonesia, the gas fields off the Dutch coast, the British North Sea, and the North Slope of Alaska. New entrants lowered the price to establish a market after which they were prepared to join the cartel and shut the door. The burden of making room for them on the original five or seven international companies increased. The price started to fall.

A Digression on Exploitation

Before I recite more of the potted history of international oil it may be well to pause briefly on a semantic point and discuss the meaning of the words *exploitation* and *excessive profits*, which feature prominently in the debate. By exploitation I mean more than "to use" as when one exploits a given resource; in the discussion of private investment in developing countries, exploitation has a pejorative connotation, closer to "abuse," or "use in some unfair fashion." It is true that one commentator who fits the sixth category of Lall's taxonomy of views on the subject, Johan Galtung, defines dependence of any kind as "exploitation." A wife who depends on her husband is exploited, as is a husband who depends on his wife. Interdependence is mutual exploitation. *Dependencia* in category five, however, is one-sided, not mutual as in trade among developed countries or two-way investment among the United States, Europe, and Japan. Some years ago Edith Penrose defined exploitation by an international company as a higher price on goods sold, or a higher profit, than the minimum it would take to stay in business (i.e., the reserve price, or the normal rate of profit below which it would in the long run move into another business). Where there are big rents, however, and the problem is how to divide them, all solutions are exploitive in this sense. At the country's reserve price the country is being exploited by the company; at the company's reserve price, vise versa. In between, each is exploiting the other. By the same token excessive profits are any above the long-run normal rate achieved through competition; that is, rents are excess profits. In a resolution of 1968, OPEC decided that "notwithstanding any guarantee of fiscal stability that may have been granted the operator, the operator shall not have the right to obtain excessively high net earnings after taxes. The financial provisions of contracts which actually result in such excessively high net earnings shall be open to renegotiation."[3]

Contract Renegotiation

Renegotiation of contracts is of course not unknown in the developed country's jurisprudence. In defense contracts, the Pentagon used to set prices tentatively and provide for renegotiation so that if these resulted in substantial profits based on cheaper costs than initially foreseen, prices and profits could be adjusted. A television or sports star who makes a big success suddenly is apt to have his old contract torn up and a new one written. But OPEC has made a fine point of renegotiation, based on any number of circumstances. When the dollar was devalued in December 1971, and again in February 1973, old contracts with time to run were unilaterally canceled and new ones negotiated. Although the contracts were written in dollars, it was intolerable to OPEC to lower the price of oil in deutsche marks, Swiss francs, or yen. Moreover it is easy to guess that countries like France, England, and Japan which made contracts to buy oil from Iran at high prices in the winter and spring of 1974 would not be granted the same freedom to renegotiate when underlying circumstances have changed and the price of oil declined from its high level of that period.

When the economic system is working satisfactorily, high profits, or perhaps they should be called excessive profits, are a signal that a particular good is in scarce supply. Potential competitors are thereby encouraged to effect entry into the industry, stepping up their exploration efforts in oil as in the 1950s and 1960s. High profits recorded by General Motors-Holden Propriety Co. Ltd. in Australia in the early 1950s, sharply criticized at the time, were competed away by new entry from other automotive companies from the United States, Europe, and Japan, to the evident benefit of the consumer. Entry may be impossible on a substantial scale. It may be impossible to find new strikes of the size and quality of those in Saudi Arabia and Kuwait. In these cases high profits (rents) will persist and will be struggled over by company and country. The company hopes for a bidding up of the value of its shares, reducing the rate of return to stockholders to a normal level; it also hopes for new and more favorable contractual arrangements when an opportunity for increased investment presents itself, and it is in position to threaten to withhold its necessary cooperation.

The country, on the other hand, raises taxes, taking over the rent in the same fashion that Henry George once proposed for the rent of land in urban settings. The country may also demand a portion of the equity of the company—25 percent, 51 percent, or the totality. In this circumstance the rent is divided between company and country, depending on the price of compensation for the part of the company sold. If the price is book value, dropping any fine points, the rents accrue to the country; if market value at normal rates of taxation, to the company. These do not represent the limits of course. In the IPC case in Peru the country entered a claim for back taxes on long distributed or reinvested profits, which wiped out the company equity. And a usual tactic is to offer to pay book value not in a single sum but over an extended period and without interest, which renders its present discounted value well below book.

The initial deal may have involved duress (a gunboat in the harbor), unequal bargaining power (between, say, tough Dutchmen and the Indians who sold Manhattan for $24 worth of beads and other trade goods), misrepresentation, extraterritoriality, bribery, corruption, lack of disclosure, and any one or more of a long list of faults which would invalidate a modern contract. Or they may not. In *American Corporations and Peruvian Politics* Goodsell finds that the *dependencia* and Marxist view, that American corportions control domestic politics by bribes, favors, domination of the mass media, and intervention by the American government to establish economic dependence of Peru on the companies, is sustained in part but refuted in part. Similarly the alternative business school hypothesis that American corporations avoid participation, minimize visibility, and bargain effectively over investment terms is verified to some extent but not totally. The most scandalous episodes recounted by Goodsell for Peru, and by Barnet and Müller in a new populist American account of the MNC, *Global Reach*, have a musty flavor and go back to the 1920s. There are an occasional IT&T Chile episode and plausible allegations such as those about the CIA in Iran in 1950 and Guatemala in 1954. Goodsell makes the persuasive case, however, that a wide variety of conduct exists on the part of American corporations, and that once the Peruvian Junta nationalized IPC, the Grace properties, the Morrison-Knudsen property, and after General Motors quit the country, the "revolutionary" government first ignored the remaining corporations and then quietly began dialogue with them to induce new investments and to make existing ones more productive.

In economics bygones are sunk costs to be forgotten. Historical wrongs, however, have a present discounted value for politicians who can win short-term victories with them. Once the politicians have gained power—which earns a rent for them—their objective function is likely to change. The economic gain from prospective development becomes more important than the political benefit of beating a dead horse, and nationalism, populism, and *dependencia* as slogans become blocks to getting business done. An insecure government like Amin's in Uganda, Allende's in Chile, and even Frei's in Chile needs to nationalize another foreign corporation each six months. Once secure, it may be necessary to disguise the fact of paying compensation for past appropriations, by converting the capital sum due into a management fee on a marketing contract. It was alleged in the press, although I have lost the reference, that Peru nationalized the Chase Manhattan Bank branch with an excessive level of compensation to assuage the Rockefeller owners of both Chase Manhattan and IPC for the derisory compensation for the latter—the story, however, makes little sense on its face given the disparity in the ownership of the two institutions. But the political benefits of nationalistic gestures and the subsequent costs of appearing to undo them may require a certain degree of political dissembling to cover economic cooperation.

Transfer Pricing

In one important respect a "wrong" is current rather than historic. Some years ago Australia found that ostensibly competing oil companies had very different profits. One, a joint venture owned fifty-fifty by Australian and American interests, earned respectable profits in Australia and paid Australian corporate income taxes. Others, 100 percent foreign owned, earned no profits in Australia and paid no income tax. Their profits were earned in the Middle East where they qualified for depletion allowances and lower taxes. Vertically integrated oil companies, where there was no need to keep local shareholders happy, tended to arrange transfer prices between stages so as to reap their profits at the crude-oil level where taxes were least. Later, a Harvard Development Advisory Service representative discovered that some pharmaceutical companies were earning no profits and paying no taxes in Colombia and paying prices on purchase of intermediate products from a Panama subsidiary, which accumulated the profits of the company in a tax shelter there.

Evidence on transfer pricing is difficult to obtain, of course, and most tax authorities are not as astute as was Constantine Vaitsos, the adviser in question. It is accordingly difficult to know how widespread the practice is. True believers from either the business school approach or from the *dependencia*-Marxist school will tend to hold different views on the same limited amount of evidence. In the United States a businessperson informs me that a ruling by the Internal Revenue Service, that transfer prices would be policed to see that they conformed to the arm's-length, competitive price, or a simulated facsimile thereof, turned virtually every American company into a model taxpayer in this respect overnight. This may or may not be so. In the underdeveloped world of the nationalist, *dependencia*, or Marxist school, pharmaceutical transfer pricing lives on in generalized form. Siphoning off the rent through transfer pricing may or may not take place but is suspected everywhere.

The tension between the economic and the political views of the multinational corporation is nowhere better illustrated, as a crucial experiment for the next months, than in the debate over whether the crunch in oil will be followed by similar squeezes in other primary products. Already in motion is a series of efforts to raise taxes on bananas, bauxite, copper, tin, and the like. If the OPEC success is purely political, it is likely to be followed by others, as C. Fred Bergsten has predicted in *Foreign Policy*. If, on the other hand, militancy is not enough, and the elasticities must be low, these efforts will not succeed. Consumption of bananas will decline relative to apples, grapefruit, oranges, and so forth, and aluminum use will decline relative to steel.

Fighting over rents is perhaps the main issue in the tension between the MNC and the less developed country (LDC). There is, however, another profound issue—the extent to which economic development should and can use market signals. The MNC responds to the market, even where it does not manipulate it. If the LDC is convinced that resources should not be allocated according to market signals, it will and should resist the MNC. Where the market does not work, even the traditional economist does not insist on using it. In economic jargon, with market failure we are in the realm of the second best. And the only valid argument for tariffs, or against direct investment, is the second best. Something is wrong with the market that gives off misleading signals. In this case it is a mistake to follow its prescription.

Market Efficiency in LDCs

Markets do not work when there is monopoly, imperfect information, failure of households, factors, or firms to respond to price signals. In these circumstances prices reflect neither scarcities nor needs, or to the extent that they do, they fail to elicit the appropriate response. For one example, take the infant-industry argument for a tariff or against foreign investment. With perfect information and perfect capital markets, local entrepreneurs would not need a tariff—or restrictions on foreign investors. They would be able to borrow to cover early losses or less-than-normal profits. Or take the Colombia pharmaceutical case: the first-best solution is to watch import prices and enforce the rule of arm's-length prices in intracompany dealings. Only if this is impossible, is it valid as second best to exclude foreign investors because of potential exploitation.

A general case can be made by the nationalists, *dependencia* school, and Marxists that the market in developing countries does not and will not represent social priorities. Consumer sovereignty is barred because of the alleged distortions of advertising, excessive product differentiation, and consumer ignorance. Foreign firms should not be allowed to borrow in the capital market that is underdeveloped, needs to learn by doing, and might be stunted in its development were it to be monopolized by foreign borrowers. Foreign firms bring in the wrong technology, responding to factor proportions in the home country and the benefits of standardization. The best is the enemy of the good. The second or third best may be good enough, or as good as one can hope for. Included in the second or third best may be wide-ranging control of foreign enterprise.

Or so the argument runs, though it is seldom so explicitly made. Nor is it always consistent with another argument that intervention in the market by developing countries is so fraught with mistakes that they must be prevented, for example, from bidding for foreign investment by an Andes Pact that limits national sovereignty and the right to intervene separately.

There is something of a contradiction between seeking to appropriate the rents provided by the market and rejecting the market altogether as a guide to what to produce, how to produce it, and for whom. Manipulation and rejection are not perhaps entirely orthogonal, but they are close to it. And those who reject the market have the task of deciding what to use in its stead. Even traditional economics is prepared to recognize that the market does not provide divine revelation of the directions in which the economy, polity, and society should move. For all its failures, however, it tends to be like democracy— better than the attainable alternatives. Populism makes a strong case against the capital, credit, money, primary product, consumer goods, capital goods, and labor market. Dispensing altogether with markets and substituting planning with quantities rather than prices, or interfering in markets based on bureaucratic or political intuition, is likely to be worse.

There is little likelihood of closing the gap between the pros and the cons. The position is brilliantly illustrated by the UN report of the Group of Eminent Persons, and especially by Part II, the "Comments of Individual Members." Since the report of Eminent Persons had a faint nationalist and populist bias, though less than the staff report *Multinational Corporations in World Development*, five of the nine individual comments (out of twenty members) came from developed countries: two from the United States and one each from Japan, Sweden, and Switzerland, and all were long, detailed, and traditional economic. The comments from the Algerian, Chilean, Indian, and Yugoslav members were short and nationalist or Marxist, but in one instance recommended the incorporation of the staff report in the report of Eminent Persons.

Where there is no meeting of minds, it seems to me useless to paper the cracks. I believe in an international body to deal with problems arising in connection with multinational corporations among the developed countries, with a broadly similar point of view. Between the developed and the developing countries, however, it seems premature. Where there is no meeting of minds, agreement on a form of words, and the creation of machinery for discussion, are idle. Let the market decide. I suggest that the Eminent Persons recommendation of a commission to run a watching brief on the multinational corporation is likely merely to institutionalize the nationalism and populism of the developing countries. On previous occasions I have urged that governments of developed countries withdraw from this field, canceling their investment subsidies, guarantees, and tax credits. Companies can then decide on economic grounds, with allowance for political risk, whether it is worthwhile to invest in developing countries, and developing countries in turn can decide whether and on what terms they want foreign investment. If the dependence is mutual, as I believe, this market will be able to strike a bargain.

Notes

1. UN Resolution 1314 (XIII) of 1958 established a Permanent Sovereignty Commission which proposed a Resolution of Permanent Sovereignty over National Resources 1803 (XVII) in 1962.

2. See UN, Economic and Social Council E/5500/Add. 1 (Part 1) "The Impact of Multinational Corporations on the Development Process and on International Relations, Report of the Group of Eminent Persons to Study the Role of Multinational Corporations on Development and on International Relations," May 24, 1974, Section IV, "Ownership and Control," and Economic and Social Council Resolution 1747 (LIV) "Permanent Sovereignty over Natural Resources of Developing Countries," adopted May 4, 1973.

3. Resolution XVI 90 of 1968.

7

Ownership and Contract in International Business

Let me start this chapter with an analytical point in economic theory. The Coase theorem, developed by Ronald Coase of the University of Chicago, states that institutions do not matter in economic outcomes, or perhaps if there are different transactions costs one way or the other, they barely matter. The contrary view of course is that of institutionalists like John R. Commons or J. Kenneth Galbraith, on the one hand, or Karl Marx, on the other, that institutions are crucial to the economic system. A recent essay by James Meade on Jaroslav Vanek's work on the self-managed firm makes the point as well. Coase would claim that it makes no difference whether the cattlemen or the sheepherders own the range. It will be used for sheep or cattle depending on which is the more efficient or profitable as a use, an outcome in its turn that depends on supplies and demands. If the cattlemen own it, but raising sheep will command a higher return, the sheepherders will buy or rent it from the cattlemen and use it to raise sheep. By analogy, it makes little difference whether the multinational corporation owns a subsidiary in a developing country or merely has a contract to manage the property. The present discounted value of the use of the property for producing copper, or oil, or transistors, or whatever, will by and large be the same despite the nature of the institutions. My tentative thesis is that corporate-owned subsidiaries are likely to be different from contracts in their effects because contracts have limits and ownership does not. I am less interested in Galbraith's technostructure, Marx's view of private property as theft, or who in fact manages the firm. And it should be noted that even the Coase theorem presupposes some institutions, such as what Adam Smith calls magistracy. There must be some set of rules

A lecture in memory of Clair Wilcox, Swarthmore College, April 7, 1977.

of order which will prevent the sheepherders from slaughtering the cattlemen to take over their range.

A brilliant article by Jürg Niehans in *Multinationals from Small Countries* (The MIT Press) knits together the theories of international trade and industrial organization with a new insight. International-trade theory, he says, has room for vertical specialization. Countries do not have to perform all the stages of production of a given product in a single country. Intermediate goods can be bought and sold internationally. Cotton textiles in England and Japan are produced with cotton from the United States. Moreover, when different stages of production are located in different countries, there is the possibility that one stage of of production will hold another up. This may be intentional—as in bilateral monopoly; the monopolist will hold up his customer, or the monopsonist will hold down his supplier. One way to alleviate the tensions implicit in bilateral monopoly is for the two parties to merge and to internalize the profits. Or the tension may be completely un-intended: new processes may be difficult to install at one stage if they require complementary investment at earlier or later stages, and the market may have difficulty in working out who invests what, dependent on the investments of others, and how the joint profits are divided. A concrete illustration, which occurred to me some years ago, is the small inefficient freight cars in Britain, especially for coal. Neither the railroads that owned the locomotives and roadbed nor the coal mines that owned the coal cars and sidings could get together to change from 10- to 40-ton wagons that required new sidings or to equip existing cars with automatic brakes, since the market was incapable of solving the problem how to divide the investment, on the one hand, or the saving in costs, on the other. In systems where the cars and sidings were both owned by the railroad, along with traction and the right-of-way, profits were internal, and the investment in improved technology was undertaken. Corporations may buy their inputs from markets without fear of being cut off from their supplies, provided those markets are broad and competitive. They may also achieve safety in limited dependence on outside purchases through maintaining inventories, though some raw materials—crude petroleum, iron ore, coal, and the like—are notoriously bulky and expensive to store. One solution to fear of monopoly or monopsony (the monopoly buyer) is vertical integration. You buy him up to control his actions.

Note that when a company advances into continuous process industry at one level, it frequently integrates forward to marketing and backward to raw materials (across national boundaries) so as to be assured of outlets for produce and sources of supply for inputs. When Standard

Oil of California discovered oil in Saudi Arabia, it looked for an assured source of marketing. This was the basis for its merger with the Texas Oil Company. The later joint venture with the Standard Oil Company of New Jersey (as it used to be called in olden times) and Mobil (then Socony, from the initials for Standard Oil Company of New York) was to get access to additional capital and perhaps, *pace* the permission gained from the Antitrust Division of the Department of Justice to buy off the competition of those international rivals. The resulting Aramco had crude petroleum, refineries, pipelines, tanks, and marketing outlets. Similarly when BP (British Petroleum) found itself long on crude oil from the discovery on the North Slope of Alaska, it bought into Sinclair and Sohio (the Standard Oil Company of Ohio) to acquire a distribution network to match its access to basic crude.

But ownership is not the only means of acquiring assurances of outlets if one has product or product if one has outlets. There is the alternative of contracts. A contract to buy iron ore may be just as good as owning the mine, especially if it is a contract both to manage production and to market output, and the prices are right. The Coase theorem looks good in the light of these examples. And one should note that though there is widespread nationalization of resource-based industry, and multinational corporations are losing ownership of subsidiaries that owned mineral rights bought or derived from exploration, many of these nationalizations are being followed by contracts to manage and market the product. Zaire nationalized Union Minière but gave it a 25-year contract to handle the copper properties. Zambia took over a majority interest in the mines of Roan Selection Trust in 1967 but undertook a 10-year management and sales contract with it, on which Roan Selection Trust received 0.75 percent on copper sales, 2.5 percent on chrome sales, 2 percent on consolidated profits, 3 percent fees on certain investment projects, and 15 percent fees on the first-year salaries of foreign personnel. I do not know whether these prices are "right," but Smith, a lawyer, and Wells, an economist, who write about them, say that the Zambian exercise is regarded by most observers as partial expropriation, but close analysis reveals that investors may have been left about the same.[1] "The corporation is one form of planning," says Lowry, "and contracts are another."[2] A corporation has value that stems in one formulation from capitalizing the stream of income it is expected to produce. Equally, contracts reduce the future to the present.[3] On this showing, the Coase theorem is neatly applicable. Institutions do not matter. If Saudi Arabia chooses to take over Aramco but permits its former owners to organize a new corporation, Stemco (derived from the first letters of Standard Oil

Company of California, Texaco, Exxon, and Mobil) to handle the logistics of planning, transporting, and marketing the bulk of the oil production of Saudi Arabia, what difference does it make, assuming that the management and marketing fees of Stemco do not differ too widely from the aftertax profits of Aramco before nationalization?[4] Or the Caltex Petroleum Corporation may readily sell its assets to the government in India, as it did for $14.4 million in the fall of 1976, and do as well by supplying the now Socialist company 1.25 million tons of crude oil from the Middle East each year for five years, and presumably thereafter under renewed arrangements.

Nationalization under these circumstances may in fact be highly desirable all around since it defuses the nationalism and xenophobia that come from foreign ownership and control, while at the same time permitting the equivalent of direct investment to transmit from the advanced to the developing country the management, technology, marketing skills, and so forth, that direct investment would have provided in a different form. Only if the developing country is short of capital and lacks the credit standing to acquire it through capital markets is there on this showing a loss from the host country buying out the investment and converting ownership to contract.

But there are contracts and contracts, and some resemble ownership in economic essentials more than others. Ownership is a diffuse relationship, as Talcott Parsons would say, whereas contractual relationships are generally specific. Sir Henry Maine, you recall, suggested that as evolution proceeded substantive relations among individuals evolved from "status" to "contract."

There is a point here for the political scientists. There is evidence that bankers don't mind rather vague engagements and diplomats detest them. I don't know why this should be. J. P. Morgan was said to make loans based on the character of his borrower, rather than to require carefully specified collateral. In a passage in his book *The Arena of International Finance*, Charles Coombs notes that university economists generally feel "distaste and distrust of informally negotiated credit arrangement . . . that probably seemed to leave too much to the human factor."[5] On the other hand, diplomats are continuously reminding us of the need of precise engagements that specify exactly who must do what, when, and that open-ended commitments are dangerous.[6] The answer to this paradox may be that money and usage in finance already are precise in nature, so that engagements can go unwritten, whereas in dealings between countries with differing interests, traditions, and responsibilities, there is enormous room for failure of minds to meet even when a form of words has been agreed. The draft charter of the International Trade Organization, which Clair Wilcox's heroic labors produced in Havana in 1948 but was not ratified by the Congress, was not in fact submitted to the Congress, because it was felt that its exceptions to tariff reductions and abandonment of quotas were too wide, leaving room for other countries to evade obligations under the charter while the United States was thoroughly committed. Vague and diffuse understandings are adequate in the family, or in the banking fraternity. Where people deal with one another at arm's length, acres of fine print in contracts may not be enough.

Even where diffuse ownership and a "well-lawyered" contract amount to much the same thing, however, there is one significant difference: in the usual case, ownership is a continuing relationship, whereas contracts bear a terminal date. This is where my interest in economic history comes in, and a small digression, that is not, I think, without relevance to the multinational corporation may be in order. Some economic historians think it made a considerable difference to the response of British and Danish farmers to the decline in the price of wheat after 1880 that Denmark had owner-occupied farms whereas British farms were usually occupied by renters. Renting, which divides the functions of capitalist and laborer, is highly efficient under conditions of fixed technology and constant relative prices. But when prices change or large changes occur in technology, the market for rentals may have difficulty in producing the important and delicate coordination of the functions of the two parties. A shift from wheat to dairy products, for example, requires substantial capital investment in barns, fencing, livestock, and the like. On wheat lands, it was clear how inputs and outputs were divided between owner and tenant. With new inputs and outputs, a new relationship was required and the market found it difficult to work out who did what to whom and who got paid how much for it. In terms of the Coase theorem, the transactions' costs were too high to be overcome.

But even where renting was well established, there was a wide difference between the annual and the long-term lease. The annual lease discourages improvements; the long-term lease encourages them. A tenant is not much motivated to improve the owner's fields by drainage and the like if the result was likely to be an increase in rent at the end of the year. An Agricultural Holdings Act was passed in Britain in 1883 to enable tenants to claim compensation for improvements, but it proved highly one-sided in operation. A tenant would have been foolhardy to bring a claim under it, contemporary observers said, because of the necessity for elaborate documentation, on the one hand, and his vulnerability to counterclaims for violations of lease restrictions and to substantial penalties on the other.[7] England, with annual leases, did not shift over from grain to animal husbandry. Scottish farmers with a tradition of 19- or 21-year leases, did so much more frequently. English agricultural observers a century earlier excoriated not only the annual lease, which did not give a farmer time to reap the benefit of his improvements, but even leases as long as nine years. On the annual lease, listen to the sarcasm of Joseph Marshall who traveled in Eastern Europe in 1769 and 1770, but whose thoughts, like so many of ours, never strayed very far from home:

How much more beneficial it is to let out an estate to farmers, for them to find the stock, cultivate the land, and employ the peasants, not only in more profit of a year, but with a view to future improvements, which must always be conducted with far more effect by people who work for their own interest, than by others who do it for a master, and a master perhaps who is always absent, or, if present, who understands nothing of the matter. What great improvements have been made in England by tenants, who enjoy a benefit during their lease, and then pay a fresh rent to their landlords on account of those very improvements![8]

On the longer contract, I commend to you the wisdom of another inveterate traveler of the period, Arthur Young:

Give a man the secure possession of a bleak rock, and he will turn it into a garden; give him a nine-year lease of a garden, and he will convert it into a desert.[9]

A peasant does not think of making his pig comfortable, if his own happiness hangs by the thread of a nine-year lease.[10]

What I am saying is that a contract with a fixed early terminal date is altogether different in its incentives from a diffuse relationship, such as ownership, or a contract with a long time to run. The conditions of work may change under ownership. The host country may change the tax laws affecting foreign direct investment, may undertake to nationalize properties, or may impose new regulations. The life of a direct investor is far from certain. Contracts moreover may be renegotiated before they expire. This is amply illustrated from the experience of OPEC, where five-year contracts to sell oil for a specific price in dollars were unilaterally torn up and replaced by new ones every few months during the early 1970s, induced by political events on the one hand, or by changes in the value of the dollar on the other. When fundamental conditions change in contracts, the right of renegotiation is present even when there is no provision for it in the fine print. Uncertainty applies both to ownership and to contracts with a long time to run.

With a contractual lease or concession about to expire, however, uncertainty is bunched in a way that can be economically distortionary. Let me illustrate from the Venezuelan petroleum concessions, scheduled to expire in 1984 which were nationalized a couple of years ago to prevent, as the Venezuelan government claimed, their ruthless exploitation. A concession that is due to expire and that is not to be extended is like a contract that will not be renewed. The contractor wants to take maximum advantage of possession while he has it. Like the man with the nine-year lease of a garden which he is confident will not be renewed, the company is content to leave it a desert. Instead of exploiting oil in the ground at the MER (maximum efficient rate) which will optimize oil recovery over the lifetime of the field, the company will be interested in recovering as much oil as possible in the lifetime of the concession, without regard to what follows thereafter. As the end date for the concession came within a decade, therefore the Venezuelan government, desirous of having the concessions in fully working order in 1984, nationalized them to forestall excessive depletion. It is of some interest that the government's time scale and Arthur Young's so closely coincide.

This issue of what transpires after the end of the contract leads me to question the suggestions of my one-time colleague Paul N. Rosenstein-Rodan and of Albert Hirschman that direct investment be undertaken with scheduled disinvestment built into the system, for example, in a concession clause that the investment revert to the host country after a specific interval of time. The difficulty that I see with such a requirement is that the investing firm, believing that it is in effect giving away the assets remaining at the end of, say, 15 years, will want to ensure that at time $t + 15$, the assets turned over to the government are nonexistent and worthless, whereas the government is expecting to receive a going concern. An economist with whom I have discussed the matter suggests that if the investing firm enjoys the profits on an investment for 10 years at a reasonable rate of return of more than 10 percent, it will not care about the loss of the assets at $t + 10$, as it will have recovered its investment fully. The assets at $t + 10$ are worth nothing to it at period t. That is of course true. But as the terminal date approaches, there is a given time for any particular rate of profit, which makes the value of the asset at the end of the contract significant for its present discounted value. When that time is reached, the firm will have an incentive to deplete or depreciate the asset faster than would be efficient for a going concern, and if possible, to zero or a negative value.

We have been discussing contracts that will not be renewed, and in which it is known to both parties that there will be no renewal. Some contracts are nonrenewable in their nature, such as an installment purchase. Others like the lease of an apartment or a union contract with an employer are normally renewed. There may be provision for renewal in the contract, or legal restrictions on termination built into the framework of relations in the community. An employer cannot change unions at the expiration of a union contract, simply by virtue of generalized "freedom of contract." What is interesting about contracts between multinational firms and host countries is that at this stage of their evolution, there is no presumption that management and service contracts which substitute for ownership will or will not be renewed when their term runs out. Whether the approaching end of a contract has distortionary effects on economic incentives or not will depend to a great extent on whether or not there is such a presumption in a given case, or generally.

The greater the presumption of renewal on more or less the same terms, the less the distortion introduced by the approaching end of a given contract. If renewal is assured, but the terms of the contract are negotiated as if starting from the beginning, we are back to the annual farm lease where the tenant has no incentive to make improvements because they will be used against him to raise the rent the following year. Nonetheless, renewal time opens up the possibility of changes in terms and conditions of the contract, with resultant uncertainty and distortion of incentives. Where renewal on the old terms is automatic, a contract is equivalent to ownership. Contracts differ from ownership, first, in whether or not they are renewed automatically or following negotiation and, second, in the extent to which the terms of the contract are extended or rewritten, and if rewritten, whether in limited particulars or from scratch.

The contracts now being written between multinational corporations and host countries are generally wide open in these particulars. There is an indication perhaps in favor of renewal and extension of old terms in the sample contract to which I come. Let me first, however, pursue another digression into economic history dealing with renewals, on virtually unchanged terms of long-term contracts, where it was understood that renewal would take place. I refer to the charter of the Bank of England, renewed many times by the British government from 1694 to the nationalization of that institution in 1945 (when ownership was substituted for contract, without producing any significant result).

Before development of a broad-based capital market, the Bank of England and the British Treasury faced each other as a sort of bilateral monopoly. The Niehans solution of merger was ruled out by the political necessity of an independent central bank, but charter renewal afforded the treasury an opportunity to squeeze a new loan out of the bank each time. During the Napoleonic Wars, when the need for loans from the central bank was especially exigent, the exchequer made an agreement to extend the charter of the bank which still had 12 years to run, from 1812 to 1833, in exchange for a loan of £3 million for six years without interest. When the loan expired in 1806, the bank renewed it at 3 percent interest at a time when 3 percent consols were selling for 60 to yield 5 percent.[11]

The Bank of France charter renewal of 1897 provided the occasion for a reduction of its requirement of discountable paper from three signatures to two, with far-reaching effects in stimulating credit expansion and economic growth.[12]

Limits set by charters or contracts may present opportunities for improvements in institutions, or in the distribution of costs and benefits between parties to the arrangements. They may lead to disturbances, as in the expiration of labor contracts which hold out the promise or threat of strikes and lockouts before a new arrangement is made between the same parties. The approach of contract end dates is disturbing, distortionary, nervous-making—whatever is the right phrase. Boundaries disturb. Limits excite. The suspension of the Bank Act of 1844 in 1847 calmed the panic rush for liquidity by eliminating the prospect that the limit to the issue of bank notes would be reached. Sir G. C. Lewis, the Chancellor of the Exchequer, discussing the bill to indemnify the Bank of England for any damages suffered by reason of suspending the Bank Act, stated that "whenever you impose a limit, there is no question that the existence of that limit, provided it makes itself felt at a moment of crisis, must increase the alarm."[13] This is analogous to the expiration of a contract, if not an exact parallel. Considerably closer is the fact that the steel cartel in the 1930s would break down as the time for renewal of the agreement approached, as each group of national producers pushed exports with subsidies to establish a better statistical base for setting its quota under the new agreement.[14]

Still other disturbing limits can be furnished by history. The French were forced to make concessions to the Germans in the Dawes negotiations, as Stephen Schuker makes clear in his book published in 1976, because the five-year limit of the Treaty of Versailles—the period during which the Germans were forced to grant free trade to

French Alsace-Lorraine—was running out, and the French were unsure that after the expiration of the period they would be able to sell their cotton textiles from Alsace in Germany or buy coke needed for Lorraine iron.[15] Moreover the British were forced to take some action on sterling in 1925, since the Gold and Silver Act of 1920 suspending convertibility was coming to the end of its five-year limit. As it happened, they took the wrong action in restoring the pound to par. Limits perturb, if you will permit that as an intransitive verb.

Let us return to the multinational corporation and to the question of ownership vs. contracts. The longer the term of contract, the more thoroughly understood it is that the contract is likely to be renewed, and the less definite the time, place, and conditions of renewal, the more the contract resembles ownership. The fact of revision of the contract is not critical. As conditions in the market change, or the bargaining power of the parties, revision of the terms between the parties is likely, whether ownership prevails or a contract.

In their study of Third World mineral agreements, Smith and Wells provide an illustrative contract which would appear to reflect their view of the positive evolution of such agreements as well as a desirable direction. The provisions of this illustrative agreement are by no means unambiguous. Part IV provides for gradual takeover of "Foreign Overseas Investors, Inc." by "National Mineral Development Corporation," piecemeal over 25 years, an initial 24 percent share, raised to 30 percent after 8 years, to 50 percent after 15 years, 70 percent after 20 years, and 100 percent after 25 years. These salami tactics may destroy the force of my earlier argument that contractual disinvestment distorts efficient operation. I am inclined to doubt it; I rather suspect that the company will turn its attention to other profit opportunities some time between the 15th and 20th years.

If we disregard the disinvestment provisions, the illustrative draft contract furnished by Smith and Wells is beautifully ambiguous as to termination date. It is drawn to run for 25 years—longer than a Scottish farm lease of 19 or 21 years—but is subject to renewal for "an additional term of ____ years on the same conditions except those relating to income taxation, royalty payments, and other financial provisions . . . and may be renewed for a second additional period of ____ years on such terms as are agreed upon by the parties."[16] These clauses suggest a continuing relationship rather than one that is expected to terminate finally, as in the case of disinvestment provision. Moreover Smith and Wells suggest the usefulness of periodic revision under a general review clause, at least of the financial articles, to make explicit what is in any event implicit in either ownership or contracts, the need for renegotiation when underlying circumstances change.[17] Nor is this one-sided. Article XXII of the draft on the agreement period, after indicating that the agreement should run for 25 years, goes on to state:

It is understood and agreed that at any time the Company may propose a substantial new investment in the Project or shall require an extension of this Agreement in order to facilitate additional financing, long-term sales contracts, or otherwise, and in any event, at least five years prior to such expiration date, the Government will give sympathetic consideration to a request by the Company to extend the terms of this Agreement to permit continuation of the Project on the basis of long-term planning and sound mining and operating practices and to assure continuing employment of those devoting their time and efforts to the success of the Project.[18]

I have no idea how persuasive these ideas and language may prove to be to host countries. They seem to me highly useful, however, in making clear the continuing rather than one-shot nature of the collaboration, if that be acceptable to the host country, and in defusing the explosive force of the terminal date in the contract.

    I wrote this chapter in the fall of 1976 because I knew I would have a busy spring. One night after that in bed it struck me like a thunderclap that I had said nothing about the impact of floating exchange rates on the difference between ownership and a contract. How far in the irresponsibility of old age does one stray from the passions of youth! It is too late at this writing to unravel the tangle. But let me make a few points of interest to economists, if not to lawyers:

1. In the absence of fixed exchange rates there is no international money, and money is needed as a public good for making contracts.

2. With floating exchange rates that are always at purchasing-power parities, ownership will be superior to contracting, since exchange-rate fluctuations will be offset by relative price changes and presumably changes in profits. With one or more fixed variables, and especially with deviations from purchasing-power parities, ownership and contracts will both be adversely affected, but contracts more than ownership.

3. There will be fanatics among economists who think that international trade and international business are improved by floating exchange rates. I differ. But of course we compare with different counterfactuals. They choose flexible exchange rates over fixed with uncoordinated monetary and other macroeconomic policies; I choose fixed exchange

rates with coordinated policies over flexible exchange rates with countries pursuing national policies autonomously.

Flexible exchange rates weaken my case, because flexible exchange rates mean an absence of international money, and money is needed as a standard for contracts.

On previous occasions I have stated that the multinational corporation is economically desirable under certain circumstances relating to the absence of monopoly, and the like, but suffers the political disability that it is regarded widely as involving control of the economy by foreigners. The substitution of contract for ownership can overcome the reality or appearance of foreign control. Contracts can be the same as other institutions, as the Coase theorem would contend, except, in the ordinary case, for the distortion of incentives and behavior set in motion by the approach of their termination. If this issue can be resolved in a way that lowers the visibility of any one terminal date, while emphasizing a continuous contractual relationship subject to change by either party as conditions call for it, progress in economic development along this dimension is possible. But in international business, as on the dance floor, it takes two to tango. Cooperation, and not confrontation, is needed for success. However specific the rights, duties, obligations, and benefits, at basis, both host country and multinational corporation must have in mind a diffuse mutuality of endeavor, stretching out some distance into the uncertain future.

Notes

1. David N. Smith and Louis T. Wells, Jr., *Negotiating Third-World Mineral Agreements, Promises as Prologue* (Cambridge, Mass.: Ballinger, 1975), p. 24.

2. S. Todd Lowry, Bargain and Contract Theory in Law and Economics, *Journal of Economic Issues* 10 (March 1976):15.

3. Ibid.

4. Saudi's Takeover Due to Encompass All Aramco Work, *New York Times*, October 8, 1976.

5. New York: Wiley-Interscience, 1976, p. 189.

6. See, for example, the negotiations between MacDonald and Herriot in 1924 in Stephen Schuker's fascinating *The End of French Dominance* (Chapel Hill: University of North Carolina Press, 1976), p. 256.

7. See discussion in my *Economic Growth in France and Britain* (Cambridge: Harvard University Press, 1964), pp. 246–247.

8. *Travels through Germany, Russia, and Poland in the Years 1769 and 1770*, from the originals (London: J. Almon, 1772; reprinted, New York: Arno Press, 1971), pp. 309–310.

9. Arthur Young, *Travels in France during the Years 1787, 1788, 1789* (New York: Doubleday/Anchor, 1969), p. 45.

10. Ibid.

11. Sir John Clapham, *The Bank of England, A History*, Vol. 2 (Cambridge: Cambridge University Press, 1945), pp. 44–45.

12. A. Dauphin-Meunier, *La Banque de France* (Paris: Gallimard, 1936), p. 130.

13. D. Morier Evans, *The Commercial Crisis of 1857* (London: Groombridge & Sons, 1859; reprinted, Augustus M. Kelley, 1969), p. 203.

14. Erwin Hexner, *International Cartels* (Chapel Hill: University of North Carolina Press, 1946), pp. 210–211.

15. Stephen A. Schuker, *The End of French Predominance in Europe* (Chapel Hill: University of North Carolina Press, 1976), pp. 215–222.

16. Smith and Wells, *Negotiating Third-World Mineral Agreements*, p. 255.

17. Ibid., pp. 127–140.

18. Ibid., p. 254.

8

Multinationals and the Small Open Economy

Of the six schools of thought on the multinational corporation set out in Sanjaya Lall and discussed in chapter 6, I propose to dismiss the business school and Marxist approaches on the two wings and to telescope the right-hand and left-hand center positions into two general categories, the neoclassical and the nationalist-*dependencia*, albeit from time to time disaggregating within one or the other position to draw subtle and not-so-subtle distinctions, for example, to note that the *dependencia* school is inclined on the whole to exclude foreign direct investment, while the nationalists focus more narrowly on selective restriction and hard bargaining with those admitted.[1]

Notice that the neoclassical position is consistent with an open economy, the pursuit of comparative advantage and export-led growth, whereas the nationalist-*dependencia* school is more likely to favor inward-looking policies, tariffs, and import substitution. The two positions, import-substitution and export-led growth, can of course be reconciled through time, the first leading under appropriate conditions to the second, and vice versa. Industries set up to replace imports may grow so efficient that they can enter export markets, and export sales may generate income that spills over into demand for market-oriented products that is satisfied in due course by new local industries substituting for imports. Paauw and Fei, studying four small open economies in Asia, discuss the transition from import substitution to what they call "export substitution," but the transition can go the other way.[2]

The neoclassical position supports buying cheap and selling dear so as to satisfy the greatest possible set of wants with a given use of

Previously published in *Journal of Irish Business and Administrative Research* 2 (1980):115–128.

resources or to minimize the resources needed to satisfy given wants. In a neoclassical world of internal factor mobility within countries, but factor immobility internationally, this calls for free trade in goods as a strong presumption. If factors are mobile internationally, there is a presumption that factors and factor services should be exported from places where they are cheap and sold where they are dear. Second-best constraints, some cultural, some political, some economic, may serve to limit migration in labor. Some countries want to shut foreign labor out; others like Ireland want to keep domestic labor home so as to prevent continued emigration that would reduce the economy, polity, and society below critical scales. In the neoclassical view, if enterprise is free to move, and with it technology, competition in goods and factor markets will be increased, factor-price equalization will be more nearly approached, and world welfare will be enhanced. Where markets function badly, however, in noneconomic space such as national defense or where, for example, an enterprise in one country would buy up a competitor in another and increase the degree of monopoly in the world industry, interference with the profit-maximizing strategy of the multinational corporation may be justified.

The nationalist-*dependencia* school objects to this case on a variety of counts. For the nationalist, bargaining power is unevenly divided between the multinational corporation and many countries, particularly those that have recently emerged from colonialism, and the outcome of the market process is therefore distorted. The *dependencia* line of thought adds a series of further reasons why market outcomes are unsatisfactory. These come down by and large to market failure in developing countries, both in economic and political markets. In economic markets traditional sectors do not respond appropriately to economic incentives until the country reaches a state of "modernization." Politically, decision makers in the developing country occasionally identify their interests with those of foreign enterprise rather than with indigenous factors, and sell out the national interest. This latter notion approaches the Marxist view that class dominates nationality, and domestic as well as foreign capitalists exploit workers. It is a subject possible to discuss, but one on which it is difficult to reach operational conclusions by rational processes rather than by acts of faith.

In *Economic Studies* Walter Bagehot asserted among the "postulates of political economy" that the assumption of internal mobility of capital and labor used by the economics developed in Britain were misleading when applied to any other place, such as the countries of the continent.[3] In a recent reinvestigation Sidney Pollard moreover is doubtful whether there was substantial labor mobility even in Britain.[4] But the neoclassical assumption of labor and capital that are reallocated by market incentives is surely out of place in early stages of development everywhere. Recent books by Shaw and McKinnon have made the point strongly that markets for money and capital must be integrated and made to function as part of an efficient policy for development.[5] The literature on economic development more frequently refers to the market for labor, and here the usual vocabulary deals with "dualism" and "enclaves."

It is possible to speak of dual economies and enclaves without addressing the question whether foreign enterprise creates the enclaves or is responsible for dualism, and I propose to put to one side for a moment these questions, along with the opposite question whether multinational corporations can overcome preexisting dualism and integrate the rest of the economy with enclaves. In *The Transition in Open Dualistic Economies*, Paauw and Fei pay little attention to the role of foreign enterprise in the early stage of exporting primary products, the succeeding stage of import substitution, or the final stage of export substitution.[6] Even in dealing with manufactured exports from Taiwan, where "at least 20 percent" of output by value comes from foreign-owned plants,[7] effects of the multinational corporation are not on their minds. Their interest in import substitution is as a means of developing indigenous entrepreneurs. Policies of overvaluation of the currency, tariffs, inflation, and concessionary interest rates are needed to transfer profits from primary-product exporters to indigenous industrial entrepreneurs.[8] They seem not to be conscious of the possibility that these policies may transfer profits from a domestic set of primary-product exporters to foreigners engaged in the import-substitution sector, or that a subsequent set of policies to effect the transition to export-led growth—undervaluation, tariff removals, concessions in taxes, and so on—may equally benefit foreign entrepreneurs without encouraging indigenous enterprise. A recent study of Article 24 of the Andes Pact has explained the requirement that to qualify for tariff concessions, firms must be in process of becoming domestically owned by the simple notion that the rents created by extension of the Andes Common Market are intended to benefit local enterprise in the Common Market and not to be drawn off by foreign firms.[9]

As noted earlier, import substitution can occur as a "natural" process and continue to the point where the industry achieves costs low enough to enable it to export. The best example I know is that of German locomotive production. For example, Prussian, Rhenish, and Bavarian railroads began in the early 1840s with imported traction, largely

British but some of it from Philadelphia. Local production began slowly, based on foreign technology, much of it stolen rather than purchased. Foreign prototypes were gradually improved; production was expanded, replacing imports; and by the late 1850s Germany was a prominent exporter.[10] There was no foreign enterprise in the industry. Tariffs were modest but perhaps not needed in so bulky and heavy a product. At the time Germany was a series of small and only partly open economies. But a small open economy that developed from exporting primary products to import substitution and then to exporting manufactures is of course Denmark. The country became rich in exporting bacon, butter, eggs, and the like. High incomes of farmers spilled over into markets for consumer goods which were satisfied by indigenous entrepreneurs so effectively that they rapidly developed outlets abroad. No policy guided the outcome, and nothing in the way of foreign enterprise.

Let us bring in foreign enterprise that we have kept in a holding pattern. Is it responsible for dualism and enclaves, as the *dependencia* school seems to think, or is it merely the vehicle for starting the transition from a traditional form of production to modernization, so that enclaves are the result of resistance on the part of traditional sectors to change, and duality the outcome when the economy and society are only half modernized?

Some years ago in a classic article Hla Myint suggested that plantations begun by Dutch and British planters in Southeast Asia produced a once-and-for-all technical change that failed to lead to further growth after an initial lift.[11] In Hirschman's terminology there were no further linkages, no stimulus to new industries to produce components for use by the plantations nor to others to process plantation output further. There was nothing about the process of raising coffee, sugar, pineapples, rubber, or whatever, that led the indigenous population to make further discoveries, whether of new product or new process. The introduction of plantations resulted in a sort of "fossilization" of the economy, in Myint's graphic phrase.

Fossilization of plantation economies might be due to the foreignness of enterprise, with its own rather rigid technology; to the nature of the products and their staple characteristics as Harold Innis would have said; or to the resistance of the particular Asian peoples to change, when some other peoples would have responded differently to the same stimuli. On the last point, I may refer to the Danish case just mentioned. Dairy products differ from colonial plantation output in many ways to be sure, and the spillover of demand is also different between independent farmers on the one hand, and low-wage labor on the other. These considerations move the contrast in favor of staple theory. Observe further in terms of staple theory the Belgian lament that their country was locked into a series of semifinished products—iron and steel bars, rods, shapes and wire, flat glass, soda ash, urea, and the like—which used technologies that had exhausted their possibilities of progress and were frozen, giving the country a slower rate of growth than countries engaged in, say, mechanical and electrical industries. A distinguished Belgian economist once complained that his country's manufactured exports of finished goods and components for finished goods were confined to standardized products. The economy was so small, he claimed, that it was impossible to achieve economies of scale except by producing the same products as those made everywhere—pure white chinaware, for example, or wiring harnesses for automobile engines which were used across a variety of models and makes.[12] But mention of white china rather gives the show away. Sweden, Finland, and Denmark are all small open economies producing tableware—silver, steel, glass, china, earthenware—that is, nonstandardized and decorated. They have no need to conform to international standards of others because they set their own. Belgian taste is presumably insufficiently refined to appeal to wide numbers of consumers abroad—compare, for example, Belgian overstuffed furniture with Danish teak or Finnish models. Export-led growth without fossilization, dualism, or enclaves is possible where a society is capable of responding positively to economic opportunities.

The last statement echoes something I wrote 25 years ago on the terms of trade.[13] The terms of trade turned against developing countries, I asserted, not because of the nature of their products, neocolonialism, or monopolies but because these countries were unable to transform. Entry in their lines was easy, exit difficult. If some exogenous shock raised prices of their exports, new entry on the part of others would bring them down again; if prices fell for any reasons, inability to effect exit would keep them low. The terms of trade now favor OPEC in the energy field, for the moment at least, because new entry is difficult and expensive.

But let us return to foreign or multinational enterprise. The nationalist-*dependencia* school by and large takes the view that MNCs stimulate dualism and enclaves and resist integration, impeding the transition to effective transformation of domestic factors. Independent technologies are cut down in infancy by insistence on the use of multinational techniques. Linkages are turned outward instead of inward.

The neoclassical answer to this is somewhat hesitant. It suggests that the MNC can create conditions under which a developing economy could transform. By itself, however, it has little or no capacity to bring it about that the economy will transform.

I have always been an admirer of the work on the multinational corporation of Stephen Hymer, although by no means have I always agreed with his conclusions. Marxist by conviction, many of his arguments were of the strong leftward *dependencia* school. One of his hypotheses was that if Canada had not admitted American and European electrical equipment companies as foreign direct investors, Canada today would have developed its own indigenous electrical technology, with one, two, or more companies engaged in competition worldwide. The conjecture is an interesting one, and one must admit the possibility of this "counterfactual," as they say in economic history—what would have happened if something else had not happened. But there are other possibilities; one is the Latin American outcome that a country tries to keep out both imports and foreign enterprise and goes without the industry. There is also the Japanese model, in which a country buys foreign technology, with the least possible amount of foreign ownership of enterprise consistent with access to the technology one wants, and then improves on it. Is it policy that determines the outcome or the nature of the country's entrepreneurship and labor?

There is something to be said for not settling on a given technology too soon. Late unification in Germany meant that such industries as locomotives began in a series of separate kingdoms, principalities, and states, each often favoring its own enterprise. This led with unification and the creation of the larger market to a choice among a variety of technological efforts. An analogy runs to the strength and diversity of German universities and music or of painting in Italian city-states, where delayed economies of scale and intense competition among small units yielded long-run efflorescence. Or one could cite the lessons learned by Rand in weapons-systems procurement, that it is a mistake to settle prematurely on a single producer of a weapon system or to freeze specifications of components. Creative uncertainty from competition stimulates technological progress.

Another case of Hymer's *dependencia* position is that it is dangerous to admit foreign direct investment because you may not be able to get it out again. The life expectancy of foreign firms is long. He used to assert that foreign direct investments were not like annuals, subject to zero-based budgeting and likely to wither when their work was done, but more like trees. On one occasion Harry Johnson went him one better by saying that they were not ordinary trees but more like

redwoods which last a thousand years. Historical evidence in transforming societies fails to support the point. Germany complained of
Überfremdung, or overforeignization, on at least four separate occasions—in the 1850s, 1890s, 1920s, and 1950s—after each of which
there was a wave of repatriation of capital. Similar repatriations have
occurred from Britain and Canada, both during the 1930s, and again
in recent years. Economic theory teaches that when a company is
worth more to someone else than to its owner, the latter will sell to
the former. When a foreign investor has lost his initial advantage
because of the diffusion of his technology, new competition in the
market, a failure to keep up with technology and design change, or
whatever, and no longer has hope of restoring the position, he sells
out. If one of the advantages he had in sourcing his products abroad
was cheap and docile labor, and that labor ceases to be cheap and
docile, he might like to sell out, but it may be that the same labor
looks neither cheap nor docile to anyone else. Hirschman is of course
correct in saying that direct investment does not reverse itself as easily
as portfolio. It is lumpy, whereas portfolio investment is divisible.[14]
But the difference is one of degree, not kind.

I argue then that foreign investment does not create or perpetuate
dualism or enclaves by anything it does. Is there anything it does to
break it down? Again one can find cases on both sides. Richard Weisskopf and Edward Wolff observe that Puerto Rico remains a fragmented
enclave economy after years of supporting foreign investment as a
means of growth.[15] More than one observer, incidentally, has noted
this case as a touchstone against which to measure Ireland. And Donald
Brash some years ago observed that General Motors in Australia labored
long and hard to bring the mechanical industry on which it sought
to depend for components up to international standards.[16]

Weisskopf and Wolff examine the Puerto Rican experience in terms
of input-output relationships. The modern manufacturing sector has
limited relations with the domestic economy for inputs but has large
input relations with the mainland United States, where it sells all its
output. The traditional primary-product and domestic-manufacturing
sector sells a small amount of output to modern manufacturing, and
feeds the latter's workers, but in turn buys the majority of its consumer
goods from the United States as imports. The economy is small, open,
but fragmented. The authors find it disturbing that some of the same
goods "criss-cross" (i.e., cheap qualities of some goods are exported
to the United States, while expensive qualities of the same products
are imported from there). But there is nothing bizarre or uneconomic
about simultaneous buying and selling of the same goods of different

qualities. It is rational for dairy farmers to consume cheap margarine and sell expensive butter, or Italian makers of high-grade olive oil to sell it to northern Europe and the United States and import the less expensive Greek product. The interest of the Puerto Rican case lies not in criss-crossed exports and imports but in the persistence of dualism and enclaves in the face of subsidized exports of manufactures from industry dominated by foreign firms.

The General Motors story bears in the opposite direction. Brash had to abandon corporate anonymity because of the overwhelming size of General Motors in the Australian economy, and it may be that this conspicuous position affected its behavior. Nonetheless, the company devoted time, energy, and money to instructing various potential suppliers how to produce effectively (i.e., cheaply and to a satisfactory standard) the various components the company needed after it acquired the Holden Propriety Co. Starting out with the rule of thumb, "Bring it from Detroit unless it is 10 percent cheaper in Australia," it later converted to the opposite algorithm: "Buy it in Australia unless it's 10 percent cheaper in Detroit."[17] I interpret the 10 percent margin as a general instruction not to bother with small differences where the cost differential would be outweighed by expense of protracted decision making. The moral of the tale, however, is that the rational corporation will source locally if it is economical to do so. A less conspicuous and a less wealthy company might not have the incentive or be willing to accept the low transitional return to improve productivity of its suppliers. Australia moreover is a big economy. What the average MNC will do in the average SOE (small open economy) is by no means evident from this example.

How does all this affect Ireland? My guess is that the more central question is whether Irish society conforms more to the patterns of adaptable and transforming economies and societies like Sweden, Denmark, the Netherlands, at least as they were some years ago, or more nearly to that of Puerto Rico. Policy choices may well be dominated by the economic material one is working with. If the society has the capacity to throw up ambitious, able, experimenting entrepreneurs, it may make little difference whether one adopts import substitution or opens up the import-competing sector by reducing tariffs and stimulates the export sector by tax subsidies and tax concessions. On the other hand, if the potentiality is not there, neither policy may work. The question that is very difficult to answer is whether there are circumstances where a small open economy would respond positively to one policy but not to the other, and whether as a general matter entrepreneurship is stimulated more by letting foreign business in than keeping it out. I greatly fear that this is one of those questions where the quantities as well as quality determine the outcome.

Before I touch on these issues, however, I would like to suggest that the Irish experience may not be generalizable, because one probably cannot repeat the experiment of a country admitted to membership in an economic community of rich countries that permits a small poor member to subsidize manufactured exports to the extent that has been done in this case. As is well known, the next round of negotiation in GATT is to be devoted to the regulation of governmental subsidies on trade flows and will outlaw export subsidies. Whether it would apply to the Irish construction subsidies or remissions of income taxes for manufactured exports is something I have no idea of, since the European Economic Community has already agreed to the Irish system. The general-equilibrium problem of assigning an incidence to such subsidies is an appalling one. Is the subsidy to employment, to exports, to consumers abroad, or to the stockholders of the firms, and does its cost rest on the Irish taxpayer, the import-competing firms in the foreign market, or whom? The U.S. Steel Company recently challenged the Internal Revenue Service in the United States, on the ground that the border-tax adjustment in EEC countries was presumptively a subsidy to exports, since it could not be shown that value-added taxes are always entirely passed forward, and none of them back on producers. Economists cannot be certain of the incidence of any tax in general equilibrium, with all the feedbacks and loops of the entire system. The new code will try to prescribe inequitable subsidies that affect trade even though their primary purpose is to aid regions, restructure industry, maintain employment, or encourage research and development. I have the feeling that the world is setting down the path that led, in the case of the Navigation Laws in Britain, to complete abandonment on the ground that they were so complex that only three people in the country understood them. It is sad to contemplate, however, that the Navigation Laws endured for almost 200 years.

It is evident from the plans of this country that you have very much in mind the necessities to break down any pluralism that may exist and to ensure that linkages from subsidized exports of manufactures by foreign firms work in this direction. The traditional sector itself has been stimulated, if that is the right word, by the freeing up of competition from imports. And the debate on whether or not the program has been a success thus far is surely addressed to the right questions. The Industrial Development Authority Regional Plan of

1972 sets out the types of industrial companies sought for Ireland. These should be

1. Irish owned or have substantial Irish participation,

2. originating outside the EEC but seeking to establish in the EEC,

3. international companies, of which all subsidiaries in such places as Ireland have a high degree of independence in policy and decision making,

4. commercially strong and have economic stability, that is, on liquidity, profitability, and growth criteria,

5. suitable industry, with some or all of these characteristics:
   low capital intensity,
   high male labor content,
   high usage of Irish raw materials, services, and natural resources,
   high potentiality for interindustry linkages,
   high profitability,
   strong growth prospects in output and international trade,
   high-skilled labor content.[18]

The list has something of a utopian character. One could examine the separate items one by one, but perhaps the most useful ones to discuss are the third and the bulk of the separate items under the fifth.

Item 3 asking for separate decision-making power in Ireland and all other subsidiaries seems to run counter to the essence of the multinational corporation. Calling for silent partners would seem to be asking for portfolio capital rather than direct investment. In franchise arrangements such as with Coca-Cola Bottling, Hilton hotels, McDonald's hamburgers, and the like, some decisions are decentralized, such as size of operations, but the franchiser rigidly lays down the standards to be met. Where a subsidiary is part of a complex international operation, the raison d'être is to integrate its operations into the wider operation. Where an extra-EEC company, say from Japan, has only one EEC subsidiary, and that in Ireland, it might be possible to meet this condition in large part. But for British and German companies, and the subsidiaries of U.S. companies which constitute the bulk of investments thus far attracted, there is little likelihood that foreign investors will establish subsidiaries in Ireland and turn them loose on their own.

When we come to suitable industries, there may be contradictions among the criteria. Low capital intensity means emphasis on food, drink, furniture, textiles, clothing, and these together with paper and printing have high proportions of women in the labor force, as may electronic and computing companies.[19] High male labor content is of course related to the desire to furnish an alternative to emigration, but large numbers of men, particularly young men, may lend themselves to labor troubles. A *dependencia* view is that one of the tasks of governments that want to attract foreign investment is to maintain political stability and a docile labor force.[20] I suppose much depends on the regional competitive situation, and a standard of docility that would be tolerated among Southeast Asian countries competing to attract a labor-intensive plant would not be completely acceptable in labor-scarcer Europe. Nonetheless, Irish experience already includes the withdrawal of a substantial Dutch employer because of strikes and kidnapping. I presume that the Irish government would tend to discourage kidnapping and strikes even in the absence of exigent foreign firms.

High usage of Irish inputs of course broadly goes with high potentiality for interindustry linkages. Dermot McAleese's *Profile of Grant-Aided Industry in Ireland* shows figures, outside of food processing, that run 60 to 90 percent for imported raw materials and components, and another dollop for packaging, transport, and materials for repair, as well as royalties, license, and interest payments.[21] Including food, import content is one-third of gross output; excluding it, the proportion rises to one-half. The foreign proportion of input expenditures of domestic firms is substantially lower. These figures seem high to me, and appear so to the author, who notes that the longer the firm stays in Ireland, the more it buys Irish materials, and that some firms may be buying technology not available in Ireland.[22] The issue is crucial. Is Ireland a "platform of space" as Frobel, Heinrichs, and Kreye describe the enclave economies of Asia and Latin America, including the free zone along the Rio Grande just south of the border? And does Ireland offer only labor, with little if any chance ever to develop manufacturing entrepreneurship and technology of its own, or will it, albeit slowly, follow the path of growth to a transforming society, integrated and capable of adaptation through export promotion rather than import substitution?[23]

The question turns on the condition and prospects for indigenous entrepreneurs. It is noted that Irish entrepreneurs do not respond effectively to the grants and subsidies that have attracted foreign multinationals.[24] The existing position is one of duality; Irish firms are smaller, do less research, export less, concentrate in the less dynamic industries like food processing, clothing, and textiles. McAleese finds satisfactory that 84 percent of the managers hired by grant-aided industry are Irish.[25] It is difficult to judge the significance of such a statistic without knowing the levels and proportions of decision-making jobs entrusted to Irish staff by their foreign employers and having some idea of whether a significant number of them will ultimately break away as risk takers as well as managers, to make the Schumpeterian distinction. One vital question is whether or not there has been any change experienced in the last 10-plus years in R. Lynn's finding, published in 1968, that 60 percent of Irish graduates at the university level leave Ireland permanently and that as of the time of his survey, 80 percent of undergraduates intended to leave for a substantial period.[26]

There is a considerable empirical literature which states that the presence of considerable direct foreign investment in a developing country is associated with low domestic savings[27] and with low rates of growth.[28] I am in no position to judge the econometrics of these studies, but I must confess to a general inchoate scepticism that the results are robust enough to use as a basis for policy. Econometricians with clear political biases may be suspected of running regression after regression until they get the result they like, with poor R^2s, just as those who like high R^2s have, in the past at least, been inclined to keep the computers crunching numbers until some relationship comes out high enough without much theory in support. I have a hard time seeing that either of these findings is applicable to Ireland, Greece, or the four Asian economies studied by Paauw and Fei—Taiwan, South Korea, Singapore, and the Philippines. Puerto Rico is a clear plus for their viewpoints, but here it would seem to me that there were other forces at work. One can argue forcibly that the multinational corporation did not integrate the Puerto Rican economy and initiate a self-sustaining process of economic growth. But it would seem to me that the causes lie not in the foreign firms so much as in the nature of the Spanish tradition in the islands and the exposure through imports, migration, and tourism, as well as the multinational corporation, to the high standards of living of mainland United States. There has been little recent discussion of demonstration effect as introduced by Ragnar Nurkse in 1953, but it may play a critical role in the relationships between growth stimulants, on the one hand, and savings and the balance of payments, on the other.[29]

I have not discussed the balance of payments of SOEs in general or of Ireland in particular. The latter hardly deserves it, as the incentives are focused heavily on exports and the growth here has been impressive. Critics properly assert that this growth is gross and that against it must be counted imported inputs, imports for consumption (in an open economy), and remittance of profits to home countries. It is perhaps worth noting that the rate of reinvestment in Ireland has been particularly high among U.S. firms. I conjecture that this is the consequence of my country's unwillingness to enter into international tax-sparing agreements. There is a double-taxation treaty of course: in "a political economy framework" this is because the Irish ruling class is committed to capitalism and does not feel threatened by foreign participation.[30] But that treaty does not allow American investors to escape income taxes on profits that escape Irish taxation because of concessions. The U.S. Treasury has been adamant in its refusal to agree to tax sparing on the ground that to do so would quickly lead to a competitive race for tax concessions to MNCs in which all countries would lose tax revenues to corporations. I would not deny that the American ruling classes, whoever they may be, are committed to capitalism, but the futility of tax concession when all jurisdictions make them is evident to anyone in the United States who has seen state and local competition in attracting industry through reductions in taxes.

The *dependencia* school presumably wants to ban foreign direct investment; the nationalist school to admit it but with the least possible concessions necessary to attract it. But of course. We all want to trade with the other fellow at his reserve price and to keep the rent for ourselves. The golden goose must be kept on laying golden eggs, but not put on any weight. It is easy to sympathize with this point of view and easy to understand why developing countries that have had highly successful foreign direct investments want to renegotiate initial concessions after success has been demonstrated. The question may be asked, however, whether Ireland can effectively withdraw concessions it has made on income taxation applicable to exports, such as were designed in 1969 to run to 1990. The question belongs more squarely in the arena of ethics than of economics, although if the initial concessions prove to be wildly generous, there could be the general case for renegotiation which the U.S. government asserts in procurement contracts and which the UN developing country group has adopted as its own. Dermot McAleese, who seems on the whole favorable to the program, indicates that it is hard to say, even *ex post*, how much of the concessions is redundant in the light of competitive capital grants in Northern Ireland and English development areas and export tax incentives in Denmark, the Netherlands, Switzerland, and Sweden. It would doubtless be helpful if the various countries of the GATT were to agree retroactively to undo their export incentives. It might be risk prone for Ireland to undertake to do so alone. And I should think that Ireland would not want to associate itself with the LDC views that contracts on the whole don't bind governments. Economic history has produced a new category for Sweden that well fits Ireland today: the "impoverished sophisticate." Sweden in the middle of the nineteenth century was a poor country with highly developed institutions that enabled it to grow very rapidly in response to new economic opportunities. One of the institutions of a sophisticate, perhaps, is a respect for keeping one's commitments.

But I must conclude: Does the MNC have a contribution to make to growth in SOEs or not, and specifically, does it have one to make in Ireland? Stoneman quotes Felipe Pazos as saying: "The main weakness of direct investment as a development agent is a consequence of the complete character of its contribution."[31] One could easily turn the remark around and the problem faced by MNCs and LDCs is that they have to bring the bulk of the skilled and sophisticated inputs with them since they cannot acquire them locally. But where the local economy has some capacity to learn, transform, and grow, it is not self-evident that the multinational corporation as such is highly stimulative or highly retarding.

As for Ireland, it is difficult to see that the MNC has slowed it down. Agriculture is improving, and the economy as a whole is responding to export-led growth. Whether indigenous entrepreneurs are responding to the opportunities thus opened up is unclear. I suppose that in these matters with enormous amounts of evidence where you stand depends on where, in the spectrum of Dr. Lall, you sit.

Notes

1. Sanjaya Lall, Less-Developed Countries and Private Foreign Direct Investment: A Review Article, *World Development* 2 (April–May 1974):43–48.

2. Douglas S. Paauw and John C. H. Fei, *The Transition in Open Dualistic Economies, Theory and South East Asian Experience* (New Haven: Yale University Press, 1973).

3. *The Collected Works of Walter Bagehot*, Vol. 11, edited by Norman St. John-Stevas (London: The Economist, 1978), p. 235.

4. Peter Mathias and M. M. Postan, eds., *The Cambridge Economic History of Europe*, Vol. 7, *The Industrial Economies: Capital, Labor, Enterprise* (Cambridge: Cambridge University Press, 1978), pt. 1.

5. Edward S. Shaw, *Financial Deepening in Economic Development* (New York: Oxford University Press, 1973); Ronald I. McKinnon, *Money and Capital in Economic Development* (Washington, D.C.: The Brookings Institution, 1973).

6. Paauw and Fei, *Transition in Open Dualistic Economies, passim.*

7. Deepak Nayyar, Transnational Corporations and Manufactured Exports from Poor Countries, *Economic Journal* 88 (March 1978):62.

8. Paauw and Fei, *Transition in Open Dualistic Economies*, p. 244.

9. Ernesto Tironi, Economic Integration and Foreign Direct Investment Policies, unpublished dissertation, Massachusetts Institute of Technology, Department of Economics, August 1976.

10. Pierre Benaerts, *Borsig et les débuts de la fabrication des locomotives en Allemagne* (Paris: F. H. Turgot, 1932).

11. Hla Myint, The Gains from International Trade and the Backward Countries, *Review of Economic Studies* 22 (1954–55):129–142.

12. Jacques Drèze, Quelques reflexions sereines sur l'adaptation de l'industrie belque au Marche Commun, *Comptes rendus de Travaux de la Société d'Economie Politique de Belgique*, no. 275 (1960).

13. *The Terms of Trade. A European Case Study* (Cambridge: The MIT Press, 1956).

14. Albert O. Hirschman, How to Divest in Latin America, and Why, *Essays in International Finance* 76 (November 1969):10–11.

15. Richard Weisskopf and Edward Wolff, Linkages and Leagues: Industrial Tracking in an Enclave Economy, *Economic Development and Cultural Change* 25 (July 1977):607–628.

16. Donald R. Brash, *American Investment in Australian Industry* (Cambridge: Harvard University Press, 1966).

17. Ibid., pp. 197–198.

18. Industrial Development Authority, *Regional Industrial Plans, 1973–1977*, Part I, Dublin, Industrial Development Authority, June 1972, p. 39.

19. Noel Farley, Explanatory Hypothesis for Irish Trade in Manufactured Goods in Mid-Nineteen Sixties, *Social and Economic Review* 4 (October 1972):19, quoted in Frank Long, Foreign Direct Investment in an Underdeveloped European Economy—The Republic of Ireland, *World Development* 4 (January 1976):57.

20. Nayyar, Transnational Corporations, p. 77.

21. Dermot McAleese, *A Profile of Grant-Aided Industry in Ireland* (Dublin: Industrial Development Authority, 1977), pp. 42–47.

22. Ibid., p. 48.

23. See Folker Frübel, Jürgens Heinrichs, Otto Kreye, *Die neue internationale Arbeitsteilung, Structurelle Arbeitslosigkeit in der Industrielandern und die Industrialisierung der Entwicklungslander* [The New International Division of Labor: Structural Unemployment in Industrialized Countries and Industrialization in Developing Countries] (Reinbek: Rowohlt Taschenbuch Verlag, 1977).

24. Frank Long, Towards a Political Economy Framework of Foreign Direct Investment, *American Journal of Economics and Sociology* 36 (1977):182; Dermot McAleese, Outward Looking Policies, Manufactured Exports and Economic Growth: The Irish Experience, paper presented to AUTE Conference, Swansea, March 28–31, 1977. See also McAleese's remark in *A Profile*, p. 49, that Irish industries seem to have low backward linkages.

25. Ibid., p. 57.

26. R. Lynn, *The Irish Brain Drain*, Dublin, Economic and Social Research Institute, 1968, quoted in Frank Long, Foreign Direct Investment, p. 73.

27. T. E. Weisskopf, The Impact of Foreign Capital Inflow on Domestic Savings in Underdeveloped Countries, *Journal of International Economics* 2 (February 1972):25–38.

28. Colin Stoneman, Foreign Capital and Economic Growth *World Development* 3 (January 1975):11–26.

29. Ragnar Nurkse, *Problems of Capital Formation in Under Developed Countries* (Oxford: Blackwell, 1953), pp. 63–67.

30. Frank Long, Towards a Political Economy Framework, p. 179.

31. The Role of International Movements of Foreign Capital in Promoting Development, in J. H. Adler, ed., *Capital Movements and Economic Development* (London: Macmillan, 1967), p. 196; quoted in C. Stoneman, Foreign Capital and Economic Growth, p. 20.

9

Origins of U.S. Direct Investment in France

In the French official literature American direct investment in France is a phenomenon that dates from the 1950s.[1] This judgment is quantitatively correct; the bulk of existing American investment in France is of postwar origin. In qualitative terms, however, one can find in the nineteenth and early twentieth centuries most of the factors that account for the recent movement, except perhaps for the sharp reduction in costs of communication and transport that have spread the movement and the "follow-the-leader" psychology. Already by 1900 there was offensive and defensive investment, investment to supplement and to supplant exports, and American firms in service industries were already establishing units abroad to hold the loyalty of their domestic customers. By 1885 in insurance, 1920 in banking, and generally by 1929, there was French concern at the American invasion of France.[2]

One of the earliest recorded direct investments in manufacturing moreover, Haviland & Co.'s porcelain factory in Limoges, illustrated a phenomenon that has only recently assumed major proportions—the establishment of plants abroad to manufacture goods primarily for the home market.

Most interest in direct investment in the literature attaches to manufacturing. In his well-known study *American Investment in British Manufacturing*, J. H. Dunning dismisses investment in "sales agencies and banking houses" during the late eighteenth and early nineteenth centuries.[3] There are a number of reasons, however, why a more complete picture of investments in sectors other than manufacturing is desirable. Up to the middle of the nineteenth century, distinctions between banker and merchant were not sharply drawn, nor were those between trader and manufacturer. Many entrepreneurs undertook all three functions

Previously published in *Business History Review* 48 (Autumn 1974):382–413.

simultaneously.[4] Finally, and not of lesser significance for our understanding of direct investment, trade and service industries add to the
generality of the explanation of direct investment based on
manufacturing.

Finance

The first significant American investment in France was that of a
banking house, Welles & Co., founded by Col. Samuel Welles of Boston
in Paris in 1816. Maurice Lévy-Leboyer gives the firm name as Welles
& Williams, indicating an association with another Bostonian, Samuel
Williams, who had a banking house in London until its failure in 1826.[5]
Both were in the business of financing European dry goods exports
to the United States. Welles had a branch in Le Havre in 1828, under
the name Welles & Greene, manned by John B. Greene of Boston.[6]
Welles & Co. served as correspondent for American merchants like
Peabody & Riggs of London and Baltimore when they bought French
and Italian goods; the firm was asked from London to honor drafts
upon it at three months to purchase fine silk, linen handkerchiefs,
collars, cravats, gloves, and veils from Paris, Lyons, and St. Etienne.[7]
In addition, Samuel Welles served as a social and mercantile center
in Paris for visiting American businessmen. Like Williams in London
up to his failure in 1826, and George Peabody in the same city from
the 1830s, "few of his countrymen failed to find their way to his
[counting] rooms, while he entertained in his home nearly every traveled
American of note."[8]

There is some doubt whether Welles & Co. can properly be called
an American direct investment. The bank was dissolved in 1841 at
the death of Col. Welles; his widow married a French aristocrat who
adopted his young son, who was then raised as a Frenchman. During
its heyday, however, it received the support of Col. Welles's cousins,
John and Benjamin Welles, who constituted the auxiliary house in
Boston to the banking house. John Welles drew his capital out of
Welles & Co., Paris, just before the troubles of 1837. Presumably other
American funds remained in the bank, whether those of Benjamin
Welles, or of another of Col. Welles's cousins, Henry Winthrop Sargent,
a member of the firm of Gracie & Sargent, the New York correspondent
of Welles & Co. Mr. Sargent retired, aged thirty-one, when the Paris
bank was liquidated at the death of Col. Welles in 1841, after the
bank had weathered the 1837 crisis.[9]

The crisis of 1837 ruined three American banks in England, beginning
with W. Wiggins & Co., Wildes & Co., and Wilson & Co.,[10] plus a

number of others—Frisch, Low & Berry, Griswold & Adams, Draper, Todd & Co., and Francis F. Dorr & Co. Williams & Co. had failed earlier, in 1826.[11] The crisis almost brought down W. and J. Brown, among the sons of Alexander Brown of Baltimore, who were aided by the Bank of England.[12] It may have dealt the *coup de grace* to Fitch & Co. of Marseilles and New York, which with Welles & Co. dominated the French trade in the 1830s.[13] Welles & Co. pulled through the crisis with help from the Bank of France. The firm had had $13,500,000 liabilities unpaid, largely to the United States, and $6,500,000 of acceptances outstanding among the public in Lyons and Paris, plus more at the Bank of France.[14]

With the dissolution of Welles & Co. after Col. Welles's death, there appear to have been no notable American bankers in France in the 1840s. In London, Peabody & Riggs evolved into George Peabody & Co., later Peabody, Morgan & Co., still later Morgan, Grenfell & Co. and shifted out of merchanting and financing shipments of dry goods, to state bonds and, at the end of the 1840s, to U.S. federal debt. George Peabody & Co. had correspondents in Paris, presumably French. Peabody's major sales of American bonds on the continent, however, were to Germany, where after 1848 American securities were sought both to hedge against further revolution and because the coupons were bought at premia by emigrants headed for the United States.[15] United States bonds were also sold in Britain, Germany, and Switzerland through branches of brokers and dealers of those countries established in New York. Lazard Frères was another such bank, in a way, although it started in New Orleans and opened branches in London and New York before establishing the head office in Paris.

An early firm which has left little trace in the record of Franco-American financial relations was Munroe & Co. This was started in 1851 as a successor to the merchandising business of its American founder. It may have specialized in silk.[16] In 1878 it was noted as one of three collectors for a charitable fund in Paris, along with Drexel, Harjes & Co. and Seligman Frères.[17] It moved gradually into stock-broking, under which designation it was recorded in the American Chamber of Commerce Directory in 1930 as a subsidiary of John Munroe & Co. of 100 Broadway, New York, with establishments in Paris, Cannes, and Pau (but it had disappeared from the directory in 1931, presumably a victim of the stock-market crash).[18] Paris and Cannes suggest a business of brokerage among American expatriates. Pau, on the other hand, is largely an English, not an American watering place, though J. P. Morgan went there on one occasion, and there is evidence that a number of very rich American single women or widows of French nobility lived there.[19] The pattern is by no means certain but would appear to have been trade, trade finance, government finance, industrial finance through bonds, stock brokerage, and then oblivion.

The next major developments in finance were associated with the Civil War in the United States. Eight Seligman brothers started out in retail dry goods in Alabama in 1838, went to California in 1849, and began as contractors in clothing, and possibly importers, in 1857. In 1862, they founded a bank, and quickly established branches in Frankfurt, Paris, and London, to market bonds of the U.S. federal government. The oldest brother, Joseph, sold bonds in Frankfurt with great success. The second brother was Jesse, the New York partner, friend of General (later President) Ulysses S. Grant and the "J" of J. & W. Seligman. William, the third brother, established Seligman Frères & Cie in Paris in 1864.[20] The firm specialized in government bonds and played a major role in the refinancing of the American federal debt during the 1870s. In June 1874 J. & W. Seligman of New York acted for the Crédit Foncier and about 15 other Continental houses in subscribing to a tender for $178,500,000 and took up half of a particular lot of $45,000,000.[21] When World War I broke out, Seligman Frères & Cie in Paris found itself in a precarious position. J. & W. Seligman in New York advanced it funds to forestall liquidation but withdrew its equity position on the ground of American neutrality. After the war the French firm became Banque Seligman, which in 1935 became Seligman & Cie, but the direct U.S. interest terminated in 1914. William Seligman, who died in 1910, was one of the leaders of the American colony in Paris at the turn of the century, and he took a prominent role in the American Chamber of Commerce there. Especially he was called on to deliver allocutions on ceremonial occasions.

The origins of the Morgan Guaranty Trust Company of New York in France go back to 1868 when the Drexel, Harjes firm was founded in Paris by Drexel & Co. of Philadelphia, its New York affiliate, Drexel, Winthrop & Co., and two individuals, Henry J. Harjes of Philadelphia and Robert Winthrop of New York. The founding firm, Drexel & Co., had originated as a Louisville, Kentucky, business in foreign exchange led by Francis M. Drexel, a German immigrant to the United States. Transferred to the broader opportunities of Philadelphia in 1838, the banking business evolved from foreign exchange to dealing in state and federal securities, along with personal banking. The firm flourished during the Civil War and developed close connections with Peabody, Morgan of London, successor to George Peabody & Co., in which Junius S. Morgan had become a partner in 1854. In 1868 it founded the Paris branch to conduct business as private bankers and to market American state and especially federal debt on the Continent. Shortly thereafter, Junius' son J. Pierpont Morgan, who had formed a small firm in New York under the name of Dabney, Morgan & Co., joined Drexel & Co. He was invited to do so by Anthony J. Drexel, the principal successor to his father, to broaden his access to the New York financial center. The firm of Drexel, Morgan & Co. was formed. In 1895 its name was changed to J. P. Morgan & Co. and that of the affiliate from Drexel, Harjes to Morgan, Harjes & Co.[22]

There is no record that Drexel, Harjes & Co. took a role in the 250,000,000 franc loan which Morgan & Co., London, placed for the French government at the end of 1870. This was before the association of Drexel and Morgan, but the episode redounded to the good reputation of Drexel, Harjes and later Morgan, Harjes & Co. The company participated in refinancing U.S. federal government debt in the 1870s. A Drexel-Morgan-Rothschild alliance took $260,000,000 worth of bonds, with Morgan selling mainly in Britain and Rothschild on the Continent.[23] The official account of the bank states that after 1873 it continued developing a market in France for the securities of U.S. companies and also became the "natural place for financial accommodation for the growing numbers of Americans visiting or living in Paris."[24]

Prior to World War I the firm engaged in underwriting and issuing securities, largely for American accounts, on the French market. It carried on its books a number of dormant accounts of important French and American industrial companies, but these, states an informal history, did their current banking business mainly with the large French banks.[25] Morgan in New York undertook to market a minimum of $100,000,000 (maximum $200,000,000) of U.S. government bonds abroad against gold coin in the panic of 1893, using the Deutsche Bank in Germany and Morgan, Harjes in Paris, along with Morgan, Grenfell of London in the syndicate. The firm also served to transfer in gold and foreign exchange, without disturbing exchange markets and without compensation, the $40,000,000 paid in 1904 by the United States to the new de Lesseps company in Paris, which sold its rights to build a canal in Panama.[26] The bulk of its business, however, was the furnishing of banking services to the colony of wealthy American residents in France and to affluent tourists.

World War I brought a major change in French–U.S. financial relations, and with it, in the activities of Morgan, Harjes & Co. J. P. Morgan & Co., in New York, was the purchasing and fiscal agent of both the French and British governments, and the Paris firm provided "the vital day-to-day contact with the French ministries."[27] In the postwar period too the French government raised private loans in the United States through J. P. Morgan, after direct Treasury-to-Treasury contact had been terminated. The firm reorganized its commercial banking facilities and observed that the older established American industrial companies, quiescent during the war, had become engaged in renewing and enlarging their plants with local credits and wanted to raise funds on the French capital market.[28] The bank changed its name to Morgan & Cie in 1926, and with the merger of the parent company with the Guaranty Trust Co., to the Morgan Guaranty Trust Co. in 1959. It celebrated its 100th anniversary in 1968.

The informal services given to American travelers by private bankers began to be replaced at the end of the century when the American Express Company opened its first foreign office in Paris in 1895. Beginning on the rue Halévy, it moved in 1901 to 3, rue Scribe, the address occupied by Drexel, Harjes & Co. from 1868 to 1873. American Express had been founded in 1850 as a result of a merger of three leading express companies: Butterfield & Wasson, Livingston, Fargo & Co., and Wells & Co. Two of the directors formed Wells, Fargo & Co. in 1852 to handle the western frontier, while American Express dealt in the East. As the railroad developed, the American Express Railway Agency was created prior to governmental parcel post in 1913, and later it became independent as the Railway Express Agency.[29] The American Express Company early started shipping cash, then turned to money orders in competition with postal money orders (1864). Interest in foreign freight began in 1888, and the activity which led to the establishment of the Paris branch was west-bound freight. But the major business quickly became the traveler's check, developed and copyrighted in 1891, after the firm's president, J. C. Fargo, had encountered difficulty in cashing his letters of credit in remote foreign parts. In the first year, $9,120 of the traveler's checks were sold, then $6,000,000 by 1900, and $12,000,000 by 1913.[30] The Paris branch was quickly followed by branches in London, Liverpool, Geneva, Rotterdam, and others. By 1929 American Express had five branches in France, and by 1972, the French subsidiary, organized as American Express International Banking, had 275 employees.

As revealed more fully later, the record is biased by being more complete for successes than for failures. One of the latter may be noted, however. In 1906, almost 100 years after the failure of Boston banker Henry Higginson in London in 1811, Lee, Higginson & Co. of Boston organized an affiliated firm in London, Higginson, Tottie & Co. which the next year became Higginson & Co.[31] In 1907 also,

Higginson & Co. of London attempted to open a Paris branch. A biography of James J. Storrow notes that this branch occupied much of his personal attention, and its closing very shortly took a place among the very few failures of Storrow's life.[32] A footnote in this biography, published in 1932, observes that the place of that branch was taken by the establishment of the French firm, Lee, Higginson & Cie in 1930. This did not last long either.

Prior to the Federal Reserve Act of 1913, national banks in the United States were prohibited from establishing branches abroad, or for that matter, outside the counties of their origin. The rule did not apply to private banks, nor to trust companies regulated by state law, and two New York banks, the Farmers Loan & Trust Company (1906) and the Equitable Trust Company (1910) existed in Paris in 1914, along with six British bank branches, two Spanish, one Italian, five Russian, and five from other nations.[33] With the passage of the Federal Reserve Act and the war, a substantial movement abroad took place. The Guaranty Trust Company of New York opened a branch in Paris in 1916. With the Bankers Trust Company and J. P. Morgan & Co., it took a leading part in organizing the French Industrial Credits of 1916, under which 165 American banks accepted credits for 75 French firms.[34] Upon American entry into the war in April 1917, existing banks expanded to serve American troops, new branches were established in ports such as Brest, Nantes, Bordeaux, and headquarters towns like Tours, and new banks entered. The number of employees of the Farmers Loan & Trust Company was 20 in 1914, then shrank to only 2 with the mobilization of its French staff, then grew to 200 in 1918. The Guaranty Trust Company staff in France reached 34 in 1917, then grew to 414 employees in Paris in 1921, plus 40 more in its Le Havre branch (started in 1919 to handle cotton imports).[35] By 1925 the business was reduced to 265 employees.[36]

The peak of American banking prior to World War II was reached in 1921, when there were eight U.S. bank branches (not counting independent affiliates like Morgan, Harjes & Co., Banque Seligman, and Munroe & Co.). By 1923, the number had shrunk to six.[37] Clyde W. Phelps explains that with the growth of trade, it was necessary to change from dealing through bank correspondents to a firm's own branches (for secrecy, to deal in dollars and limit exchange risk, to protect client secrets, and to cosset the client psychologically).[38] Paul P. Abrahams maintains that the U.S. government was interested in expanding overseas banking to push the use of the dollar worldwide.[39] The Mercantile Bank of Connecticut started operations in Paris in 1917, but it never took an important place there. Its real interests were in Latin America, but when it got into trouble over Colombian coffee and Cuban sugar, it sold off its Latin American branches to the Bank of London and South America and its Paris branch to the Guaranty Trust Company. The Farmers Loan & Trust Company branch in Paris was absorbed with the merger of the parent bank with the National City Bank. The Bankers Trust opened its Paris branch in 1920. The Chase National Bank also arrived in this period to take a leading role with Morgan, the Guaranty, and the National City.

Expansion in American banking in France has variously been viewed as offensive, as defensive, and as neutral. Clyde W. Phelps tried to explain that the banks gave French banks no competition, that U.S. banks were exclusively interested in U.S. commerce and tourists, with all internal affairs reserved for French institutions.[40] He observed, however, that French opinion during and after the war was hostile to the so-called "invasion of foreign banks," and noted that a draft law had been prepared in November 1920, though not acted on, to supplement the tax of one per mil on capital with a tax of two per mil on all operations, while forbidding to foreign banks the right to receive deposits or to issue securities for customers other than their own nationals.[41] In the United States it was claimed that American banks had to go abroad defensively: it was expected that the profits from foreign operations would be small for years to come; that the immediate profit would arise from increased domestic business growing out of the establishment of the branches for the banks' customers who were engaged in foreign trade; and that American industry could not surrender potential markets abroad to their competitors without contributing to profits that would enable these competitors to invade the United States.[42]

The depression of the 1930s thinned the ranks further, but the post-World War II upsurge filled them to overflowing. Primarily this was to serve American companies abroad, as were lawyers, accountants, advertising agencies, consultants, and the like. The banker at the head of the First National City Bank of New York's operations in Europe, located in Paris, points out that foreign banks are at a disadvantage: they have to buy their money, rather than receive it free as demand deposits.[43] Some underwriting is likely to be offensive, moving into monopolized and inefficient capital markets, and some distribution of American securities to French investors continues. For the most part the new banks and bankers are following their manufacturing customers to Europe, to be of service to them in any and all markets, with a view to holding the customers. From financing trade to the United States to borrowing abroad for the United States, lending in France, providing personal banking services to individuals, and lending to American firms in France, American financial institutions are still some distance from entering competitively into French bank lending.

Insurance

Allied to finance in the nature of the product, but more nearly like trade and manufacturing in method, American insurance companies had a brief spurt in foreign investment from 1885 to 1914. From slow beginnings as early as the early 1860s, three New York companies in particular reached by 1914 impressive totals of life insurance in force ($750,000,000 in all foreign countries), premium income ($50,000,000), foreign currency reserves ($45,000,000), and buildings. New York Life, Mutual Life, and Equitable Life constituted the "Big Three," whose advantage, necessary to foreign direct investment, lay in their aggressive selling, with high commissions paid to agents who "sold" insurance, rather than merely permitting customers to buy it. The American firms won authorization to do business in 1882 over the opposition of French insurance, banking, and railroad interests. Attempts were made in the French Chamber of Deputies to regulate the companies in 1885, 1890, 1892, and 1898, but all were unsuccessful. But in 1902 legislation was directed against them, requiring deposits in French securities, annual declarations of dividends due to policyholders, and more rigorous supervision. The large companies resisted by ostentatious purchases of French *rentes*, and an intensive propaganda campaign costing $40,000. The Armstrong scandals of 1905 in New York state led to more adverse publicity, and a new deposit law to cover old policies as well as new. Mutual Life withdrew, Equitable Life appealed to the Conseïl d'État and won its case in 1910, "partly because of the splendor of its new building." New York Life accepted the ruling, believing that the $81,000,000 of insurance outstanding in France and $13,000,000 sold in 1905 were worth it. The inflation of the war, however, made the business uninteresting.[44] By 1919, American companies had abandoned their French insurance business until after World War II, when they went abroad with further innovations, group-life insurance, and major medical policies, though in the later period they expanded through participation in majority-owned local companies rather than wholly-owned subsidiaries.

Trade

As already observed, distinctions between banking and trade were loosely drawn in the first half of the nineteenth century. Bankers and merchants financed the transaction of others, bought and sold goods for their own account and for third parties, as commission agents. As banking evolved and grew more specialized, moreover, so did trading. Commission agents, importers, wholesalers, jobbers, freight forwarders, and the like, separated themselves off. Fenwick & Co., for example, was noted as "the great importing house which played so important a part in American imports to France during the . . . three-quarters of a century" after 1894 (when the American Chamber of Commerce in France was founded). The firm was a founding member of the Chamber and was still functioning in 1969. Another founder was George R. Ostheimer, commission merchant, the Chamber's first Honorary Secretary, one of whose two sons, both members, was for many years a director.[45] In addition to specialization, however, as the scale of trade grew and qualities of goods changed, large integrated firms went in for direct buying and selling. This evolution began early with American department stores.

The first American investment in trade in France of this sort was that of Tiffany's. Charles Tiffany started his New York store in 1837, and he acquired through a new partner enough capital to send a buyer to England and France in 1841. From Paris, his partner John Young bought artificial diamonds with gold settings of a type superior to those from Germany with which the company had started. On a subsequent trip in 1848, Young and an assistant found that the market for real diamonds had collapsed because of the Revolution. Throwing away their purchasing schedule, they put all their funds into real diamonds. Shortly thereafter Tiffany decided to open a store in Paris to take advantage of sudden fluctuations in prices,[46] and to offer luxury merchandise to the many Americans traveling abroad who thought it "cosier and more reliable to pick up their more expensive mementos from a firm they could trust."[47] Tiffany, Young & Ellis, as the firm was known between 1841 and 1853, also ordered additional goods made to their own specifications in Paris. Other luxury retail establishments with shops in Paris included A. Sulka in haberdashery (which was founded in New York in 1895 and opened a Paris branch in 1910), Révillon Frères, and later Kaplan's (in furs), Durand-Ruel (art dealers), Brentano's (books), Van Cleef and Arpel (jewelry), Winston (in diamonds), and starting in Paris and moving to New York, Cartier. Tiffany closed its Paris branch in 1952.[48]

The authorship of the department store, long associated with Ariste Boucicaut's takeover of Bon Marché in Paris in 1852, and celebrated by Émile Zola in *Aux bonheur des dames*, is now in doubt.[49] There is no agreement on criteria for establishing what a department store is: on the basis of size, the Ville de Paris with $2,000,000 in sales and 150 employees in 1844 could claim precedence;[50] if the criterion is sales practices, A. T. Stewart's in New York, founded in 1823 and expanded rapidly in the 1830s and 1840s, has a strong claim, as it went in for many departments, one ticketed price, low markup, cash sales, aggressive selling, advertising, volume buying for cash, and the like, well in advance of the competition.[51] Ralph Hower insisted that the dominant consideration, however, is not the existence of departments, modern sales practices, or size, but a variety of housewares extending beyond dry goods. On this score he supported the case for Macy's, which opened its New York store in 1858.[52] For present purposes, however, what is of interest is that A. T. Stewart made his first trip abroad in 1839, and stopped buying through *commissionaires* and import houses six years later when, in 1845, he opened his own foreign purchasing department in Paris. Stewart had a Paris partner, Francis Warden, who managed an expanding purchasing operation from 1845 to 1873, establishing branch purchasing offices in every important textile center in the British Isles and on the Continent, and ultimately operating a number of textile mills in Europe for Stewart's account.[53]

Macy's relied increasingly in the 1860s on its own importations, as it eliminated importers and wholesalers as rapidly as increasing sales permitted. In 1893 it opened its own buying office on the avenue de l'Opéra, partly because of the growing volume of purchases and partly for prestige, but closed it down within three years on the ground that the separate buyers from New York must see the goods.[54]

Field, Leiter & Co., from which Marshall Field of Chicago developed, was the largest single importer into the United States, according to a Chicago newspaper report of 1906, with foreign purchases rising from $2,000,000 in 1880 to $4,300,000 in 1900 to $5,900,000 in 1906.[55] It paid three-fifths of the customs duties of the port of Chicago, which it had been instrumental in getting established in 1871.[56] The evolution of the buying process is well illustrated in Field's operations: at first in 1865 he went abroad himself in search of goods. As volume expanded, in 1868 he sent trusted employees. By the end of 1869 there was a Paris office on the letterhead of Field, Leiter & Co., but it was only a trade connection and not an independent office. In 1871 Marshall Field's brother Joseph opened a purchasing office in Manchester, and in 1872 a real purchasing office was started in Paris. The number of buyers sent abroad rose from 2 in 1875 to 21 in 1906. In the 1880s the firm expanded the two foreign operations into a network that included the Paris office for general French merchandise, a second office in Lyons for silks, and a third in Calais for lace.[57]

The Field's practice of the 1880s, however, gave way to the Macy's decision of the 1890s to rely on annual trips of buyers familiar with the needs of the customers. Commission agents, importing houses, wholesalers, and jobbers remained less preferable than direct buying, so that on the 1894 founding of the American Chamber of Commerce, it listed only two department stores with Paris buying offices: Jordan Marsh of Boston and Stern Brothers of New York, and these names with all the others were missing from the list in 1969.[58]

New York department stores and Field's in Chicago competed for exclusive agencies of European quality merchandise, especially kid gloves, chocolate, luxury china, and wines, plus French and Italian apparel. The decline of Stewart's and the rise of Field's was underlined when in 1880 the latter took over from the former the exclusive dealership of the celebrated Alexandre gloves.[59]

The next logical step after establishing purchasing offices was to undertake manufacturing. It was duly taken. It had been anticipated, however, by David Haviland, a New York importer of china from the East and England, who had been shown, in 1839, a broken teacup of unusual translucence and lightness, by a customer who wanted it replaced. Knowing only that it was French, Haviland went to France and found china of the desired quality being manufactured in Limoges. He tried to order some but found it difficult to obtain his requirements in kinds of pieces, volume, and decoration. Accordingly in 1842 he established his own plant in Limoges, the first American manufacturing direct investment in France that I have been able to find, and antedating those listed by J. H. Dunning in Britain.[60] The combination of French workmanship and American marketing made Limoges china renowned.[61] A quarter of a century later, L. Straus & Sons, importers of china, glass, and crockery which sold in Macy's and Wanamaker's in New York, R. H. White's in Boston, and in Woodward & Lothrop in Washington, D.C., acquired another china factory in Limoges, along with factories in Thuringia to make ivory and bisque novelties, and two in Bohemia for glassware and china, respectively.[62] Haviland sold 80 percent of its china through the New York importing company in 1905 and 20 percent in Paris through the Au Louvre and Bon Marché stores.[63] By 1972 only 40 percent of the Limoges output was marketed in the United States and the rest in Europe, as Haviland & Co. became truly international.[64]

Stewart's was the only department store to go far with foreign manufacture. A number of American department stores manufactured in the United States, but Stewart's operated a cotton mill in Manchester, England, a linen factory in Belfast, and an underwear mill and lace curtain factory in Nottingham. Macy's opened an office in Belfast to take charge of production of linen articles.[65]

The peculiarities of American taste led to the opening of a plant in France by American owners in one other item of consumption than china: kid gloves. Such gloves were a mark of elegance in the United States, and care was taken in department stores to stock a good brand, and if possible to do so exclusively. A. T. Stewart's loss of the exclusive agency for Alexandre gloves made by Fortin Fils et Deschamps was mentioned earlier. After Stewart's death in 1876, his successors had abandoned Stewart's practice of valuing Alexandre gloves three francs higher than other brands for customs purposes, leading finally to a customhouse charge of undervaluation, which brought unfavorable publicity to the French firm.[66] In its first year of business, Macy's claimed that its kid gloves were its own importation. Hower believed they were handled through an agent, but that at some subsequent point the volume grew to the point where direct purchase was possible.[67] Macy's adopted its own brand for La Forge kid gloves in 1877 and sold three different grades of Foster kid gloves, for which it was the exclusive agent in New York. It is not known whether these gloves were of French origin. It is noteworthy, however, that in his 1929 study *American Direct Investment in Foreign Countries*, Paul D. Dickens observed that in a few products, the presence of local raw materials or local skill had drawn U.S. investments in manufacturing, and he cites French fancy glove skins.[68] The reference is to Aris Gloves, Inc., which owns an interest in Gants Chanut, a long-lived investment which was established in 1910 and had 250 employees in the plant in 1972.[69] In 1972 Aris Gloves in New York was bought by Consolidated Foods. The subtleties of high fashion make it unclear why in one case a French manufacturer will give an exclusive agency to an American wholesaler (Stewart's, Macy's, and Field's were all wholesalers of gloves in the nineteenth century, when they were also selling them at retail), whereas in another, the wholesaler-jobber in the United States feels obliged to own the factory in France, presumably to have the product made to his idiosyncratic specifications.

The modern equivalent of Limoges china and Alexandre gloves of course is perfume and toiletries, in which American companies have taken over French firms not to make the product to suit the American market exactly but to exploit French skills and the reputation of French products.

Trade—Selling

The rise of the department store led to direct buying of foreign goods. The introduction of new goods of Yankee ingenuity eliminated the commission agent and the wholesale merchant from the selling side. The merchant system is highly efficient because of specialization in the distribution of standardized products. It inhibits technical change, which is fostered by direct contacts between the producer and the ultimate user. The merchant impedes change by telling the producer, "they don't want them like that," and telling the would-be buyer, "they don't make them like that."[70] An editor in 1884 recognized that the export house was no way to build a strong independent demand: "Sample machines lying in a far-off commission house and elegant office correspondence neatly done by a clerk on a type-writer," he wrote, "will never build up an export trade."[71] Remington & Co., which obtained the exclusive rights to sell the Latham Sholes typewriter in 1875, arranged to market through Fairbanks & Co., a scales manufacturer with outlets all over the world. Six years later it canceled the arrangement and undertook its own selling.[72] The classic example is furnished by John H. Patterson, the high-pressure salesman president of the National Cash Register company. Prior to 1895 the European business of the company was conducted through agents, and sales were minimal. In 1897 Patterson took a trip through Europe covering 15 countries and 50 cities in 60 days, and the French sales subsidiary along with many others was organized the same year. "It was not," wrote Roy W. Johnson and Russell L. Lynch, "the motion picture, or the petroleum industry, or yet the automobile that started the process often referred to as the 'Americanization' of Europe . . . the real pioneer in the movement that carried American selling methods throughout most of the civilized world was John Patterson and the NCR."[73] Patterson spent two years in London beginning in 1908. By 1914 foreign sales accounted for one-third of the company's business.[74]

Eastman Kodak, which had started manufacturing in England in 1890, was a pioneer in owning its own retail outlets. In 1902 it opened chain retail stores, first in London and then in Lyons. Twelve photographic dealers in Lyons protested. Eastman replied that the store would not subtract from their share of a fixed volume of trade, but that the publicity would expand the demand, with the result that other retail dealers would gain rather than lose.[75]

It is impressive in the literature how rapidly the move from domestic production to exports took place. Staffan Burenstam Linder's theory of comparative advantage in manufactured goods starts with development for the home market and then, presumably after a considerable period, a move to sell the differentiated products abroad.[76] The development in the local market must take place ahead of export, by definition, but it is remarkable how rapidly American manufactures entered the foreign markets and established direct selling. Producers of the reaper, revolver, sewing machine, railroad brake, adding machine, typewriter, radiator, gramophone, Kodak, arc lighting, telephone equipment, shoemaking machinery, and building elevators did not tarry in developing foreign markets. And fairly rapidly in the product cycle, as we shall see presently, they established foreign manufacturing.

In addition the list of sales organizations includes a number of products long forgotten or languishing: the Yost typewriter, Jewitt typewriter, Brill railroad car, American gramophone, American Motor Carriages, Cleveland bicycle, Consolidated tires, Dunlap hats, and Stetson hats.[77] Some gave up foreign investment prior to 1914, most before 1939. Some failed, some were driven out, some were absorbed by successor companies.

Manufacturing

The origins of American manufacturing investment in France extend earlier than the sales agencies. The idealized product cycle starts with production for the home market, patenting abroad, exports, direct selling, licensing for manufacture abroad, and ultimately direct manufacture, although the order is not necessarily always identical. Products of Yankee ingenuity like Colt revolvers and McCormick reapers were patented in France as early as the 1840s, were exhibited before Louis Napoleon and at the Paris Exposition of 1855 (following successes at the London exhibition of 1851), and were licensed for manufacture by French firms in the 1850s.[78] The Singer sewing machine license to Callebout in 1854 antedated the McCormick arrangement with D. J. Laurent of Paris and Francois Bella of Grignon in France.[79] Like the contemporaneous direct investments of Colt in London and of J. Ford in Edinburgh, neither was a success. French peasant conservatism stubbornly resisted the McCormick reaper, despite the efforts of the initial two licensees and their successor of 1862, Albaret et Cie of Liancourt Rantigny. "In some seasons," William Hutchinson wrote, "McCormick's sales in France were fewer in number than the prizes awarded him there."[80] Singer's initial licensee sold 425 sewing machines but used the 15 percent royalty owed to New York to pay off his own debts. This was the first and last time Singer sold a patent to an independent businessman. Mira Wilkins states that Singer started its own marketing in France after the expiration of the Callebout patent by the 1870s.[81] Robert Davies' history of the company abroad from 1854 to 1889 makes no mention of it, and Philip Whitcomb, noting Singer's presence among the founders of the American Chamber of Commerce in 1894, adds that the company did not begin manufacture in France until 1937.[82]

Manufacturing activities in France before 1900 included Westinghouse Air Brake (1879), General Electric and its predecessors, Edison Electric Light Co. of Europe, Ltd. and Thomson-Houston in electric lighting and arc lighting (1883 and 1892), Otis Elevator, United Shoe Machinery, Westinghouse Electric (1901), Western Electric, and American Radiator (1898).[83] Further investments up to 1914 were made by Ford, Gillette, Eastman Kodak, Carborundum Co., Ingersoll Rand, International Harvester, International Steam Pump, and American Gramophone.[84] The 14 (*sic*) companies with manufacturing facilities in France in 1914 were fewer than the number in Britain (25), Germany (22), or Canada (34).[85] All represented American innovations, predominantly in mechanical and electrical equipment. Where an invention was European, like the automobile, the investment (in an assembly plant by Ford) reflected an innovation in production on the one hand, and high rates of tariff protection on the other.

Manufacturing investment occurred in waves. After World War I there was another wave, including Corn Products, Carnation Milk, Colgate Palmolive, Atlas Chemical, and Chicago Pneumatic Tool— companies engaged in products of a second order of American ingenuity. If the story be true, one investment was inadvertent. The Norton Company in abrasives and grinding wheels, which had built a plant in Germany in 1910, was informed by a former employee that the plans on which he worked for a French factory in abrasives were identical to those which he had seen as a draftsman in Worcester, Mass. Arrest and litigation ensued, followed by a settlement, in the course of which the Norton Company ended up as the owner of a French plant.[86]

Some notable companies did not participate in the postwar wave of investment, advisedly. Both Ford[87] and General Motors turned down opportunities to buy Citroen, which came on the market in 1919, in need of rebuilding and lacking cash.[88] General Motors came in on the second wave of the 1920s but limited itself to spark plugs and refrigerators. This wave led to an outburst at the end of the decade against American imperialism, both in Germany and in France. In particular, the award of a contract for the renovation of the French telephone system to an IT&T subsidiary provoked a storm in the Senate, but was upheld.[89]

Investments by Bendix, Dana Corporation (both automotive parts), and Saint Regis Paper, all in 1930, appear to be parts of the end of the 1920s wave, parts that were delayed sufficiently to slip over into the depression. Since 1930 was a boom year for France, this delay was not unacceptable to the U.S. interest. Some substantial later investments—of Union Carbide in 1932 or Uniroyal in 1934—are more difficult to explain unless they represented long lags, a response to higher tariffs, or bargains picked up by extraordinarily liquid companies.

The complexity of timing investments in France is also illustrated by roller bearings. These are essentially an American invention and product. In 1909 the Timken Roller Bearing Company licensed a Vickers subsidiary to produce roller bearings in Britain. The British company, which became British Timken, though the American company had no interest in it at the time, licensed a French company, Société Mécanique de Gennevilliers, to make roller bearings in the early 1920s. Later in 1926, a British individual (B. U. Dewar) and American Timken bought British Timken from Vickers with a contract under which Mr. Dewar became manager. A French subsidiary was founded in 1927, also managed by Dewar, but was reorganized in 1928 as French Timken, owned first 75–25, then 50–50 by American Timken and Dewar personally. American Timken acquired Dewar's stock in French Timken in 1951 after his death.[90] An investment in France associated with an American innovation thus moved from British to American ownership over 30 years, with some cyclical fluctuations.

The pattern of owning productive assets through British subsidiaries of American companies was fairly widespread. In the typical case the British subsidiary was the first established, owing to identity of language and the "special relationship," and extension to the Continent went on from there. The pattern is exemplified in the Ford interests.[91] When Ford merged with the Mathis company of France in 1934, it had to buy back the 60 percent of its French company from its British company. The pattern of operating through London soon became unwieldy, and virtually every company ultimately chose to operate directly from the United States. If there were a European headquarters, it might be in London, or Paris, but it tended to be manned by American or international personnel. Occasionally the pattern was reversed, and the Paris office was the first in Europe. American Radiator employed the profits of its French manufacturing subsidiary of 1898 to open a German factory in 1901 and a British one in 1905.[92]

The list of American companies that once manufactured in France and have cut back is led by General Electric, Westinghouse Electric, and Ford Motor Company. All three names appear in the appendix tabulation but now are far below their peak size. In addition there are companies like Boston Blacking, which started out in cast-iron-stove polishes and moved on to chemicals, and which once owned subsidiaries in eight European countries (including France), subsidiaries since absorbed by others or liquidated.[93] In the petroleum field, another example is Caltex, discussed in the next section. There is something to the view that direct investments are immortal, but it is not a universal rule. Some shrink or die, and some, such as the manufacturing establishments shown in table A9.2 of the appendix (those with employees in France between 100 and 1,000), do not grow to enormous size.

Oil

Oil was among the earliest as well as the most important industries for investment by Americans in France. The history of the industry is highly complex and does not lend itself to rapid summary.[94] The initial effort was to sell crude petroleum to French refiners and refined products to distributors. Exactly when the Standard Oil Company (New Jersey) entered the market is not clear, but it had 50 percent of the crude market in 1893 when it formed Bedford & Cie to engage as well in refining directly, so that the selling effort probably began in the 1880s. Vacuum Oil Company, a predecessor to today's Mobil Oil Corporation, started to market petroleum and products in France in 1899, by 1900 had depots in Marseilles, Bordeaux, Nantes, Lille, Rouen, and Belfort, and in 1904 it built a plant for production of lubricants.

In the early period Esso Standard entered into agreements with French refiners to limit its interest in refining, and then to get out of it, in return for 50 percent of the crude market in France (1893) and later 80 percent (1900). The inability of the cartel to meet French requirements for fuel during World War I, however, led to its dissolution, its replacement by a government consortium, and the entry of Esso Standard into first bulk and later retail distribution of products. The French governmental counter was the formation in 1924 of Compagnie Française des Pétroles SA to take up the French participation in the Turkish Petroleum Company.[95] The major change occurred, however, with the law of March 30, 1928, which for defense purposes put a differential tax on imported products as against crude petroleum and required refiners to store substantial volumes of crude oil. Esso Standard, Mobil, and Texas (later Caltex) of the American companies bought and built refineries in France, along with Royal Dutch Shell and British Petroleum.

The Caltex company's activities in France grew out of a 1920 distribution agency of Texaco, which went into refining in France in 1932, and merged with the Standard Oil Company of California for European operations after World War II. The company disappeared from France in 1962, converting its assets into a minority interest in Union Industrielle des Pétroles, a company with a dominant state interest. This sale was made under government pressure.[96]

Services

By the 1960s a great many firms in the service industries—lawyers, accountants, advertising agencies, engineers, management consultants, and the like—had gone abroad to serve their American industrial clients, or like the banks and brokers, to serve the personal needs of the American colony. The first of these, so far as the record shows, was Dun & Bradstreet in 1872. This company, which provides information on credit ratings, had established a branch in London as early as 1857 and opened a Société à Responsabilité Limitée with a capital of 125,000 francs in Paris 15 years later.[97] That its business had not developed widely by the turn of the century is suggested in an offer to the American Chamber of Commerce, reported at its meeting of February 7, 1900, from the Comptoir d'Escompte to supply information on the financial standing of individuals and firms in France to American visitors to the Universal Exposition of 1900 who applied through the American Chamber of Commerce. In return the Chamber would be expected to give the friends and clients of the Comptoir all information in its possession regarding commerce and industries of the United States.[98]

The first prominent law office, Coudert Brothers, was established in 1879 by a firm that had been begun in New York in 1853. The father of the founding brothers had been an officer in the Napoleonic army who disagreed with the regime after the Restoration and emigrated to the United States in 1825. With the New York firm successful, one of the sons opened the Paris office primarily as a response to his love for France and Paris, and the opportunities for a practice of international law and a personal practice in wills, transfers of property, divorces, and so on, among the members of the rich American colony. Until 1946 it had few corporate clients, though it represented the Bank of France and the French government in the United States. When it did diversify, the number of its lawyers went from 6 in 1939 to 40 in 1972.[99] The leaders of the firm served in prominent positions in the American Chamber of Commerce, of which Henry Peartree was the second president and Henry Cachaud, the third.[100]

While Coudert Brothers was the most prominent, it was not alone in serving the expatriate colony. The New York *Herald Tribune*'s Paris activities were started in 1877, and many individual American doctors, dentists, lawyers, and other professional advisers (including one professor for curing shortsightedness) practiced in Paris. The American colony was estimated in 1929 as on the order of 55,000, though not all were rich. Otto Kahn had $20,000,000 in property in France when he died, and August Belmont a substantial amount. In addition many American women married into the French aristocracy and brought large dowries. The record dowry is given in one account as $7,000,000, with others noted of $6,000,000, $4,000,000, two of $2,000,000, and so on.[101]

The depression of the 1930s and World War II virtually destroyed these firms providing personal services, although they were mostly quickly reconstituted after the war. In brokerage, Bache & Co., which had started operations in France in 1936, closed down in 1940 and opened once more in 1947. Dewey, Ballantine, Bushy, Palmer & Wood (previously Root, Clark, Buckner & Ballantine) opened first in 1929, closed down in 1933, and did not return to Paris until 1965.[102]

Peat, Marwick, Mitchell & Co., a firm of public accountants who established a branch in Paris in 1906, were followed by a wave immediately after World War I, when other sizable law firms and advertising agencies came along. Engineering began with Stone & Webster just before World War II. In the 1960s there were architects, public relations firms, labor specialists, market research, armored car service, and a variety of others.[103]

Statistical Summary

The earliest estimates of American direct investment in Europe as a whole are those by Nathaniel T. Bacon for 1900 ($10,000,000) and John Ball Osborne for 1910 ($200,000,000), including United States holdings of European securities, of which there were "only a few."[104] While Paul Dickens regarded the Bacon estimate as "very careful and comprehensive" and "reasonably accurate," for Europe it was evidently far too low.[105] United States investment in France in 1929 was about one-eighth of the European total, as compared to one-third for Britain and one-sixth for Germany.[106] These relative proportions are broadly the same as the number of manufacturing subsidiaries in Europe in

Table 9.1
American direct investment in France

	1929		1936	
	Number of firms	Book value (in millions)	Number of firms	Book value (in millions)
Manufacturing	86	$ 91	77	$ 77
Distribution	56	14	55	13
Petroleum	23	25	7	40
Communication, transport	6	5		
Miscellaneous	25	9	25	14
Total	203	$145	164	$146

Sources: Paul D. Dickens, *American Direct Investment* and *American Direct Investment in Foreign Countries, 1936*, Department of Commerce, Economic Series No. 1 (Washington, D.C., 1938).

1914 cited earlier from Wilkins: Britain 25, Germany 23, France 14, if allowance is made for British subsidiaries to be somewhat larger than those on the Continent.[107] The suggestion that U.S. direct investment in France was only $1,200,000 in 1900 and $25,000,000 in 1910 is not to be believed.

The first estimate that breaks down American investment by countries is that of Paul Dickens for 1929 (table 9.1). Prior to that time the reports of the Department of Commerce in the 1920s had lumped together direct and portfolio investment, private and governmental, and those in separate countries. The figures for numbers of firms and book values for 1929 and 1936 are broken down by broad categories.

By 1950 the total had risen only to $217,000,000 of book value, broken down into $114,000,000 in manufacturing, $75,000,000 in petroleum, $5,000,000 in trade, $5,000,000 in public utilities, and $3,000,000 in smelting and refining, with total earnings amounting to $29,000,000, of which most came from manufacturing ($20,000,000) and petroleum ($7,000,000).[108] From approximately the same level in 1952, U.S. direct investment doubled in book value by 1956 and tripled by 1961, before rising to close to $3,000,000,000 in 1972.

Book values of course give a highly arbitrary and understated view of real values, although whether one should value direct investments on market liquidation, replacement, or capitalized earnings basis remains an unanswerable conundrum. In evaluating the Department of Commerce book value figure of $840,000,000 for American investment in France in 1961, Jacques Gervais calculated that this investment was worth "certainly $2,000,000,000."[109]

An educated guess would thus put the volume of U.S. direct investment in France over time, in current dollars, as

1900 $ 12 million

1914   35

1929   250

1936   250

1950   450

As this brief survey has indicated, American direct investment in France prior to the post-World War II era was significant. Many of the same factors that called forth the expansion of U.S. investment abroad in the 1950s and subsequently, both in manufacturing and in other sectors, were also present in the many instances of earlier investments in France. When American firms of recent decades engaged in overseas direct investment, they did so in the context of a long history of such activities, dating well back into the nineteenth century.

Notes

This chapter was written for a Conference of the French Association of Economic Historians on "The International Financial Position of France in the 19th and 20th Centuries," held in Paris, Octover 5, 1973. The author is indebted to many companies and individuals who have replied to letters and granted interviews. He is especially grateful to Mme. Phyllis Michaux, director of information service, American Chamber of Commerce, Paris, who made available much of the information of the Chamber, both current and historical.

1. La Documentation Française, Aperçu sur les investissements Américains en France, *Notes et études documentaires*, No. 3770, 15 March 1971, p. 3; and Les Sociétés Internationales, *Notes et études documentaires*, Nos. 3709-3710, 20 July 1970, p. 40.

2. General concern about American investment is recorded first in Britain in 1900; see Fred A. McKenzie, *The American Invaders: Their Plans, Tactics and Progress* (New York, 1901), and B. H. Thwaite, *The American Invasion: England's Commercial Danger* (Wilmington, N.C., 1902). German anxiety over *Ueberfremdung*—excessive domination of industry by foreign ownership—was recorded as early as 1852, when Gustav Meissen complained about British, Belgian, and especially French ownership of Rhineland mines. German irritation over American investment in the electrical industry was expressed in the 1890s. See Pierre Benaerts, *Les origines de la grande industrie allemande* (Paris, 1933), p. 353.

3. (London, 1958), p. 17. Dunning is mistaken in giving pride of place to the establishment in 1856 of the North British Rubber Company in Edinburgh by J. Ford of New Brunswick, N.J., for vulcanizing rubber. An earlier manufacturing investment in Britain was the branch plant established by Samuel Colt in London in 1852 to make muskets and pistols with interchangeable parts. This concern was sold to a British purchaser in 1857 at the end of the Crimean War, and failed shortly thereafter. Mira Wilkins' highly useful history of American direct investment, *The Emergence of*

Multinational Enterprise: American Business Abroad from the Colonial Era to 1914 (Cambridge, Mass., 1970), states that these two failures are exceptional as American direct investments prior to the Civil War. She has not taken account of the still-flourishing Haviland & Co. of 1842 in France, although there is a question whether that qualifies today as an American investment.

4. Fritz Redlich, Business Leadership: Diverse Origins and Variant Forms, *Economic Development and Cultural Change* 6 (April 1958):177–190.

5. Maurice Lévy-Leboyer, *Les banques européenes et l'industrialisation internationale dans la première moitiè du XIXe siècle* (Paris, 1964), pp. 432, 436.

6. Ibid., p. 436; *Adressbuch der Kaufleute und Fabrikarten von ganz Deutschland so wie der Haupt-Handels-und Fabrikarte des uebigen Europa unter der andern Welttheile* (1828), pp. 9, 19.

The liner service from New York to Le Havre was begun in 1822 by Francis dePau, four years after the initiation of the famous Black Ball Line from New York to Liverpool; Henry W. Lanier, *A Century of Banking in New York, 1822–1922* (New York, 1922), pp. 104–105. An American Chamber of Commerce in Le Havre is recorded in this period, but without details; R. G. Albion, *The Rise of New York Port, 1815–1860* (New York, 1939), p. 237. The American Chamber of Commerce established in Paris claims to be the first American Chamber abroad.

7. Muriel E. Hidy, George Peabody, Merchant and Financier, 1829–1854 (Ph.D. dissertation, Radcliffe College, 1939), pp. 17, 58.

8. Isabella Pratt Shaw, *The Welles Family and Wellesley* (n.p., n.d.), p. 23.

9. Ibid., pp. 28, 29.

10. Hidy, George Peabody, p. 84.

11. Lévy-Leboyer, *Les banques*, p. 558.

12. Hidy, George Peabody, p. 87.

13. Fritz Redlich, *The Molding of American Banking*, Vol. 2 (New York, 1951), p. 69.

Asa Fitch, Jr., is recorded in Moses Y. Beach's 1846 directory, *Wealth and Biography of the Wealthy Citizens of New York City*, 6th ed. (New York: The Sun Office), p. 10, with the statement that he was for a long time a merchant at Marseilles but was then doing a large commission business with his brother William, in Exchange Place, New York. Since the Beach directory was first produced in 1840 to provide credit information to "bankers, merchants and others" because of the disastrous experiences of 1837, there is a faint suggestion that the Fitch liquidation of the Marseilles house was connected with that panic. The directory gives the wealth of Asa Fitch as $300,000, of William Fitch as $100,000 (reproduced in Lanier, *A Century*, pp. 151ff).

14. Lévy-Leboyer, *Les banques*, p. 559.

15. Hidy, George Peabody, p. 283.

16. Cleona Lewis, *America's Stake in International Investments* (Washington, 1938), p. 193.

17. *Foreign Relations of the United States, 1878* (Washington, 1878), pp. 182–184.

18. American Chamber of Commerce in Paris, *Americans in France* (Paris, 1930).

19. Herbert L. Satterlee, *J. Pierpont Morgan* (New York, 1939), p. 150.

20. *In Memoriam, Jesse Seligman* (New York, 1894), p. 122.

21. Redlich, *Molding*, II, 367.

22. Edward Hopkinson, Jr., *Drexel & Co.* (New York, 1952); Nelson Dean Jay, informal account of the Paris office of Morgan Guaranty Trust Co., typescript in possession

of Morgan Guaranty Trust (hereafter cited as Jay typescript); John K. Winkler, *Morgan the Magnificent*, p. 46.

23. Winkler, *Morgan the Magnificent*, p. 2.

24. Morgan Guaranty Trust Co., *Annual Report*, 1967, p. 10.

A Paris Embassy dispatch to Washington on October 20, 1873, however, noted that after consulting prominent American bankers in the French capital, it could be said that the number of American residents in France "does not increase but rather diminishes" (*Foreign Relations of the United States, 1874*, p. 401).

25. Jay typescript, p. 2.

26. Satterlee, *J. Pierpont Morgan*, pp. 309, 411.

27. Morgan Guaranty Trust Co., *Annual Report*, 1967, p. 10.

28. Jay typescript, p. 4.

29. In 1899 the American Chamber of Commerce in Paris circulated its 165 members to obtain their opinions on the merits of the U.S. government starting parcel post service between the United States and France. Eighty-one replies were received, of which 71 were favorable and 8 opposed—presumably American Express and the freight forwarders. American Chamber of Commerce, Paris, *Minutes*, April 5, 1899 (bound manuscript).

30. Alden Hatch, *American Express: A Century of Service* (New York, 1950); Ralph T. Reed, *American Express; Its Origin and Growth* (New York, 1952).

31. Carl Seaburg and Stanley Patterson, *Merchant Prince of Boston: Colonel T. H. Perkins, 1764–1854* (Cambridge, Mass., 1971), p. 225.

32. Henry Greenleaf Pearson, *Son of New England: James Jackson Storrow* (Boston, 1932), p. 100.

33. Clyde William Phelps, *Le mouvement de l'extension des banques américaines à l'étranger er principalement en France* (thesis, Toulouse, Imprimerie V. Barnet, 1924), p. 141.

34. Paul P. Abrahams, The Foreign Expansion of American Finance and Its Relationship to the Foreign Economic Policies of the United States, 1907–1921 (Ph.D. dissertation, University of Wisconsin, 1967), p. 71.

35. Phelps, *Le mouvement*, p. 77.

36. Clyde William Phelps, *The Foreign Expansion of American Banks* (New York, 1927), p. 138.

37. Phelps, *Le mouvement*, p. 141.

38. Ibid., pp. 34–37.

39. Abrahams, Foreign Expansion of American Finance, p. 84.

40. Phelps, *Le mouvement*, pp. 95–96.

41. Ibid., pp. 125–126. The one per mil tax on capital (*centime additionelle à la patente*) was discriminatory in the sense that it applied to total capital of the bank, and not merely to the capital of units in France. Thus the National City Bank paid the tax on a capital of $100,000,000 for the entire bank, when it had only one branch in France, while the Société Générale, with 603 branches in France, paid a similar tax on a similar overall capital sum. In 1924, however, the National City Bank organized as a *Société Anonyme*, rather than a branch, and drastically reduced its obligation. Phelps, *Foreign Expansion of American Banks*, p. 179.

42. Abrahams, Foreign Expansion of American Finance, pp. 24, 40.

43. Jacques Koszul, American Banks in Europe, in C. P. Kindleberger, ed., *The International Corporation: A Symposium* (Cambridge, Mass., 1970), pp. 285–286.

44. Morton Keller, *The Life Insurance Enterprise* (Cambridge, Mass., 1964), part III.

45. Philip H. Whitcomb, *Seventy-Five Years in the Franco-American Economy: A Short History of the First American Chamber of Commerce Abroad* (Paris, 1970), p. 13.

46. Frank A. Southard, Jr., *American Industry in Europe* (Boston, 1931), p. xiii, lists 1850 as the date Tiffany decided to open a Paris store.

47. Joseph Purtell, *The Tiffany Touch* (New York, 1971), pp. 19–24.

48. The history of Tiffany makes a great deal of an alleged innovation in retail marketing in setting fixed prices, plainly marked on merchandise, concerning which there would be no bargaining, and attributes the immediate success of the Paris store to this technique (Purtell, *Tiffany Touch*, pp. 18, 24). It may be doubted that fixed prices were original with Tiffany, despite the fact that New York newspapers of 1837 featured the practice in headlines. George Fox, the Quaker, called for it in the seventeenth century, and Josiah Wedgwood applied it in his showrooms in the eighteenth century; see Ralph M. Hower, *History of Macy's of New York, 1858–1919* (Cambridge, Mass., 1946), pp. 26, 89. Bon Marché adopted the single price system in 1838, and the growing size of retail establishments made its spread inevitable when the store owner, or a trusted relative, could no longer take time to settle the bargain with each customer. The Tiffany investment was thus not solely or even primarily based on an innovation in retailing, although this store may have extended the system from dry goods to jewelry.

49. H. Pasdermadjian, *Le grand magasin* (Paris, 1949), *passim*.

50. Hower, *History of Macy's*, p. 73.

51. Harry E. Resseguie, Alexander Turney Stewart and the Development of the Department Store, *Business History Review* 39 (Autumn 1965):303.

52. Hower, *History of Macy's*, contains an extended discussion of the question whether Paris or New York deserves the credit for originating the department store, including an appendix (pp. 411–416) on "The Rise of the Department Store in Paris."

53. Resseguie, Stewart and the Department Store, p. 316.

54. Hower, *History of Macy's*, pp. 110, 242–243. Reference was made to "our Paris house" in the middle 1880s, but this was the buying office of L. Straus, a china-importing firm. Isador Straus (of the importing firm) bought into R. H. Macy & Co. in 1888.

55. Robert W. Twyman, *History of Marshall Field, 1852–1906* (Philadelphia, 1954), pp. 99, 178.

56. Lloyd Went and Herman Kogan, *Give the Lady What She Wants: The Story of Marshall Field and Company* (Chicago, 1952), p. 99.

57. Twyman, *History of Marshall Field*, pp. 26–28, 116, 10.

58. Whitcomb, *Seventy-Five Years*, p. 13.

59. Harry N. Resseguie, The Decline and Fall of the Commercial Empire of A. T. Stewart, *Business History Review* 36 (Autumn 1962):269.

60. Interview, Frederick Haviland, and the pamphlet, *Haviland: The History of a Name* (n.p., n.d.); see also Whitcomb, *Seventy-Five Years*, p. 15.

Like the Welles private bank, there is a question whether Haviland & Co. technically qualifies as a direct investment, since the French owners lived in France and owned as much of Haviland & Co., Importers of New York as the latter owned of them. But it falls within the spirit of direct investment.

61. A novel by Jacques Chardonne, *Porcelain de Limoges* (Paris, 1936, pp. 83, 93) records trips by a Limoges engineer to America to discuss the technical workings of furnaces and refers to the mail from America.

62. Hower, *History of Macy's*, pp. 212, 246.

63. *Custom House Justice and Haviland China* (New York, 1907), pp. 12, 33.

64. Interview with Frederick Haviland.

65. Resseguie, Stewart and the Department Store, p. 319; Hower, *History of Macy's*, p. 163.

66. Resseguie, Decline and Fall of Stewart, p. 269.

67. Hower, *History of Macy's*, p. 110.

68. U.S. Department of Commerce, Trade Information Bulletin No. 731 (Washington, 1931), p. 32.

69. American Chamber of Commerce in Paris, *List of American Firms in France* (Paris, 1972), p. 12.

70. Charles P. Kindleberger, *Economic Growth in France and Britain, 1851–1950* (Cambridge, Mass., 1964), pp. 148ff.

71. Cited in Robert B. Davies, "Peacefully Working to Conquer the World": The Singer Manufacturing Company in Foreign Markets, 1854–1889, *Business History Review* 43 (Autumn 1969):306.

72. Richard N. Current, *The Typewriter and the Men Who Made It* (Urbana, Ill., 1954), pp. 85, 103.

73. *The Sales Strategy of John H. Patterson, Founder of the National Cash Register Company* (Chicago and New York, 1932), p. 330.

74. Samuel Crowther, *John H. Patterson, Pioneer in Industrial Welfare* (Garden City, N.Y., 1926), pp. 268, 273.

75. Carl Ackerman, *George Eastman* (Boston, 1930), p. 172.

76. *An Essay in Trade and Transformation* (New York, 1961), *passim*.

77. Yost & Co. early got the domestic (but not foreign) rights to the Sholes and Glidden typewriter, which ultimately became the Remington, but later Yost & Co. gave it up and started its own company in 1880. Current, *The Typewriter*, pp. 78, 98. Little more is readily available about this company, and nothing about Jewitt.

78. William B. Edwards, *The Story of Colt's Revolver* (Harrisburg, Pa., 1953), p. 255; William T. Hutchinson, *Cyrus Hall McCormick*, Vol. 1 (New York, 1930), p. 404; Martin Tywell, *Samuel Colt: A Man and an Epoch* (Harriman, Tenn., 1952), p. 127.

79. Hutchinson, *Cyrus McCormick*, Vol. 2, p. 415.

80. Ibid., p. 685.

81. Davies, "Peacefully Working," p. 303; Wilkins, *Emergence of Multinational Enterprise*, pp. 38–39, 42.

82. *Seventy-Five Years*, p. 15.

The Vaupel & Curhan compilation [James W. Vaupel and Joan P. Curhan, *The Making of Multinational Enterprise: A Source Book of Tables Based on the Study of 187 Major U.S. Manufacturing Corporations* (Boston, 1969)] gives the date of Singer's founding in France as 1907, the method as "subsidiary formed" and the activity as sales, with a manufacturing subsidiary formed only in 1957. The American Chamber of Commerce *List* gives the date of establishment as 1872.

83. Henry G. Prout, *A Life of George Westinghouse* (New York, 1921), p. 269.

84. Exact dating of an initial manufacturing investment is difficult for the reasons illustrated in the preceding footnote. The Vaupel and Curhan compilation for 187 leading companies of 1967 and the American Chamber of Commerce *List* of 1972, covering 675 American branch, subsidiary, or affiliated companies in France (out of 1,000) are incomplete in coverage of existing firms at the time, and of course of firms that no longer exist or no longer maintain foreign investments. In addition questionnaires are not always unambiguous and respondents can become confused in interpreting. In the American Chamber of Commerce *List*, "date of establishment" is sometimes given for the French subsidiary prior to acquisition or takeover, for transfer to the parent at time of reorganization or change of name. A further ambiguity inheres in the case of discontinuous investments. Vaupel and Curhan moreover ask for exact years only after 1900. The best general statement is of course Wilkins, *Emergence of Multinational Enterprise*. Appendix I presents as accurate a picture as can be drawn from secondary sources of companies by date of investment, according to broad classes.

85. Wilkins, *Emergence of Multinational Enterprise*, p. 212.

86. Mildred McClary Tymeson, *The Norton Story* (Worcester, Mass., 1953), pp. 171–172.

87. Ford later twice bought up manufacturing, as opposed to assembly facilities, before finally selling off its Simca holding to Chrysler. It never made a profit in France. And General Motors, especially its 1920 vice-president for Europe, who later went to Ford, never thought France a good risk. Mira Wilkins and Frank Ernest Hill, *American Business Abroad: Ford on Six Continents* (Detroit, 1964),p. 367.

88. Ibid., p. 97; Alfred P. Sloan Jr., *My Years with General Motors* (Garden City, N.Y., 1964), p. 317.

89. An earlier outburst against U.S. investment, prior to 1929–1930, occurred in 1923 when German interests were bought up with dollars during the hyperinflation. This is a classic example of "market failure," like the carpetbaggers at the end of the American Civil War. See also Southard, *American Industry in Europe*, pp. 178, 226–227, 244; Octave Hamberg, *L'Impérialisme Américaine* (Paris, 1929); and Jean Bonnefon-Craponne, *La pénétration économique et financière des capitaux américains en Europe* (Paris, 1930).

90. Letter to the author, November 3, 1972.

91. Wilkins and Hill, *American Business Abroad*, p. 66.

92. Lewis, *America's Stake*, p. 303.

93. Southard, *American Industry in Europe*, p. 118.

94. See Ralph W. and Muriel E. Hidy, *Pioneering in Big Business, 1882–1911; History of the Standard Oil Company* (New Jersey) (New York, 1955), and George S. Gibb and Evelyn Knowlton, *The Resurgent Years, 1911–1927: History of the Standard Oil Company* (New Jersey) (New York, 1956).

95. Gibb and Knowlton, *Resurgent Years*, p. 510.

96. Jacques Gervais, *La France face aux investissements étrangers, analysé par secteurs* (Paris, 1963), p. 138.

97. Letter to the author from Dun & Bradstreet, International.

98. American Chamber of Commerce, Paris, *Minutes*. After some hesitation, the Chamber agreed to the exchange, despite the fact that it was contrary to its practice, because there was need for the information. It accepted the offer on a nonexclusive basis but refused to take responsibility for the accuracy of the information.

99. Interview with Charles Torem.

100. The first president, Dr. Stephen H. Tyng, represented one of the insurance companies. He had been a chaplain in the Civil War in the United States but resigned from the church over "many vexatious controversies" in religion. American Chamber of Commerce, *Minutes*, November 18, 1899.

101. George W. Herald and Edward D. Radlin, *The Big Wheel* (New York, 1953), pp. 63–65.

102. American Chamber of Commerce in Paris, *List*.

103. Ibid.

104. Bacon, American International Indebtedness, *Yale Review* 9 (November 1900):265–285; Osborne, Protection of American Commerce Abroad, *North American Review* (May 1912):673–690. Bacon (276) excludes the $45,000,000 of reserves of foreign securities held by the life insurance companies against their liabilities. He makes no mention of direct investment. Keller, *Life Insurance Enterprise*, p. 89, gives an estimte of $15,000,000 of European securities owned by U.S. investors in 1899, apart from the life insurance reserves.

105. Dickens, *American Direct Investment*, p. 37.

106. Ibid., p. 10.

107. In 1929 and 1936, United States subsidiaries in France were distinctly smaller than those in Britain or Germany:

	Country	Number of firms	Book value (in million $)	Average per firm
1929	France	203	$145	$ 700,000
	Germany	186	217	1,170,000
	Great Britain	389	485	1,240,000
1936	France	164	146	880,000
	Germany	151	228	1,500,000
	Great Britain	411	474	1,150,000

Sources: Dickens, *American Direct Investment*, p. 10; and Paul D. Dickens, *American Direct Investment in Foreign Countries, 1936*, Department of Commerce, Economic Series No. 1, (Washington, 1938), p. 3.

108. U.S. Department of Commerce, Office of Business Economics, *Balance of Payments Statistical Supplement* (Washington, 1958), *passim*.

109. Gervais, *La France face aux investissements étrangers*, pp. 53, 54.

Appendix: American Direct Investment in France to 1950

Table A9.1
Manufacturing companies with more than 1,000 employees in 1972

Date of sales affiliate	Date of manufacturing		Product	1972 employees in France	Book capital, 1970 (in million F)	Percent U.S. owned
1872		Singer	Sewing machines	4,750	64	100.0
	1879	Westinghouse Airbrake	Railroad brakes	1,775	12	88.8
1880	ca. 1913	Otis Elevator	Building elevators	5,500	36	100.0
1880	ca. 1893	Exxon (SONJ)	Petroleum products	4,899	596	82.0
	1889	IT&T	Telephone equipment	8,700	29	75.0
1890	before 1900	Studebaker Worthington	Pumps	1,200	11	100.0
1893	1909	International Harvester	Agricultural machinery	5,285	53	99.9
1893	1904	Mobil Oil	Petroleum products	2,580	249	100.0
1897	1927	Eastman Kodak	Cameras and film	8,700	972 (sales)	Almost entirely
1897	1934	National Cash Register	Cash registers	2,050	28	99.95
	1898	American Standard	Radiators	5,182	53	99.9
1904	1955	Burroughs Corp.	Accounting machines	1,900	12	100.0
1914	1920	International Business Machines	Computers	18,000	524	99.99
	1920	Norton Co.	Abrasives	2,090	81	92.0
	1920	CPC International	Corn products	2,270	53	n.g.

1921	1959	Goodyear Tire & Rubber	Tires	2,453	n.g.	n.g.
	1922	Corning Glass Works	Specialty	4,500+	n.g.	n.g.
	1923	Carnation Milk	Evaporated milk	1,200	n.g.	100.0
	1925	General Motors	Spark plugs, autos, parts, refrigerators	2,526	2	100.0
	1926	Timken Co.	Roller bearings	1,200	n.g.	100.0
1930	1934	Uniroyal	Automobile tires	1,776	28	99.9
	1930	Bendix Corp.	Automotive equipment	19,000	n.g.	n.g.
	1930	Dana Corporation	Transmission systems	3,500	n.g.	n.g.

Note: n.g. means "not given."

Table A9.2
Manufacturing companies with 100 to 1,000 employees in 1972

Date	U.S. company	Product	Employees in France, 1972	Book capital, 1970 (in million F)	Percent U.S. owned
1892	General Electric	Electrical apparatus	120	n.g.	n.g.
1898	W. W. Bliss	Mechanical presses	420	10	99.0
1901	Westinghouse Electric Co.	Electrical equipment	425	n.g.	n.g.
1901	USM Corp.	Shoe machinery	500±	5	97.0
1905	Ingersoll Rand	Industrial equipment	300	0.8	100.0
1910	Aris Gloves	Kid gloves	250	n.g.	n.g.
1910	Carborundum Co.	Abrasives	340	17	99.9
1913	Sperry Rand	Appliances	625	n.g.	n.g.
1913	Gillette Co.	Razors and razor blades	820	1	99.0
1916	Joy Manufacturing Co.	Mining equipment	229	13	100.0
1919	Coca Cola Export Corp.	Soft drinks	210	n.g.	n.g.
1921	Crane Co.	Plumbing supplies	400	19	81.0
1921	Pennwalt Corp.	Industrial equipment	252	6	100.0
1921	Lanvin, Charles of the Ritz	Toiletries	206	n.g.	n.g.
1921	E. F. Houghton	Lubricants, etc.	297	4	25.0
1923	Colgate Palmolive	Soaps	600	n.g.	n.g.
1923	Atlas Chemical	Chemicals	n.g.	n.g.	n.g.
1926	Armco Steel	Steel	600	4	99.8
1927	NVF Co.	Plastics	151	4	98.0
1927	Simmons	Home furnishings	627	7	50.0

1928	Blaw Knox Co.	Industrial equipment	350	n.g.	n.g.
1929	Crown Cork and Seal	Metallic packaging	364	n.g.	n.g.
1929	Helena Rubenstein	Cosmetics	366	5	100.0
1929	Monsanto Co.	Chemical	490	n.g.	n.g.
1930	Addressograph	Office machinery	334	2	99.0
1930	Hoover Co.	Home appliances	567	63	50 (50)[a]
1930	S. C. Johnson & Sons	Waxes	320	n.g.	n.g.
1932	Union Carbide	Graphite electrodes	630	18	56.5
1934	Ferro Corp.	Ceramic glazes, colors	349	3	10.2 (89.8)[a]
1937	Parker Hannifin Corp.	Hydraulic materials	237	2	92.0
1937	Abex Corp.	Brake linings	101	n.g.	n.g.
1937	Max Factor	Cosmetics	300	n.g.	n.g.
1946	Fruehauf Corp.	Trailers	994	13	67.0
1947	Johns Manville	Insulation	875	n.g.	100.0
1947	Fischer & Porter Co.	Industrial measures	438	n.g.	n.g.
1947	Bournes Inc.	Electronic components	350	5	75.0
1949	Foster Wheeler Corp.	Design, engineering, chemical plants	640	n.g.	n.g.
1950	Chevron Chemical	Petrochemicals	115	3	99.0
1950	Honeywell Inc.[b]	Automatic controls	690	25	100.0

Note: n.g. means "not given."
a. In parentheses, share belonging to non-Americans owned outside France.
b. Not to be confused with Honeywell Information System, capitalized at Ff 485 million, with a 66 percent participation in Compagnie Honeywell Bull, engaged in data processing equipment.

Table A9.3
Companies engaged in sales and renting only

Date	Company	Product	1972 employees in France More than 10	Less than 10
1909	Swift & Co.	Abattoir products	33	
1912	Armstrong Cork	Insulation	40	
1916	Ford Motor Co.	Automobiles	450	
1919	Smyth Manufacturing Co.	Book-binding machinery		x
1919	Brackett Stripping Machinery	Tape-stripping machines		x
1922	United Fruit Co.	Bananas	32	
1925	Dorr Oliver	Engineering		n.g.
1927	International Nickel	Nickel	30	
1930	Metro-Goldwyn-Mayer	Film distribution	97	
1935	Walt Disney Productions	Film distribution	32	
1945	International Mercury Outboards	Outboard motors	50	
1948	Pan American World Airways	Air travel	268	

Table A9.4
Companies enagaged in buying, or buying and selling

Date	Company	Product	1972 employees in France More than 10	Less than 10
1921	Conde Nast Publications	Fashions	135	
1922	Associated Merchandising	Buying Dry goods	40	
1927	*New York Times*	News gathering	n.g.	
1929	Warnaco	Lingerie	66	
1944	United Press International	News gathering	66	
1949	Aviquipo	Export-import aeronautical equipment	23	

Table A9.5
Companies engaged in finance

Date of founding	Bank or firm	Activity	1972 employees in France	
			Less than 10	More than 10
1868	Morgan Guaranty Trust Co.	Bank	481	
1875	American Express Company	Banking and travel	275	
1918	Chase Manhattan Bank	Bank	400	
1920	Bankers Trust Co.	Bank	40	
1921	First National City Bank	Bank	330	
1936– (1947)	Bache & Co.	Brokerage	19	
1938	Fahnestock & Co.	Financial consultants		x
1949	Bank of America	Bank	237	

Table A9.6
Other services

Year	Company	Service	1972 employees in France	
			More than 10	Less than 10
1872	Dun & Bradstreet	Credit ratings	130	
1877	Paris, New York *Herald Tribune*	Newspaper	n.g.	
1879	Coudert Brothers	Law firm	40 lawyers	
1906	Peat, Marwick, Mitchell & Co.	Accountants	200	
1919	Grey Advertising	Advertising	136	
1920	Price, Waterhouse & Co.	Accountants	n.g.	
1920	Porter & Dunham	Law firm		x
1920	Ernest and Ernst	Accounting	70–80	
1920	Haskin and Sells	Accounting	n.g.	
1924	Arthur Young	Accounting	n.g.	
1927	McCann Erickson	Advertising	148	
1929– 1933 (1965)	Dewey, Ballantine, Bushy, Palmer & Wood	Law		x
1939	Stone & Webster	Engineering	20–25	
1946	Parsons and Whittemore	Engineering	95	
1947	Arthur Andersen & Co.	Accounting	200	
1949	Cleary, Gottlieb, Steen & Hamilton	Law firm	n.g.	
1949	Cahill, Gordon, Sonnet, Reindel & Ohl	Law firm		x
1950	AAA World Wide Travel Inc.	Travel agency	15	

Source: The major source is the *List of American Firms in France* published by the American Chamber of Commerce in France, which deals with dates, nature of activity, and employees in 1972. The figures on capitalization are from a card file in the American Chamber of Commerce. Dating has been amplified and corrected from other sources (not all of which are themselves accurate), especially the worksheets of Vapuel and Curhan, a special printout of which has been kindly provided by the Harvard Business School project on multinational business, as well as company histories, and the like. An inevitable residue of error and ambiguity remains.

10

International Banks and International Business in Historical Perspective

Textbook myth to the contrary notwithstanding, domestic banking has many origins, not just evolution from goldsmiths. In addition to the goldsmiths, prominent in a few English banks, private banks evolved as well from tax farmers who dealt in the king's money for a time and lent out funds temporarily in their possession; from manufacturers issuing to workers tokens which continued to circulate; from scriveners and notaries; from money changers and merchants. International banking developed primarily from merchants and money changers. The money changers were for the most part unimportant, except in such a case as the Warburg bank of Hamburg (Rosenbaum and Sherman 1979). International trade and international banking were widely overlapping activities until the middle of the nineteenth century. Before that period not all traders undertook banking roles, but most bankers indulged in trade, international, domestic and even retail, and even in production. Italian bankers in the thirteenth, fourteenth, and fifteenth centuries, German in the sixteenth, Dutch in the seventeenth and eighteenth, and British in the eighteenth and early nineteenth centuries all furnish examples of a wide variety of operations:

The outstanding trait of Francesco Marco di Datini, a merchant of Prato outside Florence over the turn of the fourteenth to fifteenth century, was the variety of his activities as clothmaker, armourer, mercer, shopkeeper, import and export business, dealer in wool, cloth, veils, wheat, metals and hides, in spices, pictures and jewels. He joined the guild of cloth merchants, took over the city's tolls for meat and

Paper presented to the International Conference on Multinational Banking in the World Economy, Tel Aviv, June 15, 1983. Abridged in *Journal of Banking and Finance* 7 (December 1983):1–13.

wine, did some underwriting (in insurance), and finally against the advice of his friends, set up a bank. (Origo 1957, 78) . . . A conservative banker, Datini did not lend to princes, popes, or Communes. (ibid., 152)

Mrs. Origo comments that the great trading companies of the fourteenth century took part in every field of human enterprise: trade, industry, banking, and politics (ibid., 95).

The Tuscan bankers of the thirteenth and fourteenth centuries who loaned to the English kings did so with an eye to obtaining licenses for the export of wool (Kaeuper 1973). In the fifteenth century:

The leading staples of the Medici were wool, alum, cloth, spices, olive oil, citrus fruits, but they equally dealt in aristocratic luxuries such as silks, brocades, jewelry and silver plate, in addition to selling letters of credit to pilgrims, travelers, students, diplomats and churchmen, and handling the papal remittances from Europe to Rome. (de Roover 1966, 135, 142)

At the end of the eighteenth century and a short distance into the nineteenth, John Hope and Company of Amsterdam clung proudly to the tradition of a wide range of operations at a time when other merchant bankers were well along the path to specialization:

Hope made loans to the Russian court, and to the United States for the Louisiana Purchase, helped transfer funds owed by Spain to Napoleon by way of Vera Cruz, Baltimore, New York, London and Amsterdam. As merchants the bank dealt at first hand and second hand in "all articles: money, grain, colonial produce, ships' articles, gold, silver, drysaltery, ordnance, textiles, tobacco, tea, wine, flower bulbs, in short anything that could be traded at a profit." (Buist 1974, 53) . . .

The firm operated the monopoly of Portuguese diamonds, together with a monopoly of imports of brazilwood for dyeing, bought Talleyrand's library when he was strapped for funds, speculated in Russian hemp and flax by buying and storing it in St. Petersburg when the blockade cut off its export to the west. (ibid., 75, 212, 245)

Nathan Rothschild went first to Manchester when he left the Frankfurt ghetto and made a substantial sum speculating in cotton and cotton textiles before moving his operations to pure banking and to London (Corti 1928). At the end of the nineteenth century even J. P. Morgan bought up a distress cargo on speculation and sold it at a profit before converting to his family's more sedate mode of operation.

The Italian bankers did specialize somewhat by area. Venice dealt particularly with the Levant and Germany, exporting silver and importing spices, silk, alum. Genoa was the rival of Venice in the east, but also active in Spain, Portugal, and Lyons. When the Genoan bankers were expelled from Lyons in 1464, they moved their banking operations to the fair at Besançon, which they gradually transferred to Piacenza in Italy (da Silva 1969, I). The Tuscan bankers of the thirteenth to fifteenth century dealt more with northern Europe. With a head office in Florence, the Medici had a network of branches all over Italy: Venice, Milan, Genoa, and Pisa; abroad they had branches at London, Bruges, Geneva, Lyons, and Avignon (de Roover 1966). German and Dutch bankers seemed less specialized. The Fuggers and other South German bankers operated mainly in Bruges and Lyons but stretched south as far as Naples and Rome, and westward to Spain and Portugal (Ehrenberg [1896] 1928). Amsterdam inherited the role of the Hanseatic League—which incidentally never developed much in the way of banking and insurance—in the North Sea and Baltic, and reached down the Atlantic Coast to Nantes, Bordeaux, Lisbon, and Seville, as well as ranging to the East and West Indies.

This chapter deals with private banking and neglects the roles of public banks which were connected mainly with the provision of standard money, building capital markets for government debt, and to a limited extent supporting the great chartered trading companies such as the East India Company, the Dutch East India Company, and the French East India Company. This last connection between international business and banking was on the whole minimal—the great trading companies maintaining a market for their stock in the capital market. It proved fatal in the case of the Bank of Amsterdam (van Dillen 1934). A deposit bank, and presumably forbidden to make loans, it sought to come to the rescue of the Dutch East India Company which was sorely hurt by the fourth Anglo-Dutch War in 1782. In the course of providing this support, both institutions went bankrupt. For the most part, and despite some ostensible connection of the Sword Blade Bank with the South Sea Company, and of John Law's Banque Royale with the Compagnie d'Occident, giving rise to the South Sea and Mississippi bubbles respectively, the mercantile aspects of these operations were unimportant as compared with government finance, on the one hand, and private speculation, on the other, so that the generalization that public banks were largely disassociated from commerce and industry remains unchallenged (Dickson 1967, Carswell 1960, Levasseur 1854).

Specialization occurred gradually both in domestic and in international banking. The process can be followed in many business histories. William Braund, for example, started out in the early eighteenth century as a general merchant selling cloth in Germany and Portugal and bringing back mixed cargos. He later specialized in cloth exports to Portugal and imports of gold and silver. Gradually he gave up on exports, bought bills of exchange on Lisbon from other exporters, and with the proceeds bought specie for importation to England. Trade with Portugal flourished under the treaty of Methuen of 1704. In due course he found it less strain to focus his attention on insurance under-writing in London (Sutherland 1933). The same process can be seen a century later in the history of Brown Brothers in the Anglo-American trade. Alexander Brown migrated to Baltimore from Northern Ireland, and began his career by importing Irish linen into the United States. He later switched to exporting cotton for his own account, and financing the cotton exported by others with advances running between two-thirds and three-quarters of the value of a shipment, along with selling letters of credit on his Liverpool office to American importers of British goods. He and his sons who succeeded him at one time owned a shipping line, and the sons later dabbled in government and railroad investment. The Brown brothers spread to Philadephia, New York, and Liverpool, gave up selling cotton for their own account except to fill out a ship's load, then gave up shipping. After specializing for some years in advances on cotton exports and letters of credit for imports, the Liverpool office moved to London and took on a general banking business (Perkins 1975).

Both international business and international banking got a stimulus about the middle of the nineteenth century from the far-reaching changes in transport and communication. International banking had long been handicapped by the slowness and uncertainty of commun-ication. At the beginning of the sixteenth century usance from Genoa— the time allowed for a sight bill of exchange before payment was required—was 5 days to Pisa, 6 to Milan, 15 to Ancona, 20 to Barcelona, 50 to Valencia and Montpellier, 2 months to Bruges, and 3 months to London (Braudel [1949] 1973, I, 375). Usance between London and Antwerp was one month, a figure that lasted unchanged from the fourteenth century to 1789 (de Roover 1949, 109). Innovation in do-mestic transport proceeded earlier. In the 1630s the cities of Holland evolved a system of passenger barges, drawn in canals by horses at an average speed of 3 miles an hour. This may not have been a drastic increase in average speed, but it reduced the variance of the time taken by merchants journeying between cities on business, as it elim-inated the occasions when a sailing lugger had to wait for a favorable wind (de Vries 1979). In the international field, dependability was the purpose of an innovation that took place in 1819—the liner, or sailing vessel which left New York for Liverpool every Saturday whether it had a full cargo or not (Albion 1939). Turnpikes had sped internal transport in the eighteenth century at a rate which has been called for Britain a "transport revolution" (Deane 1965, ch. iii). By the middle of the nineteenth century, however, international transport and communications achieved a series of quantum leaps with the development of the railroad, steamship, telegraph, transatlantic cable (1866), Suez canal (1868), Alpine tunnels, and the domestic telephone (1880s) before the twentieth-century innovations of radio, transatlantic telephone, airplane, and after World War II, jet aircraft, telex, and satellite television. The first use of airplanes instead of trains for transporting central bankers in emergency was made in 1931, when President Hans Luther of the Reichsbank flew about Europe trying to borrow funds to stave off crisis, the same year that U.S. and British government officials negotiated on the transatlantic telephone for the first time. The Bank for International Settlements established by the Young Plan of 1930, and located at the central railroad junction of Europe, Basel, was from the viewpoint of transport an immediate relic of a bygone day.

The industrial revolution and especially the railroad and steamship also increased the demand for capital from business. One innovation was the spread of the joint-stock company from the mid-1850s. Domestic banking changes took place everywhere, starting with joint-stock banks in England in 1826 and 1833, and on the Continent the first "mixed bank," lending to industry beyond mere short-term financing of shipments and inventories, in the Société Générale of Brussels, founded in 1825. The real upsurge, however, came in the 50s, with the establishment of the Crédit Mobilier in France in 1852, the Bank of Darmstadt in Germany in 1856, and a host of imitations in France, Germany, Austria, Italy, Sweden, and Spain (Cameron 1961). The inspiration for this development came from Saint-Simonism, a system of thought that attached great importance in economic growth to the expansive effect of new and vigorous banks. As it turned out, intimate relations between business and banking flourished more in Germany, Austria, and Italy than they did in France after the failure of the Crédit Mobilier in 1868. The great new deposit banks of the 1860s like the Crédit Lyonnais and the Société Générale (of France) turned away from industrial lending to short-term credits on the English pattern and to securities speculation (Bouvier 1961). Some industries in Germany such as chemicals fought shy of close collaboration with banks, as Henry Ford was to do later in the United States (Riesser 1911). For the most part, however, banks and industry were intimately associated in Germany, Austria, and Italy, with interlocking directorates and bank directors voting the shares of clients' securities deposited with them.

There was a faint imitation of the Crédit Mobilier in England that failed in the financial crisis of 1866. For the most part in domestic banking the 1850s and 60s saw the development of larger and stronger banks through mergers and absorptions and the beginning of the formation of national networks. Most worked along the traditional lines financing trade and inventories, although in the north of England, a number of banks made longer-term loans to industry, sometimes disguised as short-term loans the frequent renewal of which was understood (Cottrell 1980).

In international banking the nineteenth century brought about the creation of specialized institutions like the acceptance houses and bill brokers in England, the *hautes banques* and merchant banks of Paris, Frankfurt, and Hamburg. In 1872 the Germans formed the Deutsche Bank with the express purpose of moving into the British quasi-monopoly in foreign exchange transactions. The newly formed Reich expressed disgust that the German navy bought the foreign exchange needed for overseas disbursements in London (Helfferich 1956, 53). As it turned out, the Deutsche Bank got caught up in the boom that followed the founding of the greater Reich and turned to domestic lending (ibid.). It later sought to rival British foreign banking in south-eastern Europe and Turkey but never became a formidable threat in the foreign exchange field.

The major thrusts of international banking of the period were concerned with lending to foreign sovereigns or for public works such as railroads. The Crédit Mobilier established subsidiaries in Austria, Italy, and Spain, and James de Rothschild, despite his disdain for the principles that motivated the Pereires brothers' operation of the Crédit Mobilier, followed suit. Anglo-Italian and Anglo-Austrian banks were established without conspicuous success. The period was marked, however, by a general turning of British investor interest away from the Continent after the Revolution of 1848, and the development of specialized British regional banks operating in the Far East, Africa, and Latin America.

The movement of United States banks abroad like Brown Brothers, George Peabody which evolved into J. P. Morgan, and Welles & Co. in Paris was originally motivated by trade. Gradually they turned to selling U.S. securities. Some firms such as J. & W. Seligman pioneered in the selling first of U.S. government securities about the time of the Mexican war (1846) and then of railroad bonds. A number of institutions serving tourists and American expatriates went abroad toward the close of the nineteenth century—lawyers in Paris, stockbrokers in such a watering place as Pau, and the American Express Company (see chapter 9). A number of banks set up branches in France during World War I, but most were withdrawn during or after the 1921 recession (Abrahams 1967). The beginning of U.S. direct investment in Europe can be traced back to the 1850s, but it is unlikely that American banks paid serious attention to it until the 1920s and especially after World War II.

The location of banks is generally dictated by the nature of their business. Merchant bankers were originally at ports, court bankers at the capital or seat of power. Some banks locate themselves for the convenience of their depositors, as the numerous private banks in London's West End where the aristocracy lived during the season and to which it transferred its rents from the countryside. Major banks were typically pulled to the money and capital market. The London and Westminster Bank, formed in 1833 under an interpretation of the Bank Act of 1833 which permitted joint-stock banks in London if they did not issue notes, was a combination of a money-and-capital market bank (the London of the name) and a bank seeking to serve the aristocrats of Mayfair and benefit from their deposits. In the last 20 years a new source of attraction for bank location has arisen—the multinational corporation. The movement of a number of the great New York money market banks uptown to the Grand Central area north along Park Avenue is a response to the agglomeration of head-quarters of multinational corporations there. The Chase Manhattan Bank with a new building downtown resisted the move, and tension between the two locations representing the multinational corporation, on the one hand, and the capital markets, on the other, remains unresolved, especially after the downtown location has been aided by the construction of the World Trade Center under the aegis of the then governor of New York state, Nelson Rockefeller, brother of David Rockefeller, then president of Chase Manhattan Bank. An earlier ex-ample of the magnetic attraction of multinational corporations was the winning out of Frankfurt over Hamburg and Düsseldorf as the financial center of the German Federal Republic after the enforced separation of banks by *Lander* had lapsed. Hamburg, the port, was the financial center for international trade, Düsseldorf the center of securities trading. Frankfurt had been the headquarters of the U.S. occupation forces and attracted U.S. corporations setting up subsidiaries in West Germany.

In most countries domestic banks have created national networks usually headquartered in the financial center. Banks with excess funds are drawn to the center to find outlets in the capital market; banks with strong demands for funds at home are attracted to obtain additional resources. The process is usually a long drawn out one; it may move in waves. It is seen especially clearly in Italy after unification in 1860, and in Germany following its unification in 1871 and again after 1948 when authority was turned over to the German government by the Allied occupation authorities (Kindleberger 1974). The felt need for assured sources of funds or assured outlets rests on a fear that markets may at a time of need be insufficiently broad and competitive for money to be lent or borrowed in needed amounts at existing rates.

Domestic banks may create subsidiaries abroad for separate foreign operations for the same basic reasons—mainly to find outlets for surplus funds, but on occasion to find funds to meet needs at home, and for two more reasons: to apply abroad a lending technique developed at home or even one newly developed, both gathering funds in the foreign market and dispensing them there, and to gain access to techniques of banking already developed abroad or likely to be developed there. The first of these last two reasons takes banks to less competitive markets, the second to more competitive. There is one more reason a bank may wish to establish a branch in a foreign country, that is, to have a presence there. This is called "defensive investment," investment designed not so much to make a profit in that place as to prevent a loss somewhere else, or in the system as a whole. It has been said that the First National City Bank of New York branch in Paris was at a severe disadvantage as compared to local banks, which attracted low-interest deposits whereas it had to pay market rates for funds, but went ahead because it was fearful that the day might come when some customer would want to talk to his bank in Paris and might choose to take his account elsewhere if the National City were not on hand (Kozul 1971). Defensive investment is equally a phenomenon of the multinational corporation. In a given industry, and in the short run, each company is interested in being represented in each major market lest a competitor make a great deal of money there and gain strength enough to challenge successfully in other markets.

There are also multinational corporate examples of moving to a location in order to participate in the most rapidly changing and competitive market. This is sometimes called "going up against the fastest gun in the West." Any serious money-market bank in the United States had to be represented in the Eurodollar market. A number of regional banks moved there in 1966 and 1969 during the

so-called "crunches" in order to be able more readily to borrow Euro-
dollars to strengthen reserve positions in the United States.

Niehans has claimed to find the essence of the multinational corporation in vertical integration across national boundaries for fear of
bilateral monopoly (1978). He uses a series of case studies of Swiss
multinational corporations to derive this conclusion, but a handier
illustration perhaps comes from the international oil industry. The
refiner fears being cut off from access to crude upstream; the producer
of crude in turn worries that he may be cut off from transport or
markets downstream. The effective way to overcome these fears is to
integrate vertically. If there were assured competitive markets at each
stage of production with limited price variability, or alternatively if it
were cheap to store inputs or to sell outputs forward, the possible
losses from monopoly or monopsony could be insured against in other
ways which did not run the risk of diseconomies of scale in administration. In oil, coal, bauxite, and perishable products such as electricity,
however, storage costs are high and/or forward markets undeveloped
beyond the near term.

The stockpiling alternative to vertical integration has been used by
international business in the field of finance. A firm deciding on a
capital expenditure frequently borrows the funds in the Eurocurrency
market and holds them on deposit until needed. Money can be stockpiled in this way in the same way that companies building the Alaskan
pipeline stockpiled pipe. The cost of assured liquidity, and not depending on the goodwill of bankers at a later time when money may
be tight, has been the difference between the borrowing and the
deposit rate. With floating borrowing rates this moved within a narrow
range. In any event it seems to be the case today that the risk of a
price change is less worrisome to business than the risk of inability
to count on quantity. This accounts for the acceptability of floating
rates on long-term borrowing to borrowers, and explains why foreign-
exchange risk has had such little effect in cutting off international
capital flows (Kindleberger 1978).

The first solution, vertical integration between banks and industry,
has been adopted, so far as I am aware, mainly in Japan. It is limited
in the United States to a handful of domestic cases such as the General
Motors Acceptance Corporation which finances installment paper on
sales of General Motors cars. In Japan, however, a single complex
may combine producer companies in a number of fields such as iron
and steel, shipbuilding, chemicals, and heavy engineering with a trading
company for engineering designs and marketing, and a bank plus life
and casualty insurance companies to furnish the finance. Provided

that the bank and insurance companies are successful in attracting business, the industrial complex is reasonably assured of being in a position to finance new projects as they come along.

After Japan, the relations between banks and business in Germany and Austria are the closest thing to vertical integration. The possibilities of such close collaboration were abandoned by France in the nineteenth century, and excluded by law in the United States and Italy by the Glass-Steagall act of 1933, requiring banks to separate from their investment banking affiliates, and by the 1936 Banking Law in Italy to the same effect. German and Austrian banks ran into as much trouble on their business investments in the 1930s as the Italian and American, but they were bailed out by government in the short run and allowed over the longer period to accumulate resources while armament and the war were financed by government (Hardach 1981, Nötel 1981). The intimate connections that still prevail in Germany between business and the banks after more than a century are ironically underlined by the fact that the Dresdner Bank is widely blamed for the troubles of AEG-Telefunken, the two companies sharing a common chairman in their separate boards of directors.

There is, to be sure, the possibility of close collaboration between business and banking in Italy—the official level through the governmental Istituto Riconstruzione Italiana (IRI) and the Istituto Mobiliare Italiana (IMI) in finance, the former taking over the equities in a vast number of firms in the deflationary crises of 1923 and 1933 and the latter raising funds for distribution to industry through access to government credit. It is my understanding, however, that IRI and IMI on the whole leave operating industrial firms to their own devices except in emergency situations, or where some important social purpose such as employment in Sardinia is to be served. Vertical integration between government-owned finance and industry in Italy is therefore more potential than actual.

Although U.S. banks are forbidden to have investment banking relations with commercial banks, there is a variety of interlocking directorate relationships, on the one hand, and a movement toward full-line banking outside the commercial banking field, on the other. The Prudential Insurance Company has acquired a leading brokerage house, Bache & Co., and a merger has taken place between Shearson, Hammill, a broker house, and American Express with an already wide range of financial services. Merrill, Lynch, the enormous brokerage house, has extended operations into underwriting, money funds, and, in association with a bank, a complete range of personal financial services. Citicorp is in the process of buying a failing savings and loan association on the West Coast of the United States with the intention of crossing state lines, forbidden to commercial banks, and obtaining a highly developed network of retail credit outlets in California.

A more interesting development from the viewpoint of international networks is the merger movement across national lines. For a time, early in the development of the Eurocurrency market, there was a movement to form consortia banks sponsored by leading banks in say four countries. This seems to have petered out, probably because the parent banks preferred to keep the good loans they generated for themselves, and the parents of other banks were unwilling to take only the less attractive credits. Recently, however, there have been international mergers and acquisitions, especially by foreign banks in the United States, as for example, that of the Marine Midland Bank by the Hong Kong and Shanghai Co. and the purchase of a 40 percent position in the equity of the Crocker National Bank of San Francisco by the Midland Bank of London. United States banks have long been forbidden to undertake branch banking across state lines, and in the usual case before the bank-holding company spread, across county lines. Foreign banks are under no such restriction so long as they conform to the separate laws of each state. There is a strong possibility that if many foreign banks take advantage of the gap in American banking legislation which exempts them from the prohibition against interstate banking, the regulation will be relaxed for American banks. There is talk also of relaxing the Glass-Steagall act to enable U.S. banks to constitute investment affiliates, and legislation is in process to enable New York banks to establish a sort of free zone in which they can attract international business without regulation from the U.S. authorities, after the pattern of the Eurocurrency market. Returns on these and similar changes are not all in, but it is possible to detect the sentiment that the pace of innovation in recent years—NOW accounts, CDs, money funds, the Eurocurrency market, bank-holding companies, and full-line financial operations by nonbanks—has been too rapid in recent years to enable secure judgments to be made about their consequences. At one extreme is the view that the system of regulation should be tightened up and returned to the position of a decade or so ago; at the other is the serious suggestion that any regulation of money is a disaster, and all regulation should be abandoned. Vaubel in particular argues in favor of private competitive monies on the ground that good monies will drive out bad—the opposite of Gresham's law (Hayek 1977, Vaubel 1979).

Whether banks then follow or lead international business today admits of no easy answer. National networks follow different laws and traditions, but international networks have been created by some national banking units and seem to be in formation with international ownership. Similarly, in some industries manufacturing firms have been building world networks. The movement is not universal: there are none in competitive industries such as farming or textiles, and none in coal or steel. In automobiles the intensity of international integration is being set back in depression. In chemicals, pharmaceuticals, petroleum, computers, and other electrical appliances, however, world networks continue to be filled out, although the losses in recession since 1974–75 have required many companies to sell off their best assets to keep going, and the composition of networks is in some flux. A recent modification of the theory of the multinational corporation observes that the advantage of such companies should be calculated not on the features which enable them to make their separate investments, but on their capacity overall to arbitrage on a world basis (Kogut 1983). The same is true of world banking networks. To return to the original question, it is likely that where bank networks are aggressive in building world networks, and industry focuses on single projects and defensive investment, banks lead and industry follows. On the other hand, where industry is aggressive and banks are defensive, the order is reversed. I see no way to determine which the dominant tendency is now, and I suspect that it is subject at the moment to substantial change.

Two types of world banking networks can be distinguished, at least in theory. Citicorp claims to operate with the first, an integrated world network in which the dollar goes round the world each day and world activities are dominated from New York. All branches are exposed to the possibility that they may be directed with little or no notice to transfer a sizable proportion of their lendable funds to another branch. The other type that applies to most banks is to assign a certain amount of capital to a branch, and to make changes slowly, step by step, expanding successful branches by small increments as the system gains resources and contracting less successful ones the same way. Although the two systems are different in theory, they probably converge in practice. The same distinctions were originally made by a major oil company in capital budgeting, with the head office in New York notionally bringing to that city the net cash flow of all the branches in the world, especially, depreciation, depletion, and profits, and allocating capital expenditures to separate branches and subsidiaries on the basis of the year's prospects as if each unit in the world were starting de novo. In practice each unit was expected to survive from year to year and in fact to grow at the average pace of the company, except when some prospect changed significantly for the better or the worse. The same implicit conflict exists in the World Bank, where theoretically new loans could be concentrated anywhere that substantial opportunities were presented, though in reality the Bank is divided into area divisions, each with a fairly well-established portion of the total funds, and most countries in good standing can expect to be accorded loans on a regular basis. The fear that a region might lose its share of the available capital to another region probably accounts for the decision to set up the development banks with soft money for social-overhead-capital projects on a continental rather than global basis.

Are banks more or less international than firms? Some years ago I suggested a classification of degrees of internationalism for industrial firms (which did not meet with favor in the literature and has not been adopted). Three categories were distinguished: (1) national firms with foreign operations, (2) multinational firms, and (3) international firms. The distinction rested in theory not on size or system of organization as such, though there are students of management who use such criteria, but on behavior. In foreign exchange, for example, the first group was disposed to feel completely easy only in its own currency and minded going long but not short of foreign currencies. The second group, trying to be a good citizen of every country in which it had operations, was reluctant to go short of any currency. The international corporation on the other hand was prepared to maximize worldwide by taking long positions in strong currencies and short in weak, without regard to which currency was that of the firm headquarters (Kindleberger 1969). In employment the first group hired mostly its own nationals in positions of responsibility, the second nationals of the host countries, the third the best people it could find regardless of nationality. Similar classifications could be made for capital budgeting, new products, location of research and development, and a host of other functions.

It is probably fair to say that there are no truly international corporations by these criteria. All to a major or minor degree are conscious of government policy of the home country, and find themselves exquisitely embarrassed when they are pulled two ways by two different governments as in the case of the GE rotors for the compressors for the Soviet pipeline. Henry Ford once transferred a major sum to England to buy the minority shares in Ford of England and was publicly scolded by the Eisenhower administration for so doing because the U.S. balance of payments (in 1960) was weak. Some years later Royal Dutch Shell sold £140 millions of cash on hand in London for dollars to protect its net worth and was told by Her Majesty's government that the action was unseemly. The home country counts even for the giants.

There are probably no truly international banks, either. I have not attempted to devise criteria on which a scale of internationalism for banks could be rated. The foreign-exchange criterion is unsatisfactory, since most banks have learned on the basis of such episodes as the speculative losses of the National City Bank of Brussels in the 1950s that short-term monetary assets and liabilities in separate currencies are best balanced if not hourly at least at the end of the day: Total liabilities owed to foreigners? Or to foreigners and compatriates outside the borders of the country of headquarters? Number of branches? Rank in assets in each country among foreign banks, in each country outside the home country? Howard Reed has ranked financial centers by various criteria and divided the centers into categories, but not the banks (1982). Even though one can classify banks as local, regional, money-market, and international, the lines between the truly international banks and those regional and national banks with foreign branches or representation are hard to draw. A few banks continue to specialize in foreign operations without forming worldwide networks (i.e., the First National Bank of Boston in Latin America). And even world banks are examined by national authorities since these authorities have a residual responsibility for the world operation of banks headquartered in their jurisdictions under the Bank for International Settlements concordat of 1975 that followed the Herstatt episode. That agreement has been thrown into some doubt by the Bank of Italy's unwillingness to accept responsibility for the Banca Ambrosiano's Luxembourg subsidiary, on the ground that it was not a branch.

I suspect that there is no way to judge whether the 20 leading banks of the world measured by assets are more or less international than the 20 leading corporations on the *Fortune* world 500 list. It is clear, however, at the moment that banks are probably becoming more international, as foreign banks come to the United States, even if some American banks with interests abroad shrink them a little, and that there is at the moment a decline in the spread of international firms.

World banks are sufficient in size and number, however, that monetary policy should be made on a world basis, starting no doubt with money supplies, interest rates, and moving perhaps ultimately to such questions as regulation and taxation.

One final point. I very much doubt that the rise of international banking and business networks in the next period of recovery, and those that succeed it, will ever eliminate the need for the local knowledge which is the advantage of the local bank or the local firm. The return to general nonspecialized business and finance that comes with world economic integration still requires someone to specialize in understanding local credit and local ways of doing business. Not everything in the way of relevant knowledge can be punched into the computer and transported with complete understanding to company or bank headquarters, as the troubles of the Continental Illinois, the Chase Manhattan, and the Seattle First National Bank in the Penn Square fiasco illustrate. Some specialized networks will continue to develop, subordinate to the world network: I have been told that Aberdeen acquired its oil-lending techniques direct from Houston rather than by way of London and New York which would canalize the money flows. Whichever leads in the increasing nonspecialized world, banking or business, there will be no getting away from the need for a minimum of specialization by some unit or units in local knowledge.

References

Abrahams, Paul P. 1972. *The Foreign Expansion of American Finance, 1907–1921.* New York: Arno Press.

Albion, Robert G. 1939. *The Rise of New York Port (1815–1860).* New York: Scribners.

Bouvier, Jean. 1961. *Le Crédit Lyonnais de 1861 à 1882.* 2 vols. Paris: SEVPEN.

Braudel, Fernand. 1949. *The Mediterranean and the Mediterranean World in the Age of Philip II.* Vols. 1, 2. Reprint New York: Harper & Row, 1973.

Buist, Marten G. 1974. *At Spes Non Fracta: Hope and Co., 1700–1815.* The Hague: Martinus Nijhoff.

Cameron, Rondo. 1961. *France and the Economic Development of Europe.* Princeton: Princeton University Press.

Carswell, John. 1960. *The South Sea Bubble.* London: Cresset Press.

Corti, Egon Caesar. 1928. *The Rise of the House of Rothschild.* New York: Blue Ribbon Books.

Cottrell, P. L. 1980. *Industrial Finance, 1830–1914, The Finance and Organization of English Manufacturing Industry.* London: Methuen.

Da Silva, José-Gentil. 1969. *Banque et crédit en Italie au XVII siècle.* Vols. 1, 2. Paris: Editions Klincksieck.

Deane, Phyllis. 1965. *The First Industrial Revolution.* Cambridge: Cambridge University Press.

De Roover, Raymond. 1949. *Gresham on Foreign Exchange.* Cambridge, Mass.: Harvard University Press.

De Roover, Raymond. 1966. *The Rise and Fall of the Medici Bank.* New York: W. W. Norton.

De Vries, Jan. 1978. *Barges and Capitalism: passenger Transportation in the Dutch Economy, 1632–1839.* Philadelphia: Benjamins North Am.

Dickson, P. G. M. 1968. *The Financial Revolution in England: A Study in the Development of Public Credit, 1688–1756.* New York: St. Martin's Press.

Ehrenberg, Richard. 1896. *Capital and Finance in the Age of the Renaissance.* Reprint New York: Harcourt Brace, 1928.

Hardach, Gerd. 1981. Banking and Industry in Germany in the Inter-War Period 1919-1939. Paper submitted to a conference of the Banco di Roma held at MIT, October 23-24.

Hayek, Friederich A. 1977. *Choice in Currency, A Way to Stop Inflation.* Occasional Paper no. 48. London: Institute of Economic Affairs.

Helfferich, Karl. 1956. *Georg von Siemens.* Krefeld: Serpe.

Kaeuper, Richard H. 1973. *Bankers to the Crown: The Ricciardi of Lucca and Edward I.* Princeton: Princeton University Press.

Kindleberger, C. P. 1969. *American Business Abroad: Six Lectures on Direct Investment.* New Haven: Yale University Press.

Kindleberger, C. P. 1974. *The Formation of Financial Centers: A Study in Comparative Economic History.* Princeton Studies in International Finance no. 36. Princeton University Press.

Kindleberger, C. P. 1978. Price and Quantity, Especially in Financial Markets. In C. P. Kindleberger, *International Money.* London: George Allen & Unwin, pp. 256-266.

Kogut, Bruce. 1983. Foreign Direct Investment as a Sequential Process. In C. P. Kindleberger and David Audretch, eds., *The Multinational Corporation in the 1980s.* Cambridge, Mass.: The MIT Press, pp. 38-56.

Kozul, Julein-Pierre. 1971. American Banks in Europe. In C. P. Kindleberger, ed., *The International Corporation,* Cambridge, Mass.: The MIT Press, pp. 273-289.

Levasseur, E. 1954. *Recherches historiques sur le système de Law.* Reprint New York: Burt Franklin, 1970.

Niehans, Jürg. 1978. Benefits of Multinational Firms for a Small Parent Economy: The Case of Switzerland. In T. Agmon and C. P. Kindleberger, eds., *Multinationals from Small Countries.* Cambridge, Mass.: The MIT Press, pp. 1-39.

Nötel, Rudolf. 1981. Money, Banking and Industry in Interwar Austria and Hungary. Paper submitted to a conference of the Banco di Roma, held at MIT, October 23-24.

Origo, Iris. 1957. *The Merchant of Prato.* New York: Knopf.

Perkins, Edwin J. 1975. *Financing Anglo-American Trade: The House of Brown, 1800-1880.* Cambridge, Mass.: Harvard University Press.

Reed, Howard C. 1982. *The Preeminence of International Financial Centers.* New York: Praeger.

Riesser, Jacob. 1911. *The Great German Banks and Their Concentration in Connection with the Economic Development of Germany.* Washington, D.C.: National Monetary Commission.

Rosenbaum, Eduard, and A. J. Sherman. 1979. *M. M. Warburg & Co. 1798-1938, Merchant Bankers of Hamburg.* New York: Holmes & Meier.

Sutherland, Lucy. 1933. *A London Merchant, 1699-1774.* London: Oxford University Press.

Van Dillen, J. G., ed. 1934. *History of the Principal Public Banks.* The Hague: Martinus Nijhoff.

Vaubel, Roland. 1977. Free Currency Competition. *Weltwirtschaftliches Archiv* 113: 435-459.

11

Book Review: Barnet and Müller, Global Reach

For a while it looked as though I would get by without reading this book. When the proof sheets were gratuitously sent me last August 1974, I read for ten minutes and decided "Not for me." Then the *New Yorker* two-part summary appeared in the fall of 1974, and my name was mentioned. Friends lent me the issues; I verified the fact that I had been quoted, found a statement of such reckless McCarthy-like attack that I noted it in something I was writing ("The extent to which the [oil] crisis was the result of conspiracy [by the petroleum industry] may not be known until the historians are given access to the oil companies' equivalent of the Pentagon Papers" (repeated in the book on p. 222) and resolved that I did not need to read it. Simon and Schuster sent one advance copy of the book in December 1974, which I shelved unread, and another in January 1975, which I gave away. Last spring I was asked to review it at a sizable fee for the house organ of a large corporation. That was easily resisted. A request from *Christianity and Crisis* seems based less on making a case and more on genuine puzzlement as how to view the issues raised by *Global Reach*. In the end I had to read it.

It is not an easy book to read. I suspect that the average purchaser reads no more than a third of it before finding more absorbing ways to occupy him- or herself. The first hundred pages or so contain a staccato barrage of factual statements and quotations in what I call *Reader's Digest* style (often used in sermons and in my view highly objectionable as prose): "Chief Executive Roundtable discussion paper notes . . ." "what IBM's Maisonrouge calls . . ." "The Dow cafeteria in Midland, Michigan offers . . ." "David Rockefeller and other global executives are calling for . . ." "says Pepsico president Donald

Written in 1975 at the request of *Christianity and Crisis*. Unpublished.

Kendal ..." "Henry Heltzer, chairman of 3M believes ..." "Lee L. Morgan, executive vice-president of the Caterpillar Tractor Company, thinks ..." "Carl Gerstracker says, ..." "Maisonrouge says ..." "A. W. Clausen of Bank America [sic] believes ... " "CPC International believes ..." "says José de Cubas, senior vice-president of Westinghouse ..." (from pp. 62–65). Slow going.

After the first hundred or so pages in this vein—largely one surmises the work of Barnet, the political scientist—we come to economic analysis with a dizzying barrage of numbers: national incomes, sales, profits, statistics on trade, the balance of payments, concentration ratios, and the like, evidently the work of Müller, the economist. An economist myself, I should have relaxed, but the author piles the reader's plate to the point of total indigestion. For example: "foreign deposits of the biggest banks are now two-thirds of their domestic deposits ... Almost all foreign deposits, according to Andrew Brimmer of the Federal Reserve Board, are in the hands of 20 multinational banks. Indeed just four banks ... have about 38 percent of all foreign deposits ... In the early 1950s, corporations on the average had $8 of cash for every $10 in short-term debt. In the 1969–1973 period, corporations had so extended their debt that they held only $2 cash for every $10 of current liabilities ... Thus in 1973, according to the Federal Reserve, nine New York City banks, six of which belong to the Rockefeller-Morgan group, accounted for more than 26 percent of all commercial and industrial lending in the United States (There are 220 banks, according to the Fed, which do virtually all the corporate lending in the country). About half of all the money lent by these New York superbanks goes to global corporations ..." and so on until the head spins.

Global Reach for all the indigestibility of its prose has a message. It is that the large U.S. corporations operating worldwide are a menace. For all their vaunted interest in growth, these corporations, Barnet and Müller believe, are responsible for hunger, unemployment, pollution, business depression, difficulties of macroeconomic management, energy problems, transport troubles, currency crises (though not all short-term capital movements come from them, p. 286), widening gap in levels of living between developed and developing countries, alienation of workers at home and abroad, the demise of competitive markets, unequal income distribution, and economic injustice. This powerful bill of particulars is a little uncertain as to whether to include inflation as another consequence (for "yes," see pp. 269 and 289, and for "no," see the complex footnote on pp. 448–449). In a final chapter the authors urge a rather vague program of planning, local control of business, backyard steel plants, prohibitions on the power of firms to exploit their mobility: "yet how this is to be done is by no means clear."

Despite their universalistic title the authors are much more interested in U.S. corporations and operations in Latin America than in the operations of U.S. corporations in other parts of the world, especially Canada and Europe, or operations in the United States of corporations sited in other developed countries. The index is untrustworthy (there are only three references to Müller's other work, but I counted nine unindexed citations, and the same was true of other economists indexed), but if we assume that it understates possible index entries evenly, it is significant that there are one citation for Australia, three for Canada, five for France, nine for West Germany, and 12 for Britain, whereas Chile has 16, Mexico 29, and Brazil 33. It is not clear whether the European and Japanese corporations undertaking investment in the United States can be held to assist the obsolescence of American labor, poor nutrition of American families, unemployment, balance-of-payments difficulties, and the like.

The argument is riddled with contradictions. United States corporations are enormously powerful at home but subject to grave weakness abroad at the hands of countries such as those belonging to OPEC (the Organization of Petroleum Exporting Countries); they shift money out of the United States but do not bring it to the countries where they undertake investments abroad; they destroy jobs both at home and abroad, except in "export platforms"—a phase which bemuses them, where coolies in Hong Kong, Taiwan, Singapore, and so forth, work for wages, given within a few pages (303 to 312), as 14 cents an hour, 30 cents an hour, 40 cents an hour, 50 cents an hour, $2 a day. Corporations take a long view of planning but are subject to the tyranny of the quarterly balance sheet and profit statement; they are monopolists of technology, but part of their difficulties arises from being quick to sell off technology; they are monopolists who can charge any price they please but have to use cheap foreign labor in order to be able to compete. Developing countries have solidarity, but their national individualism is strong. And so on. I was particularly troubled by the contradiction in the statements: "In Argentina, the First National City Bank charges in some cases a negative interest rate (This is the result of charging an astronomical sounding 30 percent interest in an economy with an inflation rate of 60 percent)" (p. 141). A few pages later (p. 154): ". . . scarce financing is retailed to the general public in the form of consumer debt at exorbitant interest (in Colombia a prominent economist has estimated that the actual interest rate charged

by Sears, including hidden charges, is in excess of 30 percent a year)."
No mention of the rate of inflation in Colombia.

In a technical journal I would dwell on some professional weaknesses.
Here it is sufficient to single out: failing to understand that demand
elasticity is increased by competitive supply; falling for Prebisch's long-
exploded view of the terms of trade of Latin America; suggesting that
Keynesian analysis has in it a central place for the rate of interest
(which it in fact ignores); ignoring potential imports in discussing oligopoly and concentration in the American automobile industry; believing that the United States can borrow net from the Eurodollar
market . . . The list could be extended. Worth particular mention,
however, is the identification of U.S. unemployment in shoes and
textiles with the global corporation, with which it has nothing to do,
as there are no MNCs in competitive fields like shoes and textiles.
Barnet and Müller oppose competitive imports. They oppose monopoly
for enterprise but want it for manufacturing workers, embracing the
"cheap-labor argument" against labor-intensive imports, a view that
has been categorized by economists as fallacious since the day of Adam
Smith. In fact they sneer at it: "free trade has become part of the
holy writ of the American consensus" (p. 319). They set out uncritically
the AFL-CIO arguments for restricting imports of goods and exports
of capital and technology but leave alone exports of goods and imports
of capital and technology.

Barnet and Müller, and one assumes their 4 main helpers and 14
other assistants and crusaders, have carpentered together a nonbook,
not a synthesis but a synthetic product, slick, well packaged, and
promoted with all the skill of the Madison Avenue huckster-publisher.
Their text is heavy with attacks on advertising, which would have
been less objectionable had not the book been the object of a hard
sell, designed to put it on the best-seller lists. The authors object to
American products that lack merit but load their pages with 90 pages
of footnotes, "not meant to burden the general reader" but meant to
paid for by him. The first ten pages of footnotes cover 123 pages of
text but thereafter there are roughly ten pages of notes for 25 pages
of text, referring superficially to everything under the sun. I must
confess that in the ten or so weeks after publication, I kept an eye
on the *New York Times* best-seller list and took a certain amount of
satisfaction from the fact that despite the hard sell they did not make
it.

In reviewing this work which I found so little appealing, it is important
not to fall into the trap of questioning the representativeness of the
evidence it offers, rejecting the extreme conclusions it draws, and then

rushing to the defense of the multinational corporation and the assertion that there is no problem. Demagoguery obscures truth by polarizing issues. There are many problems. Revelations after the book appeared of political contributions by U.S. corporations abroad, some legal but of dubious ethics, some outright bribes out of slush finds, mean something is wrong even if the multinational corporation cannot be held responsible for all the ailments of the world, including the common cold. The evidence uncovered by Constantine Vaitsos on transfer pricing in pharmaceuticals in Colombia, later extended to other products in Colombia and to Peru and Ecuador in the Andes Pact may not bear the weight of the elaborate conclusions that Barnet and Müller would like to build on them but reveal inexperienced national bureaucrats taken advantage of by sophisticated businessmen. Defensive investment which the authors mention twice but do not explain—foreign investment under oligopoly may be excessive where each firm invests at low or zero profit to forestall progress by competitors—builds industry to inefficient scale, thereby wasting resources and blocking development.

There are thus real economic issues embodied in the multinational corporation, but *Global Reach* so overreaches the mark that it is impossible to sort them out. There are moreover political issues such as the tendency of politicians in difficulties to focus on short-run appeals to xenophobia at the cost of long-run potential gains in well-being. An excellent book that addresses this problem realistically is Charles Goodsell's *American Corporations and Peruvian Politics* (Cambridge, Mass.: Harvard University Press, 1974), which is worth ten *Global Reaches* and will sell one/one-hundredth the number of copies.

The wider and fundamental issue, however, is that the area efficient for economics is generally larger than that best served by political and social units. The optimum economic size for many products is the world—although Barnet and Müller would deny this. The optimum social area is often very small, small enough to give people a sense of participation. In between the optimum political area is likely to be large or small, depending on whether the political unit is seeking glory or merely survival without trouble.

Tension between the optimum economic unit and the optimum political and social unit, the large and the small, is inevitable. Most economists would take the view that it is necessary to construct some international functional agencies to cope with the distortions and divergences of large economic units from optimal conduct. Barnet and Müller go in the other direction and would cut down economic institutions to the optimum social scale. It is a romantic, essentially

Populist notion of backyard steel plants, computerized small-batch production of manufactures, and hydroponic apartment-house production of foodstuffs which would enable the world to increase real income in the cozy atmosphere of cottage industry.

The basic intellectual sin of the True Believer, however, is to load all the problems of the world on one institution, as the good people of Salem did with witches or the Fundamentalist does with Satan. Barnet and Müller hate the multinational coporation, and this makes them feel good. But it fails to advance the solution to real problems.

12

Book Review: Magdoff, The Age of Imperialism

The only interest in Magdoff's book—in full, Harry Magdoff, *The Age of Imperialism: The Economics of U.S. Foreign Policy* (New York: Modern Reader, 1969)—is to see what radical youth have adopted for their bible in the interpretation of U.S. economic foreign policy. Taken at face value, the book is a rather empty collection of statistics and string of quotations, all from respectable sources, which are intended to make the point that U.S. economic foreign policy is unrelievedly evil. The Marshall Plan had its sole purpose in preventing Europe from becoming socialist; foreign aid to less developed countries is to keep these countries dependent; U.S. policies in the stabilization of international money are designed to use the dollar as a main instrument of control over the capitalist world. The argument, however, is asserted as self-evident rather than reasoned. No use is made of the rigorous test of analyzing counterexamples. And the whole text is a botch of contradiction, misstatement of fact, analytical error, and empty rhetoric.

As difficult counterexample, take Japan. The United States has aided Japan, Japan has access to the U.S. capital market, uses the dollar, and gets its self-defense from the U.S. military. Is Japan a puppet of the United States? The answer to anyone who reads the press is pretty assuredly no. United States exporters would like to knock down Japanese tariff barriers and quotas but cannot. United States direct investors would like to get in on the ground floor of the growing Japanese economy with economic stakes but are being stalled. The Department of State finds itself obliged to make concessions to Japan on Okinawa. Magdoff's *Age of Imperialism* looks curious in the light of U.S.–Japanese relations, . . . or French, or German, or Swedish.

For contradiction, take Magdoff on oil. This is discussed throughout the book as an example of the new imperialism run without colonies

Previously published in *Public Policy* 9 (1971):513–514.

but with giant firms. "The structural difference which distinguishes the new imperialism from the old is the replacement of an economy in which many firms compete by one in which a handful of giant corporations in each industry compete" (p. 15). But compare Lenin of 1916: "The principal feature of moderate capitalism is the domination of monopolist combines of the big capitalists. These monopolies are most firmly established when *all* the sources of raw materials are controlled by the one group."[1] On page 35, the handful becomes "a leading firm or group of leading firms," and oil is the classic illustration. By page 191, we are up to 12 oil companies in the list of leading 50 industrial concerns engaged in international economic operation; by page 193, it turns out that there are 24 firms that hold 93 percent of the total foreign assets in oil, but by page 195, we are back to oil as an illustration of monopoly. Where has Magdoff been while first Standard of California, then Texas, then Gulf, Sun, Tidewater, Atlantic Richfield, Indiana, Occidental Petroleum, and the others have entered the foreign oil arena, and British Petroleum has come into the United States? From a world of two major oil firms in the 1920s—Shell and Standard of New Jersey, with Socony Mobil a lesser factor—the world has moved to some 20 or 30 firms which have an impact in world oil. Nor does Magdoff so much as hint at the fact that the Middle East countries and Libya have seen their revenues from oil increase from roughly $1 billion in 1960 to more than $6 billion in 1969.

The book cannot make up its mind as to the extent to which the United States is driven abroad by the need for raw materials. On page 32, there is a section devoted to the new drive for raw materials," in which Magdoff follows the Latin American line (also developed by Claude Julien in *L'empire americain*) that the U.S. interest in foreign economic policy is in obtaining raw materials cheaply (but at high profits) for the inexorable U.S. economy which has run out of supplies. A few pages later (p. 38), it turns out that the theory of imperialism is not concerned with investment in underdeveloped countries. Magdoff refers to the Paley Commission (p. 196) but chooses to quote the statistics showing increasing net imports of raw materials, rather than the conclusion that these could readily be reversed by a small rise in domestic prices.

Magdoff also embraces other elements of the traditional Latin American analysis of international lending, that the United States somehow exploits Latin America by "taking more out of it in profits than it puts back in new loans." It is surely not incumbent on a reviewer to destroy this tired fallacy, beyond saying that if one makes an investment, say in ten shares of General Motors, one is not obliged to reinvest in GM a sum equal to the annual dividends for the rest of time, nor is one exploiting General Motors if one spends the income.

Finally, the chapter on finance is particularly weak. Magdoff favors a Leninist view of imperialism which relies on finance capitalism, based on a falling rate of profit at home, and in which the major difficulty is intense competition among the capitalist financiers and countries, leading to war. Long series of tables and quotations from conventional sources, combined with such assertions as "The most extravagant and unparalleled use of financial power for control over other parts of the world is that exercised by the United States since the second world war" hardly prove the Leninist thesis. The industrial powers are not at war with each other. One can say many things about the Vietnam war but not that it proves much about the imperialism of finance capitalism.

In short, an unimpressive effort that will, however, be cited widely by the faithful. Economists might, however, be interested in the level of analysis indicated in footnote 53 on page 113, in which Magdoff responded to the (my) argument that the dollar-exchange standard, a single money, was desirable for efficiency by stating "Efficiency for what? This the good professor sees purely in terms of the efficiency of capital transfer and of carrying on existing trade relations. To be sure, the dollar-exchange system is a truly efficient device—especially for mobilizing the resources of world capital to finance the war of devastation against the people of Vietnam." One is reminded of the wartime story of the American officer shown through a well-designed airplane factory who asked his Soviet guide why the long line of finished airplanes at the end of the assembly line lacked propellers. "What about the lynchings in the South?" was the answer.

Note

1. V. I. Lenin, The Mature Marxist Theory, 1916, in D. K. Fieldhouse, ed., *The Theory of Capitalist Imperialism* (New York: Barnes and Noble, 1967), p. 107.

13

Plus çà change—*A Look at the New Literature*

I started out to include in this collection my introduction to Stephen Hymer's posthumously published thesis, written in 1960, appearing in 1976, but was dissuaded by my MIT Press editor and by two referees. That was a personal account and appreciation of the man who revolutionized the theory of direct investment, and it was controversial. It was called "simply splendid" in print, and one friend thought it my most effective piece of writing; another friend of both Hymer's and mine regards it as an embarrassing and inexcusable intrusion. But the multinational corporation without Hymer is Hamlet without the Prince. I now turn from the person to the doctrine.

Dogmageschichte or the history of ideas does not have much to recommend it, particularly when the ideas are recent and pride of originality is disputed. There is a strong temptation to fall to the level of debate over the relative social merits of Harvard and Yale, as I was perhaps guilty of doing in scolding Thomas Horst in the *Journal of International Economics* (1974) for having ascribed the "advantage theory" of direct investment to Richard Caves (1971) instead of to Hymer. Horst magnanimously ceded the point in his part of a four-pronged review of the Hymer thesis (1977, 396), in which he said that Hymer was more than a few years ahead of his time. But the reason for returning to "hawking the thesis . . . and publicly chastizing those who forget it" (ibid., 395) is that a spate of recent publications—*The Future of the Multinational Enterprise* (Buckley and Casson 1976), *A Theory of Multinational Enterprise* (Hennart 1982), and *New Theories of the Multinational Enterprise* (Rugman, ed., 1982)—purport to offer new and distinct theories. These go under such names as "internalization," "transaction costs," "diversification," and "appropriation," although Magee who is the author of the last is explicit that this view that the multinational corporation is a device for appropriating rents unobtainable through the market is a "natural evolution" of the work of Hymer and others (1977, 317). A recent review of the new theories asks whether those of the 1970s and early 80s provide a distinct alternative to "the" theory in vogue at the end of the 60s, and holds that the answer must be in the negative (McClain 1983, 296). Candor requires me to disclose that Magee and McClain are, like Hymer, Ph.D.'s from MIT.

It is perhaps overblown to credit Hymer with a Kuhnian revolutionary transformation of the field, with subsequent work consisting not so much of new theories but extensions, recommendations, filling out of detail, and especially the translation of Hymer's work into the vocabulary gaining currency in other parts of economics—overblown because the theory of direct investment is not such a cosmic aspect of economics to be worthy of discussion at the level of Thomas Kuhn. It nonetheless represented a sharp discontinuity. One can form a notion of the impact of Hymer's contribution by following the rhetoric of the discussion of direct investment in the successive editions at five-year intervals in my *International Economics*. The chapters on the subject in the 1953 and 1958 editions under "Suggested Reading" both start: "The literature on direct investment is sparse" (pp. 361, 410, respectively). In the 1963 edition in which my debt to Hymer's thesis was acknowledged in two places, this sentence is replaced by "The literature on direct investment has only lately begun to expand." Attention is called to the pioneering work of Penrose (1956, 1959), Byé (1958), Dunning (1958), and Behrman (1962), much of which was reaching for a new explanation of the phenomenon but not quite grasping it. Hymer's impact is on the text of the chapter. Whereas the 1953 and 1958 editions discussed direct investment in terms of foreign trade— investment to expand imports or to substitute for imports—by 1963 the discourse ran in terms of industrial organization: horizontal and vertical integration across national boundaries, the peculiar advantages of international coordination of economic activity within the corporation, and the like.

The Hymer argument in its emphasis on market imperfections was general, but the illustrations used many of the words and virtually all the ideas that have now emerged as the "new theories." Caves' widely cited 1971 article stayed narrowly in the industrial-organization track worked by Hymer that he derived from Bain. In his most recent survey in the Cambridge University Press series, Caves uses the "transactional approach": the multinational enterprise operates in an internal market in which transactions costs are lower than they would be in open arm's-lengths markets (1982). One of the transactions costs strongly emphasized by Caves is the cost of information. Information is mentioned by Hymer at three places ([1960] 1976, 34, 41, 50), and he often approached the same idea in talking of "better communications" within a firm (ibid., 221).

My memory runs that Hymer wrote of "coordinating" operations in different countries more effectively within the firm than the market could do, but I fail to find these words in his text. We doubtless discussed it, and the notion appears in my 1963 chapter (p. 411). In production processes using bulky inputs, difficult to store, often for continuous processes where interruptions are expensive, vertical integration across national boundaries enables savings to be realized by producing, shipping, and using such inputs as crude petroleum, iron ore, bauxite, and the like, within the firm. If markets were thick at various stages of production, broad futures markets existed, or storage in inventories was cheap, the need for vertical integration would be lessened as a firm could depend on markets for inputs without high cost and without fear of being held up by a monopolist. The point about coordination also arises in technological change, though Hymer does not deal with it. It can happen that an innovation at one stage of production requires ancillary technical change, new investment, or change in scale at other stages up or down the production process, and that the market finds it impossible to achieve such coordination of investment and innovation when the separate stages of production are owned separately. I came on these ideas, or at least used them, in writing about the size of coal wagons on British railroads and the difficulties that the tenant-occupied farm in England had in changing from raising grain to animal products—in contrast to the owner-occupied Danish farm (1964, 141ff, 247). My colleague Morris Adelman for a long time resisted the notion that vertical integration was anything more than horizontal integration at various stages of production. Ultimately he changed his mind and conjectured that had the coal mines of West Virginia, the Norfolk and Western railroad, the port of Hampton Roads, and coal-marketing organizations in Europe been owned by a single company, it would have paid that company to make the necessary coordinated investments at the several stages so as to substitute 250,000 ton bulk carriers for the tramp ships engaged in coal exports—or at least to substitute ships with a deep enough draft to clear the Chesapeake Bay tunnel at high tide (Kindleberger 1969, 21). There is little discussion of this sort of technical interrelatedness in multinational enterprise, even where research and development are given as the advantage that the MNC possesses.

Transaction costs are also key to Hennart (1982) who takes off from a penetrating article by McManus (1972) and maintains that transaction costs, information costs, and bargaining costs are all reduced in the multinational corporation as compared with competitive markets. Bargaining costs approach the question of coordinating operations or technological change at various stages of production, and represent something not in Hymer's text, if present in the discussion about him at all.

Rugman thinks transactions costs are just another way of saying "internalization," the word used to describe the "new theory" of the University of Reading (England) school led by Dunning and including Buckley, Casson, and Rugman himself. The word "internalization" is not in Hymer, although it is hard to see much difference between this and his emphasis on vertical and horizontal integration for "joint maximization" ([1960] 1976, 48, 71). I do not find "internalization" in the 1963 or 1968 chapters of the textbook, but *American Business Abroad* states: "Like government planning in Rosenstein-Rodan's 1943 article on balanced growth, vertical integration converts external economies to internal profits" (1969, 20).

Dunning has gone beyond straightforward internalization to combine it with location theory—that branch of economics that deals with where various processes are likely to be located—and called it an "eclectic theory" (e.g., 1981, chs. 2, 4). He developed the concept in 1976 at a Nobel symposium in honor of Bertil Ohlin. Professor Ohlin's best-known work, *Interregional and International Trade*, analyzes the relations between location theory and international trade theory, so that it was natural for Dunning in a paper written for the symposium to extend his work on the theory of direct investment to encompass location theory (1977, ch. 12). But location theory was part of the theory of direct investment long before Hymer's Kuhnian transformation of direct investment. The 1953 edition of my textbook had a short section on tariff factories, stressing the obvious idea that they were more readily attracted by tariffs on market-oriented and footloose industries than on those that were supply oriented (1953, 191–192). The ideas in my case were borrowed from Haberler (1937) but of course go much further back.

As already noted, Magee's theory of appropriability is explicitly acknowledged to be an extension of Hymer's, who, as it happened, used the expression "to appropriate" at least three times: "Control is desired in order to appropriate fully the returns on certain skills and ability" (1976, 25), and "These imperfections (in the market for technology) prevented the appropriation of all the returns to the advantage (otherwise than through the multinational corporation)" (ibid., 97; see also ibid., 26).

Niehans' theory of the multinational corporation as a response to fear of monopoly and/or monopsony—for which he makes no claim as a new theory—is of course congruent with Hymer's work, although he developed it empirically from a detailed study of five major Swiss multinationals (1977). For example, Hymer used the expression bilateral monopoly continuously ([1960] 1976, 24, 38, *passim*) and also sequential monopoly (pp. 49–50).

Another motive for direct investment is diversification. The financial aspects of this are pushed by Agmon and Lessard without, however, claiming that it is a new theory (1977). The essence is that, with their information, firms are more diversified investment vehicles for many investors than internationally balanced portfolios. Hymer observed that diversification is one explanation of the cross investment observed in the multinational corporations but noted that it can also explain two-way movements in portfolio securities ([1960] 1976, 7, 40–41). I interviewed the comptroller of the Corn Products Refining Company, one John W. Scott, Jr., in 1950 when I first became interested in foreign operations of domestic companies and traveled frequently to New York to give a course at Columbia. I learned that the company was interested in foreign operations very widely, on the theory—in a period of widespread exchange control—that at any one time some part of the world at least would be both profitable and prepared to remit earnings to the United States. Two salient excerpts from my personal notes read:

To a considerable extent the remittance of dividends, in cases where exchange regulations permitted, was ordered to offset changes in company domestic earnings (as in 1936–37), and used as a balancing mechanism . . .

CPRC would contemplate new foreign investment in dollars only when the likely return would run to 25 or 30 percent. This would be in local currency. Their thought is that a wide spread of foreign investments is useful since a dollar shortage in one area which makes remittance of dividends impossible is likely to be offset by prosperous conditions in another area . . .

The emphasis on foreign-exchange controls makes it out of date for the 1980s, but the notion that foreign investment is a form of diversification cannot be counted as new.

But the recitation becomes tiresome. Is there anything important in the current literature that is not explicit in Hymer? One major contribution was Raymond Vernon's product cycle (1966) which grew out of the dynamic trade theories of John Williams (1929), Hoffmeyer (1958), and was spelled out particularly by Burenstam Linder (1971). The role of direct investment is derived from the product cycle in international trade. Innovations occur and are diffused; then just as the trade advantage is on the verge of being lost, the firm may go ahead to hold on somewhat longer to its market against domestic competition. The relationship to appropriability is indirect.

Another contribution is defensive investment, introduced into the 1963 edition of my textbook on the basis of the inspiration of Lamfalussy's study of domestic investment in Belgian textiles (1961). A firm may invest abroad not to earn a return on its marginal outlay there but in order to prevent a loss on some other portion of its operations at home or worldwide. The idea is implicit in Hymer in his insistence on the "jointness of profits of the enterprises at home and the enterprises abroad, which makes it difficult or impossible to measure the profitability of direct investment" ([1960] 1976, 71). He was moreover highly conscious of cross investments that were critical in distinguishing portfolio (despite diversification) from direct investment (ibid., 16, 18, 119–121, 174). He did not, however, go as far in the thesis — though he made the point often later — of defensive investment as Knickerbocker (1973) who saw entire industries reproducing themselves from one market to another so as to forestall an end run by a single competitor producing large profits that might then be used against the others. Nor was he as explicit as Graham with his theory of cross investment as an exchange of threats (1974): *A* investing in *B*'s backyard, and *B* in *A*'s in order each to be on hand to retaliate in the event that the other firm made an offensive move.

But enough. One ought to keep in mind that the theory of direct investment — whoever produced it — is not that robust when companies in almost the same circumstances act in diametrically opposed ways and when decisions whether to invest abroad or not are changed frequently. At one time Volvo had its mind made up to come to the United States and Volkswagen, having acquired a plant years earlier, sold it because it had made up its mind not to come to this country. In the event Volvo backed out, and Volkswagen charged in, to the latter's substantial regret later. For a time two firms in the same industry, looking much alike, Campbell's Soup and Heinz, behaved very differently: Heinz was all over the map, Campbell merely in the United States and Canada. That later changed. But in the early stages Campbell did well, was content with its profits, and scanned a narrow horizon while Heinz with too much competition at home looked for the soft touches abroad. Or try St. Gobain and Pilkington, French and English companies both in flat glass, each with an innovation: St. Gobain built a plant in the United States, and Pilkington licensed its technology. The decisions are close, as Hymer's discussion of which way to go—export or invest, import on the open market or invest in one's own unilateral production abroad, or license or invest—amply demonstrates. It is true that the slope of the curve has been tilting toward the investment option away from exporting, buying in world markets, or licensing technology. But the old theories and the new theories are still better at explaining what has happened than at predicting how a given company will behave in particular circumstances.

This excursus has been limited to theories of direct investment. Most of the authors involved are interested at the same time in policy, as Hymer in his dissertation was not. Among the more interesting recent books on policy is *American Multinational and American Interests* by Bergsten, Horst, and Moran (1978). But they stay with the 1960s brand of theory as they set it out in the chapter "Industrial Structure, Competition, and Antitrust."

References

Agmon, Tamir, and Donald R. Lessard. 1977. Financial Factors and the International Expansion of Small-Country Firms. In Tamir Agmon and C. P. Kindleberger, eds. *Multinationals from Small Countries*. Cambridge, Mass.: The MIT Press, pp. 197–219.

Behrman, Jack N. 1962. Direct Private Foreign Investment: Nature, Effects, and Methods of Promotion. In R. F. Mikesell, ed. *U.S. Private and Government Investment Abroad*. Eugene, Oregon: University of Oregon Press.

Bergsten, C. Fred, Thomas Horst, and Theodore H. Moran. 1978. *American Multinationals and American Interests*. Washington, D.C.: The Brookings Institution.

Buckley, Peter J., and Mark Casson. 1976. *The Future of Multinational Enterprise*. London: Macmillan.

Byé, Maurice. 1958. Self-financed Multiterritorial Units and Their Time Horizon. In International Economic Association, International Economic Papers no. 8, New York: Macmillan. Original version in French, 1957.

Caves, Richard. 1971. International Corporations: The Industrial Economics of Foreign Investment. *Economica* 38:1–27.

Caves, Richard. 1982. *Multinational Enterprises and Economic Analysis*. Cambridge: Cambridge University Press.

Dunning, John H. 1958. *American Investment in British Manufacturing Industry*. London: George Allen & Unwin.

Dunning, John H. 1977. Trade, Location of Economic Activity and the MNE: A Search for an Eclectic Approach. In Bertil Ohlin, Per-Ove Hesselborn, and Per Magnus Wijkman, eds. *The International Allocation of Economic Activity*. London: Macmillan, pp. 395–418.

Dunning, John H. 1981. *International Production and the Multinational Enterprise.* London: George Allen & Unwin.

Graham, E. M. 1974. Oligopolistic Imitation and European Direct Investment in the United States. Unpublished dissertation. Graduate School of Business Administration, Harvard University.

Haberler, Gottfried. 1937. *The Theory of International Trade.* London: Macmillan.

Hennart, Jean-François. 1982. *A Theory of Multinational Enterprise.* Ann Arbor: University of Michigan Press.

Hoffmeyer, Erik. 1958. *Dollar Shortage, and the Structure of U.S. Foreign Trade.* Copenhagen: Ejnar Munksgaard.

Horst, Thomas. In A Review Symposium of Stephen H. Hymer, *The International Operations of National Firms* by Carlos J. Díaz-Alejandro, Jagdish N. Bhagwati, Thomas Horst, and Robert Rowthorn. *Journal of Development Economics* 4:395–397.

Kindleberger, Charles P. 1953, 1958, 1963, 1968. *International Economics*, Homewood, Ill.: Richard D. Irwin.

Kindleberger, Charles P. 1964. *Economic Growth in France and Britain, 1851–1950.* Cambridge, Mass.: Harvard University Press.

Kindleberger, Charles P. 1969. *American Business Abroad: Six Lectures on Direct Investment.* New Haven: Yale University Press.

Kindleberger, Charles P. 1974. Review of Thomas Horst, *At Home Abroad: A Study of the Domestic and Foreign Operations of the American Food-Processing Industry. Journal of International Economics* 4:396–397.

Knickerbocker, F. T. 1973. *Oligopolistic Reaction and Multinational Enterprise.* Cambridge, Mass.: Division of Research, Graduate School of Business Administration, Harvard University.

Magee, Stephen P. 1977. Information and the Multinational Corporation: Appropriability Theory of Direct Foreign Investment. In Jagdish N. Bhagwati, ed., *The New International Economic Order.* Cambridge, Mass.: The MIT Press.

McClain, David. 1983. Foreign Direct Investment in the United States: Old Currents, "New Waves," and The Theory of Direct Investment. In C. P. Kindleberger and David Audretch, eds., *The Multinational Corporation in the 1980s.* Cambridge, Mass.: The MIT Press, pp. 278–333.

McManus, John C. 1972. The Theory of the International Firm. In Gilles Paquet, ed., *The Multinational Firm and the Nation State.* Don Mills, Ontario: Collier Macmillan Canada, pp. 66–93.

Niehans, Jürg. 1977. Benefits of Multinational Firms for a Small Parent Economy: The Case of Switzerland. In Tamir Agmon and C. P. Kindleberger, eds., *Multinationals from Small Countries.* Cambridge, Mass.: The MIT Press, pp. 1–39.

Ohlin, Bertil, 1933. *Interregional and International Trade.* Cambridge, Mass.: Harvard University Press.

Penrose, Edith T. 1956. Foreign Investment and the Growth of the Firm. *Economic Journal* 66:220–235.

Penrose, Edith T. 1959. Profit Sharing between Producing Countries and Oil Companies in the Middle East. *Economic Journal* 69:238–254.

Rugman, Alan M., ed. 1982. *New Theories of the Multinational Enterprise.* New York: St. Martin's Press.

Vernon, Raymond. 1966. International Investment and International Trade in the Product Cycle. *Quarterly Journal of Economics* 80:190-207.

Williams, John H. 1929. The Theory of International Trade Reconsidered. *Economic Journal.* Reprinted in American Economic Association, *Readings in the Theory of International Trade*, Philadelphia: Blackiston, 1949, pp. 253-271.

14

Statement before the International Finance Subcommittee of the Senate Banking, Housing, and Urban Affairs Committee

February 22, 1974

I am honored to testify before the subcommittee on Senator Stevenson's bill on foreign investments in the United States that calls for a census of all foreign investment in the United States and for registration of new ventures, but fail to see that there is a problem which requires legislative intervention. As an economist, I believe that there are many issues which it is appropriate to leave to the market, though I am not so doctrinaire as to believe one should never interfere with market forces. The question of foreign investment in the United States is one to leave to the market. If a Volvo company decides that it is more efficient, that is, more profitable, to assemble cars in this country rather than to ship them from abroad, it is either right or wrong. If it is right, both it and the U.S. public gain; if it is wrong, it alone loses, and the American public may or may not gain but in any event does not lose. If Gimbels is worth more to a British buyer than to its American owners, it is appropriate for the latter to sell it to the former and invest the proceeds in higher paying ventures.

In a statement to the press on January 20, reported in the *New York Times* for January 21, Senator Stevenson expressed his concern about foreign investment, that

Foreign buyers are driving up land costs in many areas, and foreign ownership of natural resources like coal mines, timber and farmland can divert critical raw materials overseas instead of into the United States market.

I differ from the chairman. Foreign investment is by no means unique in its effects on the prices of U.S. goods and factors—land, labor, and capital. It makes little difference to land costs whether we export coal to Japan or the Japanese buy a coal mine, whether we import steel from Japan made with U.S. coal and U.S. scrap, or the Japanese produce that steel here. The price of labor in the United States is raised through foreign investment, and I assume that the chairman approves of that.

Moreover foreign ownership of land in no way derogates from the sovereign power of the U.S. government to direct the flow of the products of U.S. resources. If the government chooses to halt the export of soya beans—which I regard as a serious economic and political mistake—it can do so regardless of the nationality of the ownership of the land within the U.S. boundaries on which said beans were produced or the nationality of the farmhands. We have seen an illustration of this lately when Arab countries directed U.S. companies with producing properties within Arab states *not* to export oil of Arab origin to the United States, and they did not. Residents of the Arab countries have to obey Arab decrees, and foreign residents of the United States have to obey the laws of the United States.

It is not my place to make a further legal argument, but I observe that the United States is bound by its many treaties of friendship, commerce, and navigation to treat foreign enterprise on the same basis as American enterprise with respect to the conduct of business in the United States—with certain exceptions covering cabotage, transport, and communications, etc. Foreign enterprise is subject to state regulation in banking, as is American, and to the same antitrust, SEC, FTC, FDA, and so on, regulation. It may be noted that other countries which have agreed to give U.S. business national treatment have not always done so: France is perhaps outstanding in discriminating when it was bound by treaty not to discriminate, but the national-treatment clause of FCN treaties is not everywhere disregarded, and even if it were, the United States remains bound by it so long as the treaties are not denounced. You may find some irony that it is entirely legitimate for a country to discriminate between foreign and domestic goods, that is, laying tariff duties on the former which are not applied to the latter, while binding themselves not to discriminate between foreign and domestic enterprise domiciled within the United States. Such is the practice, however, and this country has benefited greatly from it over the years. It is to my mind unbecoming a major country to insist on its rights when it is to its advantage, and to withdraw the reciprocal rights extended to others at the moment a major claim is made upon them.

The thought is expressed in some quarters that the recent sharp rise in the price of oil, and the prospect that some oil-exporting countries will earn more foreign exchange than they can fruitfully spend on imports gives rise to a likelihood of new and voluminous foreign investment in the United States which warrants controls. Representative Dent, I believe, has introduced a bill which would limit foreign owner-ship in any U.S. corporation to 5 percent of the equity, and may possibly have in mind the need for a barrier against foreign takeovers of U.S. corporations through the massive funds which Arab nations are expected to accumulate.

It is right to recognize the complex new situation in world capital markets created by the tremendous increase in the price of world oil, but there is a grave question whether hasty action of the sort proposed would help rather than confuse the situation, and especially whether it would not create new uncertainties and disorder in capital markets which would make matters worse. There is a strong self-correcting mechanism in well-functioning markets, as are those in this country. The likelihood of a foreign country buying up a major U.S. corporation in the open market—if, for the sake of the argument, we regard this as undesirable, as in reality I do not—is small. The more stock such a country buys, the higher it drives the price of the stock outstanding. As other owners see what is taking place, they hold back for still higher prices, and the action is self-defeating. Early purchases might be well disguised—as Russian intentions in wheat were hidden from the grain dealers for a time. But there were limits as to how much wheat the Soviet Union could buy, and limits to how much of General Motors, Exxon, Gulf Oil, and the like, that Kuwait or Saudi Arabia can acquire. Whether such acquisitions are good or bad for the country moreover would depend on what was happening as a result through the rest of the economy.

I leave aside as not germane to the issue at hand the possibility of a rollback in prices which I think highly likely, and soon. Assume, however, as does the Morgan Guaranty Trust Company in a recent publication that oil-exporting countries will earn $85 billion in 1974 and spend no more the $35 billion on imports of goods and services. Is it likely that the $50 billion difference will be invested in the con-suming countries, and would this create a problem? How large a problem, in particular, would this be for the United States, although the Congress of the United States cannot be indifferent to the problems of other countries or the possibility of damage to the world monetary system? Among the other countries especially are the non-oil-producing developing countries, for example, India, Pakistan, Bangladesh, and the poor and famine stricken countries of Africa, whose debts the oil-producing countries are unlikely to accept and in which countries the oil producers are probably unwilling to invest.

A lot of suggestions have been put forward to meet the $50 billion "gap." The developed countries might pay for oil with gold, with newly issued SDRs, with newly created dollars which the consuming countries borrowed in the Eurodollar market, with short- or long-term debt issued to the oil exporters by the consuming countries or through financial intermediation by the Eurocurrency market or Eurobond market, or by real assets (or equities) sold in oil-country ownership, such real assets being either outstanding or newly created. How this is done makes a considerable difference to the international monetary system and to the state of the U.S. economy, but I cannot see how, under any circumstances, it will help to enact legislation affecting the right of foreign countries to acquire real property or equities in the United States or the terms on which they do so. In the event the solution to the problem of paying for oil will probably not take a single form: gold, liquid assets, debts, equities or real assets, but an amalgam of all (except possibly gold). To restrict the access of foreigners to U.S. shares would inhibit the solution; to go to special lengths to facilitate foreign purchases of U.S. equities is unnecessary in the light of the wide latitude presently existing.

A discussion in detail of the implications of the rise in the price of oil for the monetary system and the U.S. economy may lie outside the scope of the subcommittee's investigation, but one important point is surely relevant. It makes a considerable difference to the outcome over time of oil-producer investments in the United States whether they add to net capital formation in this country or not. If we buy oil by going into debt or selling off assets now owned by residents of the country to foreigners, we are in effect consuming our capital. There are no new earning assets to pay the interest on the new obligations or to provide the profits due to the new foreign owners of American equities or productive assets. We shall be having the same sort of experience as the Indian peasant who goes into debt to the moneylender to buy food in a famine. Luckily we are rich and can accept a loss in wealth. The Indian peasant has no wealth and must borrow more to pay the interest, falling deeper and deeper into debt.

If, on the other hand, the country pays for its oil by diverting consumption from other production, releasing resources which are employed by the oil producers within the country to build new facilities, the new productive assets will pay the interest or profits, and we shall not have to reduce our real income in the future to service the debt. The reduction, to be sure, will occur currently, as we cut down on the consumption of other items to pay for the oil. But on this score there is every reason not to interfere with the capacity of foreigners to undertake new productive investments in the United States.

Let me conclude by expressing my concern that the United States along with many other countries in the world is suffering from a wave of neomercantilism, xenophobia, or know-nothingism which, if unchecked, is likely to plunge the world into a damaging race of *suave-qui-peut*, devil-take-the-hindmost, every man for himself. The United States used to be the leader in efforts to stabilize the world. Many people in this country seem now ready to disregard the public good of internationalism for the private (and dangerous) end of nationalistic gain. Since the time of Adam Smith almost 200 years ago, economists, or most economists, have been preaching that intervention in markets for the sake of nationalist gain is likely to be self-defeating. Restriction breeds retaliation, and retaliation defeats the initial restriction, leaving the world and each country worse off. I realize that many of you are under pressure from your constituents to take short-range, nationalist, and xenophobic action, as the American public finds the rapid change in the world economy puzzling and bewildering. I recommend strongly, however, that you exercise the leadership which the world today so much needs, and in this particular case refrain from striking out blindly to legislate on the international market for securities as it affects the United States.

15

The International Corporation in the Late Sixties and Early Seventies

The international corporation, as I shall call the phenomenon under discussion in this conference—otherwise known as the supranational, the transnational, or the multinational corporation, or sometimes, with intent, the domestic corporation with foreign operations—is a subject on everyone's lips, and not always favorably. Foreign governments and citizens are ambivalent as I shall demonstrate. They love it for its contribution to output and hate it for its foreignness. Even Americans are occasionally antithetical. Take a sentence by my MIT colleague (in linguistics), Noam Chomsky:

When I make some arbitrary statement in a human language, say, that "the rise of the supra-national corporation poses new dangers for human freedom," I am not selecting a point along some linguistic dimension . . .[1]

Political subconsciousnesses in this country are thus preoccupied with the international corporation even when the conscious mind is otherwise engaged.

Economists have long been interested in the subject under the heading of "direct investment," that is, the investment of capital across national boundaries in the form of equity ownership accompanied by control. Early analysis of direct investment concentrated on the variability of debt service—when no profits were earned they did not have to be remitted—or on the accompaniment of the factor, capital, with technology, useful in economic growth. More recently, economists

Background paper prepared for a conference on the Multinational Corporation, Office of External Research, Department of State, March 1969.

have concluded that direct investment belongs less to the subject of capital movements—often there is little or none as funds needed for investments are borrowed locally—and come to regard it as an exercise in monopolistic competition. Investments abroad do not occur in highly competitive industries. In oligopolistic industries they are made both ways, with Jersey and Palmolive-Colgate in Britain and Shell and Lever Brothers in the United States, each firm policing the backyard of its major competitor. Direct investment is usually undertaken when a firm has a monopolistic advantage in another market, using that term in a clinical rather than a pejorative sense, or is about to lose one.

But these investments typically both increase and reduce monopoly, making their net impact hard to judge. A large foreign firm entering a national market breaks up the local monopoly of small noncompeting domestic firms, just as a chain grocery or drugstore adds to competition in the small town. Often vertically integrated at several stages of production, it also makes entry difficult. And when a few firms in an industry become vertically integrated, others are likely to follow suit in fear of being excluded from access to raw materials, transport, or markets. The vertically integrated firm is sometimes more efficient than atomistic markets at successive stages of production, especially in industries where technology is changing and it is necessary to co-ordinate investment at different stages, or in those where productive operations must be closely coordinated because of the cost of main-taining bulky inventories. But vertically integrated industries are difficult to enter, and with entry restricted, oligopolistic competitors tend to eschew price competition which would pass the benefits of greater efficiency forward to the consumer.

Host countries are not nearly so much at the mercy of the inter-national corporation as they sometimes indicate. Typically they main-tain high tariffs and then complain when the efficient inframarginal foreign firm makes high profits. As any second-term student of eco-nomics can demonstrate geometrically, one way to reduce the mo-nopoly of foreign firms protected by a tariff is to lower the tariff and admit imports. Tariffs to stimulate domestic concerns may today result mainly in attracting foreign suppliers previously supplying the market through exports. Infant-industry policy must therefore be amended to include not only tariffs but prohibition of foreign investment in the designated activity. If the tariff is merely to encourage production within the national territory, the remedy is first to attract the foreign firm through a tariff and then to lower the level of protection.

In the second place many foreign countries encourage or at least tolerate a level of domestic monopoly which seems high by U.S. standards. There is something—though it is impossible to measure how much—to the proposition that one of the reasons for U.S. firms to go abroad is that they are unable to expand much further in their own domestic industry because of antitrust policies. Conglomerates and direct investment are thus part of the same tendency for corporate managements to invest their earnings rather than pass them along to the shareholders. Double taxation may be partly responsible for this, but so is the corporate value system which places such a high status on the growth of sales and assets. Most foreign surveillance of direct investment is carried out by foreign-exchange control authorities. In one of the few countries where administration is in the hands of the fair-trade authorities, Japan, the thrust of regulation is to keep out foreign firms to prevent competition with small and inefficient domestic firms or at least to keep others out until more large, efficient firms capable of competing can be built.

An important consequence of the monopolistically competitive feature of the international corporation is that it is virtually impossible to lay down codes of treatment or even rules of conduct of general validity. Circumstances alter cases. Japan objects to 100 percent foreign ownership of local enterprises, but if that is the only way it can attract certain vital sorts of technology, it will make exceptions for them. India insists on foreign corporations selling 30 percent of their equity to local investors, but again the rule will be relaxed for companies of great attraction which refuse to enter on any other basis. In the Anglo-Saxon tradition governance should be by laws rather than by men. The administration of the international corporation, however, is to a great extent a bargaining process in which decision must be made case by case. When a monopoly buyer faces a monopoly seller—called in economics bilateral monopoly—there is no determinant outcome. This makes the phenomenon a difficult one to study.

These introductory remarks are not intended to discuss economic problems at any depth. I shall do no more than mention the balance-of-payments problems posed by the international corporation, except to note that both the home and host countries complain about the difficulties they give rise to, which will make skeptical a reasonable man who believes in symmetry. The basis of the asymmetry is partly poor economic analysis but primarily the concentration of the home country in the short run, when the investment takes place, and of the host country in the long run, when profits are being reaped and repatriated. If each were to take a reasonably balanced view, it is hard to see how the direct investment could worsen the balances of payments of both parties.

My attention turns rather to the political aspects of the international corporation. I do this not as a political expert but *faute de mieux*. The international corporation raises political problems, and especially problems of foreign policy that political scientists by and large have ignored. Indeed, the international corporation may be said to threaten the nation-state, as one perceptive political scientist has said does international technology closely associated with the international corporation.[2] The international corporation brings an intruder into the body politic, whether the foreign policy of another state to which the corporation responds, as is sometimes claimed, or merely a force with a domain that extends beyond the nation-state and therefore eludes or frustrates its will.

There is a functional basis for antipathy between the nation-state and the international corporation, which I shall come to presently. Much of the dislike, however, is instinctual. More and more as I study the international corporation, I am impressed by the visceral reactions of populations to foreign control, and I conclude that many reactions to foreign firms are at an elementary level. Before we acquired education and sophistication in economics, most of us were by nature monopolists, Populists, mercantilists, misers, and above all wanted to have our cake and eat it too. In the political area the instinctual drives are if anything less amenable to relaxation through the application of rationality. Man is a peasant, with a love for his good earth—the territorial imperative recently celebrated by popular writers—and a xenophobe who resents and resists foreign ownership and control. The international corporation threatens the community. It is they who are trying to do things to us.

To a certain extent the ambivalence that is felt with regard to the international corporation is of the "have-our-cake-and-eat-it-too" variety. The international corporation brings capital and technology, which are wanted, but foreign control, which is feared. It is too simple to say that in the love-hate relation between the host country and the international corporation, the love is economic and the hate political. Some of the hate is economic; the state as a whole may fear monopoly; some elements in it resist competition; Populists fear especially foreign banks; mercantilists worry lest foreign firms fail to export sufficiently; and so on. But there is little political love for the foreign firm. When the state is disaggregated, it may be that labor welcomes the infusion of foreign capital (in a developed state), or domestic capital is favorable to foreign entrepreneurship in less developed countries where the bourgeoisie is not strong enough to make its own way. On the whole, however, the view of the international corporation held politically is negative.

One exception may be noted. In the United States no one thinks about foreign firms at all. During the war there was much excitement, most of it juvenile, over the alleged military and intelligence activities of German firms. For the most part, however, foreign firms here are accorded national treatment (except in coastal shipping, communication, transport, etc., where they are excluded) and are ignored. United States-owned firms abroad, however, are typically noticed. This is partly because they are foreign, partly because they are American.

One could expatiate on the objections to American corporations on strictly socioeconomic grounds — their flouting of local customs, pushiness, high wages and salaries, impersonality, etc. — although the basis for these criticisms is rapidly disappearing where it has not long been displaced by adaptation to local conditions. More significant for our purposes are the accusations that the corporation has a political role, or the government an economic one. The simple-minded Marxian view is that U.S. foreign policy is designed by big business in this country to serve its exploitive interests. Never a colonial power, the United States has perfected neocolonialism, or in today's world neo-imperialism, to draw tribute from the world in the form of cheap raw materials and high profits from manufactures produced abroad. United States foreign policy is dollar diplomacy. The State Department's "support" for apartheid in the Union of South Africa is dictated by Charles Engelhard's interest. Cuba, the Dominican Republic, the Hickenlooper amendment applied in Sri Lanka and Peru, even the excessive reaction of the State Department to the Mercantile Bank case in Canada all show the U.S. government dancing to the industrial establishment's tune.

Equally radical, but more interesting, is the view that the relation of master and servant implied by the Marxist interpretation should be reversed. Government does not respond to corporate bidding, but the contrary. Along with the CIA, the Pentagon, and the foreign service, the corps of American businessmen abroad is an instrument of U.S. foreign and domestic policy. Through it the government of the United States extends its grasp into foreign sovereignties, ordering firms outside its jurisdiction to conform to American precept in questions of blockading Cuba and mainland China, remitting profits to the United States, antitrust policy, antinuclear proliferation, and so on. Foreign countries have been weakened in their capacity to conduct an independent foreign policy by the intrusion on their soil of significant entities who owe allegiance to another sovereign power and especially, in some variations, a power with imperialist designs to dominate the world.

Few of those who hold this view would admit that there is anything to be said for the other side of the argument. If host countries have a right to maintain independent foreign and domestic policies, so does the United States. It is understandable if the United States reacts to the frustration of a policy of, say, cutting off U.S. sales of manufactures to Cuba through Cuban purchasing of products from U.S.-owned companies abroad, by trying to prevent such sales. Functionaires in charge of trading with the enemy, balance-of-payments restrictions, antitrust policy, and the like, are not interested in imposing U.S. domination on the world so much as in carrying out their assigned tasks in the face of a check imposed by an actor escaping the jurisdiction. United States attorney Robert Morgenthau's investigation of U.S. security transactions carried out through Swiss numbered accounts may be resented as an intrusion of the United States into Swiss jurisdiction, but existence of different sovereignties poses an issue where the cost of shifting from one to another has become trivial. The sovereignty of the United States could be undermined if it were unable, in any way, to pursue abroad those who act in contravention to U.S. purposes.

Galbraith has noted that the rise of big business in the United States led to the development of countervailing institutions of big labor unions and big government. In the international sphere big business has thus far elicited neither response but mainly a negative political attitude, often accompanied by economic permissiveness or in some cases guidelines for good corporate citizenship which on the whole mean conduct no different from that of national firms. The international corporation in its turn has tended to sink into a passive good citizenship everywhere in the world, failing to perform its economic function of reallocating activities worldwide from high- to low-cost locations but maintaining, and even expanding, activities everywhere without regard to their profitability. National policies will sometimes leave interstices in which the international corporation can act free of any supervision or restraint; they will sometimes overlap and push the corporation in different directions. (Corporations respond to conflicting authorities much as children learn to thread their way through the divergent orders of separate parents, teacher, coach, etc.) Often, as in the field of taxation which is widely regulated by treaties of double taxation, they will be nearly joined. The need, as I see it, is for more such harmonization of existing policies, or elaboration of new, so as to permit the corporation to pursue its task of improving world efficiency in competitive conditions and without extending monopoly. The prospect of supranational government strikes me as so remote as to be uninteresting in today's circumstances. The need must therefore be met on an international basis by agreement among nation-states.

The issues calling for resolution concern the behavior of the international corporation, on the one hand, and the intrustion of one state into the sovereignty of another through the corporation, on the other hand. I see no prospect of assisting the corporation when it is being attacked in different ways by two separate states on political grounds. If the Coca-Cola company, for example, is not allowed to operate in the United Arab Republic if it sells in Israel, and will be boycotted by Israel if it maintains its operations in the United Arab Republic, it is doubtful that any international body can get the two sovereign powers to agree to let the company operate in both; the company must choose. I am also skeptical that an international body should require a country, which sets high store by its independence and therefore resists the entrance of foreign firms, to open its doors. Acting to a considerable extent in response to the importuning of the United States, the OECD has applied pressure to Japan to admit more foreign business. Where Japan wants entry for Japanese firms abroad, it makes sense for other countries to ask for reciprocity. But I see no economic or political imperative that calls for international action to urge Japan to open up. Individual companies may bargain for entry, and many do. But if Japan wants to stay clear of the international system in some respect, it seems to me an essential attribute of sovereignty that it be allowed to.

By the same token any country that chooses for its own reasons to keep foreign firms out, or domestic firms in, would not need to justify its action before such an international tribunal. Discrimination by industries would be acceptable, though perhaps not discrimination by countries. The main economic reasons for prohibiting the entrance of foreign firms can be classified under the same heading as the reasons for levying tariffs: defense, infant industry, antimonopoly, and second best, including in the last category concern for the balance of payments that the country is unable to cope with by first-best techniques. In the long run one would want to see the adoption of the principle of laissez faire in international investment as in tariffs, but as Bismarck made clear, in a world of unequal economic strength, laissez-faire is a weapon of the strong.

What is required then is not a set of rules for international corporations, or for countries regarding international corporations, but a forum where policies that affect the international corporation, especially taxation, financial disclosure for the benefit of security holders, and antitrust, can be harmonized in a number of respects and where governments can negotiate with one another or on a regular basis over the intrusion of one country's sovereignty into another's in such matters as blockade, balance-of-payments regulation, domestic antitrust policy, and so on. It should be possible for a country in such forum to question the appropriateness of an international merger, such as the Alcan acquisition of Aardal og Sunndal Verk from the Norwegian government which reduced competition in the world aluminum industry. But the major purpose would be to resolve issues between countries, recognizing both the right of the host country to have its sovereignty maintained relatively inviolate and that of the home country not to have its policies frustrated by citizens who flee the jurisdiction.

Whether the General Agreement on Tariffs and Trade is sufficiently sturdy as an international organization to take on this assignment is something on which I do not have a clear view. The first requirement is an international study group to make recommendations regarding the scope of harmonization of policies and of the forum for the resolution of particular cases. Such a group might at the same time be asked for its recommendation regarding machinery of agreements. I suspect, however, that in anything as important as envisaged here for business in this country, it would be necessary to proceed by treaty in which the views of separate interests could be expressed not only in formulation but again at the time of ratification.

No economist is an expert on procedure, and I have already disqualified myself as a political expert. From the narrower vantage point of a technician, however, it seem highly likely that the international corporation will be a source of foreign-policy confusion and international dispute, which are best met head on. There is another view: that the negative response of nation-states to the firm when it goes abroad will result in the firm adapting completely to the local situation and seeking the quiet life, that is, giving up the attempt to maximize profits worldwide and accepting what comes where it comes. Perhaps. The professional deformation of the economist, who is a believer in profit maximization, however, leads him to doubt it.

Notes

1. Noam Chomsky, Language and the Mind, II *Columbia Forum* 11 (Fall 1968): 24.

2. See Robert Gilpin, *France in the Age of the Scientific States*, Princeton: Princeton University Press, 1967.

16

Toward a GATT for Investment: A Proposal for Supervision of the International Corporation

with Paul M. Goldberg*

The Problem

Since the end of World War II, the world has witnessed a spectacular growth in the number and size of international corporations. During the period 1950 to 1968, U.S. private investment abroad grew from $19 billion to $101.9 billion, and overseas private investment in the United States grew from $8.0 billion to $40.3 billion. These figures represent fivefold increases and annual growth rates of 10 percent.[1] Before the U.S. mandatory investment controls were instituted, the National Industrial Conference Board projected that by 1975 the United States and the rest of the world each have a gross national product of about $1 trillion per year. Of the rest of the world's $1 trillion, 25 percent would come from branches and subsidiaries of U.S. corporations and an additional 10 percent would be at least partially the result of U.S. portfolio investment. At the same time 20 percent of the United States's $1 trillion would be "European—or Japanese—tinged."[2]

The world's experience with the phenomenon of the international corporation is short enough to render precarious any serious prediction as to its future shape. Indications are, however, that the "two-way

Previously published in *Law and Policy in International Business* 2 (Summer 1970):295–325.

*J. D. University of Washington; doctorate in international business, Sloan School of Management, Massachusetts Institute of Technology. Member of Massachusetts Bar.

street" for European investment is rapidly widening and that overseas investment in the United States will undergo the faster growth in the next decade. It is not unlikely that in the absence of some regulatory scheme the culmination of present trends will be a world organization of individual industries with market shares roughly identical in all major markets.

Such a situation may leave individual nation-states relatively helpless in the face of a powerful, closely interlocked, and geographically mobile network of industrial enterprise. As the management of local economies becomes impaired, governments will become less effective in stabilizing employment, redistributing income, and providing social overhead capital. A reasonable analogy is that nations, in the face of increasing effectiveness of international corporations, will be as ineffective in governing themselves as today's cities.

Even at present the international corporation raises serious complications for political institutions. Because the corporation operates within a wider domain than that of the nation-state, it is capable (within limits) of reallocating world resources and evading national jurisdictions. Since the international corporation is able to react to changes in governmental regulation or taxation by moving from one jurisdiction to another, its mere presence is often perceived as a threat by home and host countries alike. Some students of the problem believe that the power of international corporations poses a threat to world order. The economist is concerned that takeovers across national lines will reduce world competition. The political scientist worries that the international corporation acts as a vehicle for the intrusion of the policies of one state into the jurisdiction of others. Last, and perhaps least, the international corporation itself is concerned lest it be subject to double taxation, double and diverging regulation, and double jeopardy.

Reduced to its simplest terms there is an inherent conflict between the objectives of the international corporation and the nation-state. The corporation strives to rationalize operations so that production occurs where costs are lowest and sales are made where prices are highest. Given good coordination, industrial activities can be managed to take advantage of cost differences in labor, capital, tax rates, and market conditions. Further refinements can be achieved through adjustments in transfer pricing as goods move from one subsidiary to another. The nation, on the other hand, seeks to have the corporation return the greatest net benefit to its jurisdiction. That is to say, the host state would be happiest when the international corporation manufactures and exports locally to the point where its contribution to the gross national product minus repatriations of earnings to the parent are at a maximum. Although this view may be somewhat shortsighted in that it fails to account for benefits that do not show up on the national income accounts, such as technology transfer, it is a fair representation of the policy objectives of most host countries. Needless to say, the likelihood of worldwide correspondence of corporate and political objectives is low.

For some time now, commentators in the field have put forward suggestions for the resolution of the nation-state/multinational enterprise dilemma. Analysis of these suggestions reveals a spectrum of positive actions that the world as a community could take to reduce these conflicts. The purpose of this article is to outline the scope of previous suggestions, set forth a new proposal, and document those specific areas in which we feel that it would be most effective.

We limit ourselves to problems that involve an international corporation, a host country, and a home country where the parent corporation is located. This excludes a substantial class of problems that may be regarded as involving almost exclusively the domestic jurisdiction of the host country: requirements affecting the hiring and firing of local and foreign labor, access to the local capital market, conditions for investment with respect to export, research, and so on.[3] We also exclude the traditional problem of expropriation and its compensation, an issue on which the International Bank for Reconstruction and Development has developed a vehicle for dispute settlement.[4] Although expropriation does involve conflict between host and home countries via the international corporation, the long history of international negotiation on the issue suggests that there is little to be gained from merging this apocalyptic problem with the issues that arise in the day-to-day operations of the international corporation.

Fortunately the substantial and recurring problems involving the international corporation are found only in a handful of areas: taxation, antitrust policy, balance of payment controls, export controls, and securities regulation. We briefly discuss these problem areas as symptomatic of the overall dilemma. Each has a common denominator: the international corporation is either unregulated, having slipped between the cracks of national jurisdiction, or is cabined by the overlapping regulation of two countries having varying political or economic goals.

The Problem Areas

Taxation
The substantive problem of taxation as it affects the international corporation is twofold and is typical of the "underlap–overlap" problem.

In the "underlap" case the corporation structures its operations to avoid substantial taxation; in the "overlap" case it cannot avoid being taxed on the same earnings by more than one jurisdiction. The former case works to the corporation's advantage, whereas the latter works to its detriment. Both situations have long been considered by governments, host and home, in an effort to inject order into the world system of taxation.

The possibilities of "underlap" have been substantially reduced by the closing of overseas income loopholes. In the United States much of this was accomplished by the Revenue Act of 1962.[5] For corporations this act added the "Subpart F"[6] provisions which, in certain cases, tax the income of foreign subsidiaries of U.S. corporations even if such income is not remitted to the United States. Since these provisions did not block the door to tax avoidance entirely, tax havens still operate but not so widely as they did before 1962.[7]

Today corporations must be able to avoid Subpart F rules if they are to make effective use of tax havens. From an economic viewpoint such operations are inefficient. The subsidiary in the Grand Cayman Islands or Curaçao has (in all but a handful of cases) no commercial reasons for operating there. The sole purpose is tax avoidance. And as the loopholes in the United States become drawn more tightly, the paths through them become more difficult to discover and maintain. This means a greater diversion of resources to legal, accounting, and financial overhead that could be properly applied elsewhere. Because these overhead services are very expensive, companies below some critical size cannot afford to purchase them and are thus barred from international investment activities. These services therefore act as a form of subsidy to the larger firms. Declining costs of travel and communications, however, are lowering the threshold at which this subsidy to larger firms, and barrier to entry of smaller firms, applies.

The "overlap" problem has been gradually curtailed over the years as part of an international competitive process.[8] Host countries offer restricted tax reductions in certain instances to attract foreign investments, much as the several states of the United States do to attract domestic investment. This process, when pursued vigorously by host countries in competition with one another, merely succeeds in reducing their tax revenues from foreign investment without achieving real-locative effects. When carried to its logical extreme, the process tends to produce additional tax havens. Since tax abatement is hardly uniform among host countries, distortionary results occur as tax levels become a significant factor in the investment location decision.

Corporations have been ingenious in avoiding the "overlap" problem whenever possible. One common device is a system of transfer prices based on arbitrary rather than competitive or market-determined prices. By this scheme a corporation can effect a transfer at a national boundary for the purpose of diverting income between jurisdictions.[9] A related device of course is the use of multiple operating, holding, and financing subsidiaries for centralized technology transfer, borrowing, and purchasing activities.[10]

In view of such tactics it is not surprising to discover that there is a highly involved series of bilateral treaties between home and host countries to eliminate double taxation for the international corporation (and citizens as well). These agreements do not provide total relief from host country taxation but do limit such taxation to mutually agreeable levels and applications. There are literally hundreds of these treaties in existence today and unfortunately very little uniformity among them.[11]

However, even when the "overlaps" and the "underlaps" have been adjusted, and taxes computed and assessed, the problem of collection remains. In itself this is one of the thornier issues in the international area. Needless to say, many valid tax assessments go uncollected simply because the taxpayer is beyond the jurisdictional reach of the levying country or because the costs of collection outweigh expected receipts. Generally speaking, foreign governments cannot bring suit in the company's home country for collections, since states customarily do not enforce the tax or penal legislation of other states.[12] Because of the universality of the problem tax commissioners of various countries have begun to cooperate in the administration and collection of taxes from international corporations. Only one serious proposal has been put forth for formal organization in this area.[13] The plan suggests a system of intergovernmental cooperation in collection, in training of tax officials, and in the exchange of information. It was based on personal interviews with tax administrators around the world, all of whom are apparently favorably disposed toward the enactment of such a scheme.

Antitrust

For the most part antitrust enforcement has been confined to regulation of domestic industries and their overseas operations. Any act by a foreign corporation outside of the boundaries of the aggrieved state goes largely unregulated. The reason for this hiatus is found in problems of both adjudicative and legislative jurisdiction. International law has adopted fairly uniform concepts of adjudicative jurisdiction.[14] Basically these amount to the necessity of having the person "found" within its territory before a state can assert jurisdiction over him. Once he is found, unless restricted by treaty, the state has absolute jurisdiction over the defendant, be he domestic or foreign. For the United States the rule was laid down more than a century ago by Chief Justice Marshall in *Schooner Exchange v. McFadden*, when he said, "The jurisdiction of the nation within its own territory is necessarily exclusive and absolute. It is susceptible of no limitation not imposed by itself."[15]

Legislative jurisdiction is a far less uniform concept in the international arena.[16] At the outset therefore we find that jurisdiction creates a built-in gap in global antitrust enforcement. Over the years governments have made various attempts to bridge that gap, and they have not always been successful. Attempts at antitrust enforcement, just as in tax cases, are severely contested by the allegedly guilty firms and by their own states. In a case that has become a classic in its field, the U.S. government tried to enforce a decree handed down by its own courts requiring Imperial Chemical Industries, Ltd. to reassign certain patents from British Nylon Spinners, Ltd. to DuPont.[17] BNS sought an injunction in British courts to prevent ICI from complying with the order. The British courts refused to recognize the order because the acts which gave rise to it, although illegal in the United States, were quite legal in the United Kingdom and issued the injunction.[18]

More recently, ICI has figured in another case involving the extraterritorial enforcement of antitrust decisions. In July 1969 the Commission of the European Economic Community (EEC) fined ICI and nine others $490,000 for allegedly fixing prices in aniline dyestuffs.[19] Since ICI is a British firm, the legislative jurisdiction of the EEC must be based on the same "protective" approach that underlies the U.S. view of antitrust enforcement, a result often criticized in the past by European jurists. The same holds true for three other of the ten firms implicated, Geigy, Ciba, and Sandoz, all of which are Swiss. Although no British courts are involved in the case as yet, the British government has informed the EEC, via diplomatic note, that its attempt to fine a company based outside the EEC "exceeds the limit fixed by the recognized principles of international law."[20]

In a comment on this case *The Economist* posed the following consideration:

What the law says is obviously complex, and it is up to the courts of law to decide the ICI case. In the meantime, governments must decide what they want the law to be in the future. Do they want it to encourage local subsidiaries to hide behind the legal immunity of parent companies? Or do they want it to help anti-cartel agencies to discipline international firms? Clearly there is a danger of governments using cartel powers to help local businesses, but equally there is a danger, if parent companies are untouchable, that the countries with large business empires overseas, like the United States and Great Britain, will use immunity to further their interests. Britain indeed has tried too often to shelter under the excuse that subsidiaries are somehow not their masters' voices, Rhodesian sanctions being a case in point. It is time to stop the see no evil.[21]

The ICI case illustrates the point that even when the facts of a case show conclusively that anticompetitive acts have in fact occurred, it is frequently impossible either to punish the guilty actors or to prevent continuation of the acts in question. Just as important, however, as *The Economist* article suggests, are the situations in which the only nations with jurisdiction refrain from exercising it. For example, consider the case of the acquisition of Aardal og Sunndal Verk, a Norwegian aluminum smelter.[22] Aardal was acquired from its former owner, the Norwegian government, by Alcan, a Canadian company. Clearly an acquisition of this magnitude reduces world competition in aluminum. The Norwegians felt that any smelter operating independently of a supply of ingot was in a financially precarious position. Since they believed that shelter from the vagaries of the world aluminum market justified further concentration in the industry, they handed over the smelter without hesitation. Insofar as the Canadian government was concerned, the strengthening of one of its own companies vis-à-vis the rest of the world by an overseas acquisition was highly desirable.

Similarly France may or may not have been terribly concerned whether it is IBM or GE which took over Machines Bull in the first instance. But, as one of us has suggested in a previous publication, two vastly different results from a world point of view will follow depending on which U.S. company is the acquirer.[23] In the case of IBM, competition in the computer industry would be severely reduced. Conversely, a marriage of GE and Machines Bull brings together two firms with differing quantities of capital, research and development activities, and marketing strengths. Together they would provide competition for IBM, whereas either one alone could not.

An international economist therefore wishes to see some regulation of international mergers, working agreements, and anticompetitive practices that is not hamstrung by present-day jurisdictional rules. At the same time he would desire an institution to assume jurisdiction on behalf of the world when individual nation-states refuse to do so. At the very least the time has come to end the double standard in international antitrust for the treatment of imports and exports. Cartelization of exports is prevalent among the great trading nations of the world, including the United States.[24] In a world interested in reducing tariff and nontariff barriers to trade, such distinctions are clearly out of place.

Because of the great national differences in policies, both legislative and judicial, it is not surprising to find that there has been little success in international antitrust cooperation. Serious attempts at such co-operation began after World War II with the proposed International Trade Organization charter, which provided for agreement by states to take local action whenever anyone restricted production or interfered with any of the charter's provisions.[25] Following the demise of the International Trade Organization, several attempts to fill the void of worldwide antitrust regulation were launched.[26] Two were global in nature (UN Economic and Social Council, ECOSOC, and the General Agreement on Tariffs and Trade, GATT), and three were confined to Europe (Council for Europe, European Coal and Steel Community, and the European Economic Community).

In 1951 the United States proposed that ECOSOC establish an ad hoc committee to prepare an international agreement to prevent restrictive international trade practices.[27] The resolution was adopted, and a committee appointed. Two years later it filed its report which ironically was based largely on the ITO proposals.[28] The report called for an agreement by all nations to condemn and to prosecute restrictive practices in international trade and for the creation of an independent agency to receive complaints, analyze the facts, and make procedural recommendations to the relevant member countries. The report was circulated among member nations and received generally favorable comment. In 1955, after a change of administration, the United States dealt a second blow to international antitrust cooperation by withdrawing its support in favor of unilateral national action.[29]

After prolonged debate on the topic the GATT, in 1960, adopted an agreement providing for a consultative procedure among member nations. It called for any affected nations to call on others as appropriate to work out a satisfactory solution. The secretariat was to be informed whether the results were satisfactory or not, and in the latter case it would so inform the member nations, presumably to generate some multilateral pressure on the recalcitrant states.[30] These mild provisions have never been invoked.[31]

Balance-of-Payment Controls

The major industrial nations are increasingly concerned with the effect of direct investment upon their balance-of-payment positions. Although economists are by no means uniform in their analysis of the effect of such investments, many nations have enacted regulations to control the associated financial flows. The recent spiral of regulatory enactment was initiated by the publication of "voluntary guidelines" by the United States in February 1965.[32] In simple form, these "guidelines" called for restraint on the part of U.S.-based corporations in exporting capital and diligence in repatriating profits.

Almost immediately, other nations, particularly in the Commonwealth, adopted procedures to deal with the new U.S. government policy. Australia, for example, reacted strongly to its noninclusion in the list of nations singled out for special treatment (Canada and Japan). Australian financial institutions were ordered not to make fixed-interest loans and capital issues to foreign-based firms until the U.S. position became clarified.[33] As soon as the initial shock wore off, and the Australian government discovered that the U.S. regulations were not unduly severe, the controls were relaxed.

Second-round Australian internal regulations in the capital field became more concerned with the domestic new issues market than with the balance of payments. Control in this area was effected by distinguishing on an ad hoc basis between old and new foreign firms. New firms were restricted to raising locally that portion of their total debt structure that was equal to the percentage of their equity that was local. The regulations were issued by the Reserve Bank and enforced through the commercial and merchant banking system. No restrictions applied to old firms.[31]

In Canada the Voluntary Credit Restraint Program also produced reactive measures, despite Canada's exemption from the balance-of-payments regulation. Government guidelines, entitled "Some Guiding Principles of Good Corporation Behavior in Canada" emphasized, among other things, that foreign-owned firms were to push exports and procure locally "where economic to do so," regardless of the requirements of foreign governments.[35]

Finally there was clash between the voluntary program and the government of the Republic of France which also asserts jurisdiction over the foreign remittance practices of French subsidiaries of foreign companies.[36]

Early in 1968 the Johnson Administration felt that the international position of the dollar had weakened significantly in the face of continued balance-of-payments deficits, domestic inflation, and the devaluation of sterling. In an express effort to reduce net capital outflows by $1 billion, in 1968, the President enacted the "mandatory controls" on January 1, 1968.[37] Clearly these regulations were another presumptuous intrusion into the financial policies of host countries. With the sequence of home country action and host country reaction that has occurred, many companies have found themselves caught in a "cleft stick," unable to comply with both sets of regulations simultaneously. Consequently, a three-member Foreign Direct Investment Appeals Board was set up to handle complaints based on these inconsistencies.[38] In such instances the United States has little alternative but to work out an acceptable compromise since the host country always has the upper hand.

The obvious response to these difficulties has been the expansion of the Eurobond market.[39] By borrowing in this market, the international corporation can transfer capital to the host country without running afoul of either home or host country regulations. The Eurobond market is in reality a two-tier market. The actual borrowers are the international financing subsidiaries of major home country corporations. For the U.S company this usually means a tax haven corporation with nominal net worth.[40] What makes its securities marketable is the guarantee of the parent that debt service payments will be made on time. The intention of course is that enough cash will flow through the financing subsidiary from overseas operating subsidiaries to maintain the payments. In view of the likelihood of this prospect, the Office of Foreign Direct Investment (OFDI) issued General Authorization No. 1 which allowed parent corporations to make debt-service payments under a guarantee if the parent had previously certified to the Secretary of Commerce that it had no reason to believe that the financing subsidiary would be unable to make such payments. For the most part Eurobond borrowings are paid back without recourse to these provisions, which were instituted mainly to allay fears of lenders as to the parent's technical inability to make good on a guarantee.[41]

Since Eurocurrency is simply currency circulating outside of its country of issuance, there is no fixed geographic base for Eurobond registration and they can be issued in any country in the world. U.S. companies naturally issue outside the United States and thus avoid OFDI and Securities Exchange Commission (SEC) regulations simultaneously. Most Eurobond offerings are made by quite substantial corporations to quite substantial lenders. At present, with the market limited to sophisticated investors and borrowers, there may be no real need to regulate such offerings. The borrower can adequately determine for himself the commercial desirability of his borrowing terms, and the lender can likewise assess the security offered for the loan. As the market develops, however, the credit rating of the borrower will be lower, and the identity of the lender will be more like an average investor than an oil-rich sheik. Somewhere in the not too distant future, regulation will be necessary to protect all parties.

If supervision of the Eurocurrency bond market were to be assigned to some sort of international agency, it might be possible to provide for withholding of income tax on such bonds in such a way as to halt tax evasion or stem the use of what are, in effect, interest-free loans involuntarily made by governments to taxpayers, who buy the bonds on which withholding is not required, through Delaware or Luxembourg corporations. The administrative difficulty, in the case of bearer bonds, is to know to which government the taxes withheld should be paid.

As previously mentioned, the Eurobond market will eventually develop to the point where small borrowers can utilize it. At present they are effectively excluded. The mandatory controls provide an escape route through the *de minimis*[42] provisions whereby any industrial investor can transfer up to $1 million overseas without need for compliance with the regulations. Unfortunately, there is still a gap between the very small overseas investor who remains below the million dollar level and those who can float a Eurobond issue. As with tax havens there is a distortionary effect on the size of firms operating internationally due to artificial regulations.

Present-day institutions that deal with balance-of-payments problems, such as the International Monetary Fund (IMF), Working Party No. 3 of the Organization for Economic Cooperation and Development (OECD), or the Group of 10 are restricted to governments and to macroeconomic effects. By and large the concerns of private firms do not feature in these proceedings. What is needed is a forum where the impact of balance-of-payments regulations on separate firms can be resolved, especially where the pressure from two or more countries on a single firm pushes it in different directions.[43]

Export Controls
Among the most controversial issues is the attempt by some countries, and specifically the United States, to impose its foreign policy on other nations through the foreign subsidiaries of domestic corporations. For example, consider the case of Fruehauf-France, S.A., of which Fruehauf (U.S.) owns a two-thirds stock interest. In December 1964 Fruehauf-France signed a contract with Automobiles Berliet, S.A., another French company, for the delivery of 60 vans for shipment to the People's Republic of China. In January 1965 the U.S. Treasury Department ordered Fruehauf (U.S.) to suspend execution of the contract as it was in violation of the U.S. Transaction Control Regulations.

On January 12, 1965, the president of Fruehauf International in-formed the French subsidiary of the Treasury Department's order, and on January 28, 1965, he formally directed the subsidiary to rescind the contract.[44] Fruehauf-France approached Berliet on the matter of rescission. Berliet refused to annul the contract and informed Fruehauf-France that it would be held liable for all ensuing damages. The French minority directors, fearing that a unilateral repudiation of this sort would weaken its position with Berliet, its largest customer, brought suit in France against the American directors and Fruehauf (U.S.).[45] On February 16, 1965, the court appointed a temporary administrator to head Fruehauf-France for three months and to execute the contract.

The decision was appealed to the Court of Appeals in Paris, which affirmed the lower court's decision on May 22, 1965.[46] Among the considerations cited were the damages which Berliet would have suf-fered by its break with the ultimate buyer. Fruehauf (U.S.) had given no indication that it was willing to accept these as its own. Furthermore commercial relations between Berliet and Fruehauf-France would most likely have been terminated, with Fruehauf-France facing an overnight loss of over 40 percent of its business. It is indeed likely that it would have been forced to cease operations, causing the unemployment of over 600 workers.

Looking at developments in France, the U.S. Treasury Department noted that the U.S. directors had attempted to replace the original director-general with one who would comply with the directive from Fruehauf International. Furthermore the U.S. directors had promptly challenged the French court's appointment of a temporary adminis-trator. It concluded that neither Fruehauf (U.S.) nor the American directors of Fruehauf-France were able to control effectively the ac-tivities of the company. Consequently the Treasury Department rea-soned that its administrative jurisdiction which was grounded on "control" no longer existed. It rescinded the order, and Fruehauf-France performed.[47] After the incident was concluded, all parties re-sumed amicable relations. Berliet was still Fruehauf's best customer, although it has refrained from passing on any more proscribed con-tracts. Fruehauf of course suffered a considerable loss on the contract due to legal and travel expenses, executive hours diverted, and delays in delivery.

This is not an isolated incident. Many have involved Canada and the United Kingdom, which have no regulations restricting trade with the Communist bloc. The Watkins Report recognizes that governments have a national propensity to see that their policies are not frustrated by citizens who escape their jurisdiction for the purpose of undertaking some action which they could not do at home.[48] At the same time Rubin has admitted that the U.S. Treasury Department's interpretation of the regulations under the Trading with the Enemy Act[49] has become "rather stiff and doctrinaire" and has given rise to "considerable irritation abroad."[50]

Several possible escapes from this sort of clash exist. The first and most obvious is for governments to seek to gain adherence to their views by approaching other governments which, if they concurred, would apply similar legislation or regulations within their own jurisdiction. This is the path of harmonization. This approach was pursued in the Coordinating Committee (COCOM) limiting the export of strategic materials to the Eastern bloc, under the Battle Act and similar legislation.[51] When foreign policies differ, however, harmonization is of no avail. Nevertheless, as a principle of international relations, it is still desirable to pursue the government-to-government means of extending the reach of a national policy before issuing directives to domestic corporations for communication as instructions to their foreign subsidiaries.

Second, it may be possible to draw a number of fine distinctions which can serve as guides to conduct. For example, the availability of the goods in question could be taken into consideration. When France wanted to buy a computer from the French IBM subsidiary for use in its nuclear weapon program, the United States instructed IBM not to proceed with the sale because it wanted to curtail the proliferation of such weapons. If a similar computer was readily available from alternative sources, it would be a loss only for IBM and the United States when France bought elsewhere. Such considerations were incorporated into the Export Administration Act of 1969.[52]

Similarly, many old established trading relationships exist between U.S. foreign subsidiaries and third countries. Some of these third countries were bloc countries, and considerable disruption has been caused to host country trade patterns because of restrictions on trading with the enemy. An issue of considerable importance is the history of the subsidiary. Was it formed expressly to sell goods to bloc nations or has it been trading with bloc nations a long time?

These issues are reflected in current Foreign Assets Control regulations.[53] Three are worth noting:[54] (1) U.S. subsidiaries abroad are *not* prohibited from exporting to Cuba, whereas firms located in the United States are; (2) U.S. subsidiaries abroad may export non-COCOM goods to the Soviet bloc; and (3) U.S. subsidiaries abroad may export certain non-U.S. origin technical data to countries other than China, North Korea, and North Vietnam that U.S. firms may not export.[55]

Nevertheless, it is evident that differences in foreign policy between the home and host country can make life uneasy, difficult, or even intolerable for an international corporation as it is pulled in different directions simultaneously. Some observers feel that there is a natural asymmetry of pressure in that the home country can more readily expand its policy in the host, rather than vice versa. Perhaps this is a result of relative assets in cash jurisdiction. However, it is not evident that Switzerland can push the United States around through Nestlé, even though 90 percent of its assets are abroad. In any event a forum to which a company could appeal from conflicting pressures, or to which a country, host or home, might seek relief from policy intrusion, would seem to be a promising means for conflict resolution in this area.

Securities Regulation

A controversial issue which has been smoldering for some time is the extraterritorial effect of statutes and regulations regarding transactions in securities.[56] If a nation has the requisite constitutional authority (such as our interstate commerce clause), there is little doubt that it can regulate its internal securities markets. Serious jurisdictional questions arise, however, when attempts are made to assert control over foreign nationals who are parties, in a more or less peripheral manner, to domestic securities transactions. Similar conflicts arise when the *only* domestic contact is the nationality of the purchaser.

Securities transactions can be modeled as a three-party process involving the buyer, the issuer, and the market in which the securities are traded. There are eight permutations of these three parties when they each can be either foreign or domestic. For simplicity, the role of the investment adviser has been disregarded although disputes have arisen involving domestic purchasers and foreign advisers.[57] Considering the United States to be the domestic country, we have the following situations:

Buyer	Issuer	Market
US	US	US
US	US	F
US	F	US
F	US	US
US	F	F
F	US	F
F	F	US
F	F	F

The jurisdictional implications will now be discussed briefly.

US–US–US

This is the pure domestic case; no problems arise.

US–US–F

This case is more hypothetical than real. A U.S. issuer selling on a foreign exchange will usually refuse to sell to a U.S. buyer to avoid compliance with SEC regulations. What he does is intentionally place himself outside the ambit of U.S. regulation by selling only to foreign buyers (the F–US–F situation). This latter scheme is expressly permitted by an SEC rule[58] which authorizes the operations of overseas capital corporations as domestic subsidiaries of U.S. parents. Most Eurobond offerings of U.S. companies use this or a similar vehicle as described earlier.[59]

US–F–US

This is the most controversial situation. Clearly supervision of this case makes sense when the foreign issuer seeks out U.S. buyers via a U.S. exchange. There is no reason why he should be treated more leniently than a domestic issuer. This view was upheld in the recent case of *Schoenbaum v. Firstbrook* where the U.S. Court of Appeals for the Second Circuit said:

> We believe that Congress intended the Exchange Act to have extra-territorial application in order to protect domestic investors who have purchased foreign securities on American exchanges and to protect the domestic securities market from the effects of improper foreign transactions in American securities. In our view, neither the usual presumption against extraterritorial application of legislation nor the specific language of Section 30(b) show Congressional intent to preclude application of the Exchange Act to transactions regarding stocks traded in the United States which are effected outside the United States when extraterritorial application of the Act is necessary to protect American investors.[60]

By a recent amendment to the Securities Exchange Act,[61] and Commission regulations thereunder,[62] foreign issuers whose shares are held by 300 or more U.S. persons, even if traded only on the over-the-counter market, are required to register with the Commission or to furnish detailed information to it. These regulations come into play even if the issuer did not seek to have his shares traded in the United States, or even if he took active steps to prevent their being traded in the United States. Registrations and disclosures of this type are particularly obnoxious to foreign companies who operate in a confidential environment relatively free from public surveillance. These requirements also reach to "insiders" as principal shareholders or operating officers in ways almost totally unknown abroad.

The overseas reactions to the regulations when proposed were succinctly reviewed by *The Economist*:

These views of the U.S. securities industry [in opposition to the regulation] coincide broadly with those of many foreign governments and issuers. Canada, for one, has filed a stiff protest with the State Department, complaining that the SEC actually proposed to extend U.S. law into the affairs of Canadian companies. Canadian companies have complained that they will now find themselves subject to SEC regulation whenever Americans independently purchase more than the minimum 300 shares of their companies on a Canadian exchange. The Japanese question the legality of the rules under international law and suggest that the disclosure the SEC is seeking should be obtained, if at all, through government-to-government negotiations. Among individual companies complaining is Rolls-Royce.[63]

F–US–US

This is another highly controversial area which affects the operations of overseas based and registered companies who make use of the U.S. exchange to buy U.S. securities for foreign purchasers. A notable example is The Fund of Funds operated by Investors Overseas Services (IOS) of Geneva. The Fund of Funds deals exclusively in U.S. mutual funds for foreign shareholders. By virtue of its overseas base of operations and foreign registration, the Fund of Funds (and other IOS activities) have generally avoided SEC supervision. However, in *Roth v. The Fund of Funds, Ltd.*,[64] the plaintiff brought a short-swing profit suit against the defendant who qualified as an insider by virtue of greater than 10 percent holdings of Dreyfus Corporation common stock. The court assumed jurisdiction over the defendant because of the situs of the wrong—the New York Stock Exchange. Although correct on standard conflict principles, this decision is certainly threatening to foreign investors who may find their assets sequestered by virtue of U.S. administrative and judicial procedures. It is possible that a more progressive "contacts" test would have led to a decline of jurisdiction by virtue of the peripherality of the situs when compared to facts such as the nationality of the defendant and *its* shareholders.

F–F–US

This is another hypothetical situation. It is rather unlikely that a foreign purchaser will entangle himself in the web of U.S. securities regulation when he could purchase the same securities in more unregulated environments abroad.

US–F–F

Even though the relevant statutes and regulations are designed to protect the shareholder, U.S. courts have consistently refused to assume jurisdiction where the only U.S. contact was the nationality of the shareholder. However, in an unusual reversal of its own position, the Federal Court for the Southern District of New York reanalyzed the jurisdictional facts and found the requisite contacts in *Ferraioli v. Cantor.*[65] The court based its reversal on the domestic activities of the issuer, even though it was a foreign corporation. Since the fraudulent activities had taken place at least in part within the United States, a sufficient basis for jurisdiction was established under traditional territorial principles.

F–F–F

This is the purely foreign case. There is no jurisdiction.

Jurisdiction in these cases is most clear where use is made of a U.S. stock exchange. Such jurisdiction can be quite offensive to a corporate issuer who had no intention of having his securities traded locally. Furthermore he may be unable to avoid such jurisdiction when convertible issues, warrants, or rights are involved and freely traded. There has been little actual experience in this area of international securities conflicts, and most law has been judge-made. Some form of governmental coordination is clearly required.

Existing Approaches

At one end of the spectrum of approaches to the problem these issues underscore is to do nothing about it. It is argued that the problems involved are not of primary importance, and they can be solved in the day-to-day working of normal diplomacy. This is the view of Seymour J. Rubin, a practicing attorney, part-time international negotiator for the U.S. government and astute commentator on these problems. Rubin sees a trend toward natural harmonization of national policies. For example, he perceives the antitrust views of the EEC and the United States as being more alike than not.[66]

In further support of his position, Rubin cites the U.S. mandatory control program on capital exports which caused great concern among foreign nations when first instituted, especially among "Schedule C" countries which were slated for a cutback in direct investment and an increase in repatriation of earnings. Yet, when Undersecretary of State Nicholas Katzenbach informed Michel Debré, the Finance Minister of France (a Schedule C country), of the content of the new regulations, M. Debré announced that the French government was prepared to support the U.S. plan, even though it conflicted quite clearly with French foreign exchange controls, because of the weakness of the U.S. balance of payments.[67]

Another example is found in Canadian-United States antitrust co-operation. Following a number of cases where the United States ordered U.S. corporations to produce records of Canadian subsidiaries, to the indignation of both the public and the private interests concerned, an informal agreement on policy in such matters was negotiated between U.S. Attorney General Rogers and Minister of Justice Fulton of Canada. This agreement, popularly referred to as the Antitrust Notification and Consultation Procedure, provides for informal harmonization of action in antitrust matters involving both countries.[68] In a variety of other areas, moreover, U.S. courts have shown themselves sensitive to the problem of intrusion into foreign jurisdictions and have not compelled action that would be contrary to the law of other countries.[69]

George W. Ball, now chairman of Lehman Brothers International, Ltd., is the spokesman for the opposing end of the spectrum.[70] He feels that international incorporation is the optimal, if not the only, solution. The Ball proposal envisions the creation of a body of supra-national law under which the global parent would be incorporated. This body of law would be a comprehensive companies law and would include, inter alia, antimonopoly provisions and guarantees against uncompensated expropriation. The parent, no matter where its head-quarters are physically located, would operate under these provisions in an environment that is void of local interference on substantive corporate matters. The advantages that would accrue to an international corporation under this proposal appear to be increased freedom with regard to mergers, capital transfers, and trade and investment decisions.

The basic problem with the Ball proposal is that it simply cannot be achieved in the foreseeable future, although the authors agree that in the long run it contains the most merit. Ball himself suggests that worldwide incorporation would likely be an extension of a regional plan, such as an EEC company. Unfortunately there does not seem to be much progress being made within the EEC toward regional incorporation.[71] The reasons for this lack of progress are clear enough — the political problems standing in the way of an EEC company convention are enormous. Consider just these three issues: (1) should there be worker representation on the supervisory boards, (2) what should the tax status of an EEC company be, and (3) which groups should be allowed access to European incorporation? Although there has been a body set up within the EEC to consider these issues, the fact remains that little resolution of them has been achieved thus far.[72]

An intermediate path between the Rubin and Ball approaches is through international agreement on specific matters. Table 16.1 summarizes post-World War II efforts in this connection, listing agreements affecting international investment by scope and format. The infinite array of domestic regulation in the fields of tax, foreign-exchange controls, limitations on investment in certain areas, and so forth, has been intentionally omitted.

Only one serious attempt has been made to reach an agreement that is both multilateral in format and comprehensive in scope—the draft charter of the International Trade Organization.[73] Although it is not possible to discuss the ITO at length, the draft covered a wide number of aspects of world trade: employment; economic development; commercial policy including tariffs, quantitative restrictions, exchange controls, subsidies, antidumping, and trademarks; restrictive business practices; commodity agreements; dispute resolution; and others.[74] Its production consumed four years of informal work during World War II and two years of formal negotiation after the war by representatives of over 50 nations. Three major conferences were required to put the document in final form for submission to national legislative bodies for ratification. Although a few countries ratified it almost immediately on completion, each ratification was contingent on subsequent U.S. ratification. The treaty was quietly withdrawn from Congress as soon as it became apparent that ratification would not occur. Other countries then lost interest, and two years later the ITO was a dead issue.[75]

As the scope of a multilateral agreement narrows, its probability of ratification increases. The narrowing can be achieved either in content or through geographic limitation. A glance at table 16.1 shows that the successful restricted scope–multilateral format agreements were either limited to a specific problem (e.g., tariff reduction, international monetary matters) or to membership limited to the developed countries of Western Europe. Of this type there are as many successful arrangements as unsuccessful ones.[76]

A fourth suggestion that we feel is worth noting has been put forward by two young economists.[77] Briefly, they propose the organization of industries along product lines within the national boundary in accordance with the socialistic model. Such a plan would certainly make the extent of the enterprise coterminous with the state so as to provide the necessary political authority over the investor. They fail, however, to examine the performance of economies operating on this principle, notably those of the Soviet bloc. The economic costs in achieving efficient resource allocation among two or more Socialist

Table 16.1
Post-World War II agreements to promote international investment

Format	Scope Comprehensive	Restricted
Multilateral	*International Trade Organization* (ITO)[a]	International Monetary Fund (IMF)[b]
		International Bank for Reconstruction and Development (World Bank)[c]
		General Agreement on Tariffs and Trade (GATT)[d]
		UN Conference on Trade and Development (UNCTAD)[e]
		UN Committee on International Trade Law (UNCITRAL)[f]
		European Coal and Steel Community (ECSC)[g]
		European Community (Common Market)[h]
		European Free Trade Association (EFTA)[i]
		International Center for the Settlement of Investment Disputes (ICSID)[j]
		ECOSOC antitrust venture (UN Economic and Social Council)[k]
		GATT antitrust venture[l]
		Organization for Economic Cooperation and Development *tax proposals, insurance scheme,* and *property rights convention*
		Sohn-Baxter Treaty[m]
Bilateral	Treaties of Friendship, Commerce and Navigation (FCN Treaties)[h]	Tax treaties[n]

Note: Those proposals that have not been approved are printed in italic type.
a. See U.S. Department of State, Pub. No. 3117, *Havana Charter for an International Trade Organization* (Commercial Pol. Series 113, 1948).
b. Articles of Agreement, Dec. 27, 1945, 60 Stat. 1401 (1946), T.I.A.S. No. 1501, 2 U.N.T.S. 39, *amended* May 31, 1968, T.I.A.S. No. 6748.
c. Articles of Agreement, Dec. 27, 1945, 60 Stat. 1440 (1946), T.I.A.S. No. 1502, 2 U.N.T.S. 134.
d. Oct. 30, 1947, 61 Stat. A3, T.I.A.S. No. 1700, 55 U.N.T.S. 187. For text as currently amended see 4 GATT, *Basic Instruments and Selected Documents* (1969).
e. UNCTAD was established by resolution of the U.N. Economic and Social Council and endorsed by the General Assembly in 1962. See UNCTAD, *Basic Documents on Its Establishment and Activities* 1, 4 (1966).
f. Established by General Assembly Resolution 2205 (XXI) 1966, XXI GAOR, Supp. N-16.
g. Treaty Establishing the European Coal & Steel Community, April 18, 1951, 261 U.N.T.S. 140 (1957).

Table 16.1 (continued)

h. Treaty Establishing the European Economic Community, March 25, 1957, 298 U.N.T.S. 11.

i. Convention Establishing the European Free Trade Association, May 3, 1960, 370 U.N.T.S. 3.

j. Convention on the Settlement of Investment Disputes between States and Nationals of Other States, [1966] 1 U.S.T. 12070, T.I.A.S. No. 6090, 575 U.N.T.S. 159.

k. See U.N. Economic & Social Council, Report of the Ad Hoc Committee on Restrictive Business Practices, U.N. Doc. E/2380 (1953).

l. See GATT, Decisions of the Seventeenth Session, Dec. 5, 1960, GATT Doc. L/1397.

m. OECD, *Draft Double Convention on Taxes on Income and Capital* (1963); OECD, *Draft Double Taxation Convention on Estates and Inheritances* (1966). OECD, *Report on the Establishment of a Multilateral Investment Guarantee Corporation* (1965) [(draft may be found at 8 *Harv. Int'l L. J.* 328 (1967)]. See also Martin, "Multilateral Investment Insurance: The O.E.C.D. Proposal," *id.*, at 280. OECD, *Draft Convention on the Protection of Foreign Property* (1967), reproduced in 8 *Int'l Leg. Mat'ls* 117 (1968). See Sohn & Baxter, "Responsibility of States for Injuries to the Economic Interests of Aliens," 55 *Am. J. Int'l L.* 545, 548 (1961) (draft convention).

n. *E.g.*, Treaty with the Netherlands, March 27, 1956, [1957] 2 U.S.T. 2043, T.I.A.S. No. 3942, 285 U.N.T.S. 231.

o. *E.g.*, Income-Tax Convention with Trinidad and Tobago, Dec. 22, 1966 [1967] 3 U.S.T. 3091, T.I.A.S. No. 6400.

countries are ignored, as are the human costs in the loss of individual rights.[78]

The Proposal

Consider now those issues that involve two or more states as well as the investor. Their roots clearly lie in managerial decisions taken by private companies, such as repatriation of profits as opposed to local reinvestment. The ensuing actions are regarded as detrimental by at least one of the countries involved and are perceived as conflicts of government policies even though they stem from private corporate decisions. Fortunately, the conflicts are serious in only those handful of areas that we have discussed: taxation, antitrust policy, foreign-exchange and export controls, and securities regulation. Because these conflicts are universally accepted as posing a problem for solution, the authors are optimistic that meaningful progress toward resolution of multiparty disputes can be made in the near future. Although there is little hope for a resurrection of an ITO-type code, it seems likely that a contractual arrangement could be developed from agreement on a few fundamental concepts of substance and procedure. Then, as a seminal body of accepted principles emerge, broader and deeper agreement as to foreign investment practices would be generated. Perhaps after a guarded and gradual start gathered momentum, an international treaty of substantial coverage could be accepted by the nations of the world.

At the outset it must be emphasized that all that is called for is a forum for the problems related to the international corporation and some procedures that could enhance dispute resolution in the two- or two-plus-country case. This means agreement on only the most fundamental of levels and a willingness to work toward global solutions to a global problem.

The authors are mindful of the fact that multilateral agreements are most difficult to launch. They also are aware of the success that GATT has achieved in a relatively narrow, but commercially important, area. In our opinion difficulties are certain to arise if too much is attempted too soon. The ITO failed in part because it was an attempt at codification at the outset, a scope far greater than was possible either then or now.[79]

What is proposed here we believe to be more acceptable in scope. We suggest an approach directed toward the formation of a General Agreement for the International Corporation, similar to the General Agreement on Tariffs and Trade. We urge that governments agree to the formation of a preparatory commission to draft in detail the few principles on which agreement is needed and to establish the limited international machinery it requires. Specifically we suggest that an international group of experts and staff be impaneled for a period of up to two years to consider the problem of regulation of the international corporation. Their goal would be the creation of an international agreement based on a limited set of universally accepted principles. This agreement would be structurally similar to GATT.

It is envisioned that questions could be submitted to the agency set up to administer the agreement by either countries or companies. The agency would then investigate the facts and the issues presented. Recommendations to take or to cease action would be issued, but there would be no compulsion to abide by them. If it succeeds in acquiring a reputation for thorough analysis and impartiality, the agency would in due course be able to have its decisions accepted voluntarily by participants. As its status in the world community improves, the agency could act as an ombudsman for corporations and countries seeking relief from oppressive policies.

Sponsorship, budgeting, and other administrative problems we leave to others. The costs of such a procedure may look fairly high and the results fairly low. In our opinion, however, international supervision is a much more preferable solution than complete laissez faire or a return to nationalism. Degrees of possible international supervision differ. A thoroughly worked out international system, as proposed by Ball, seems utopian at this time. It is necessary to start nearer the laissez faire position and to evolve a system, through trial, error, and the establishment of precedent. But it is necessary, in our judgment, to act. The sooner a start is made, the sooner the world will be on a path toward global efficiency in resource allocation, production, and distribution of goods.

Notes

1. Devlin & Cutler, "The International Investment Position of the United States: Developments in 1968," *Survey of Current Business*, Oct. 1969, at 24.

2. Rose, "The Rewarding Strategies of Multinationalism," *Fortune*, Sept. 15, 1968, at 100.

3. The writers are unsympathetic to the strong pressures that the Organization for Economic Cooperation & Development (OECD) and the U.S. government applied to Japan to open its market to direct investment from the United States and Western European countries. See, e.g., Address by Hon. John T. Connor, Sec'y of Commerce, before a Joint Meeting of the American Chamber of Commerce in Japan and the Japan-America Society to Tokyo, July 8, 1966, "Expanding the Fabric of U.S.-Japanese Economic Relations," 55 *Dept. of State Bull.* 215, 219 (1966). If a country wants to keep out foreign investment in infant industry, national-defense, or antimonopoly grounds, it would seem legitimate for it to exercise its sovereign powers to this end. The country trades increased national control against imports of capital and technology. But of course it cannot in turn expect to be entitled to opportunities for foreign investment as a matter of right. Presumably, if the proposals of this paper result in regulation of the international corporation, some of the bases for resistance to foreign investment would be eliminated, but not the xenophobic ones.

4. Convention on the Settlement of Investment Disputes between States and Nationals of Other States, [1966] 1 U.S.T. 1270, T.I.A.S. No. 6090, 575 U.N.T.S. 159.

5. Pub. L. No. 87-834, 76 Stat. 960 (Oct. 16, 1962).

6. *Internal Revenue Code of 1954* §§951-64, 26 U.S.C. §§951-64 (1964).

7. Prior to 1962 U.S. citizens and U.S. corporations paid no income tax on foreign income. The most significant tax loophole left by the Revenue Act of 1962 is the provision that permits a foreign subsidiary to receive foreign dividends, royalties, licensing fees, and other nonoperating income and maintain this income's tax free status provided at least 70 percent of the foreign subsidiary's income is derived from legitimate functions. In other words, if the foreign subsidiary can comply with the 70 percent rule, all of its income is beyond the U.S. income tax laws. *Id.* §954. See Beardwood, "Sophistication Comes to the Tax Havens," *Fortune*, Feb. 1969, at 95.

8. The home country response to host country taxation has been the foreign tax credit. Most developed countries have enacted some form of legislation in this area. They are limited to certain types of taxes paid abroad and in the amount of credit

available. According to U.S. law, for example, only income, war profits, and excess profits taxes are creditable. *Internal Revenue Code of 1954* §§901(b)(1), 26 U.S.C. §§901(b)(1) (1964). Excise taxes and value-added taxes are not. The limitation rules are too intricate to describe here, but they basically limit the credit to a percentage of the tax paid equal to the corporation's taxable income derived from foreign sources divided by its total taxable income. *Id.* §904. See generally P. Musgrave, *United States Taxation of Foreign Investment Income* (1969). Consequently the smaller the overseas income of a corporation in relation to its total income, the less effective the credit becomes.

The credit is available only in cases where the corporation pays the tax directly, where a subsidiary of which it owns 10 percent or more of the voting stock pays the tax or where a secondary subsidiary of which the primary subsidiary owns 50 percent or more of the voting stock pays the tax. *Internal Revenue Code of 1954* §§902(a), (b). The rules of the United Kingdom are similar in concept but substantially more complicated due to the system of income taxes, profit taxes, and capital allowances. See *CCH British Tax Guide* §12. The net result, however, is that even after allowance for the credit, foreign taxes are still a significant distortionary factor in overseas investment decisions. For a discussion of policies leading to tax neutrality, see P. Musgrave, *supra*, ch. VII.

9. However, some corporations get caught in a "double squeeze" when both the home and host countries attempt similar reallocations of income and expenses from their own points of view. In the petroleum industry, for example, royalties paid to producing states are computed on the basis of the national price, and downstream transfers between affiliates are made at the price also. In 1963 the Australian Commission of Taxes attempted to revise downward the price at which the local Shell subsidiary purchased crude even though the royalties paid were not creditable against the Australian income tax. Petroleum Press Service, Oct. 1966, at 363.

10. See, e.g., Neufeld, *A Global Corporation—A History of the Development of Massey-Ferguson, Limited* (1969).

11. United Nations, *International Tax Agreements* (compilations). The OECD completed in 1963 a draft uniform law for bilateral tax treaties. One of its chief objectives was the standardization of terminology. Because of the magnitude of the problem involved in renegotiation of all the existing tax treaties, little attention has been paid to it. Some of its definitional concepts, however, have been incorporated into treaties executed since its publication. OECD, *Draft Double Convention on Taxes on Income and Capital* (1963). See also 2 *Law & Pol. Int'l Business* 232, 243, n. 36, 255 (1969) (U.S. tax treaties).

12. The U.S. government came under the onus of this doctrine in a recent decision by the Supreme Court of Canada. In the case of *United States v. Harden,* Can. Sup. Ct. 366, 41 D.L.R. 2d (1963), the Court denied enforcement of a consent judgment rendered by a U.S. district court on a claim for taxes. The Supreme Court of Canada held that the foreign cause of action did not merge into the foreign judgment. Accordingly a foreign revenue claim could not be enforced directly or indirectly. There is, however, the possibility of avoiding this doctrine via international treaties. The validity of this method was affirmed in the *United States v. Van der Horst,* 270 F. Supp. 365 (D. Del. 1967). The court found that international treaties may be consummated which, at the discretion of the sovereign, will permit the foreign government to collect taxes from the citizens of the foreign country who are using

the other country to escape taxes. An illustration of this mutually beneficial arrangement is the U.S. tax convention with the Netherlands which provides:

[The] Contracting States undertake to lend assistance and support to each other in the collection of taxes which are the subject of the present Convention, together with interest, costs, and additions to the taxes and fines not being of a penal character.

Income-Tax Convention with the Netherlands, April 29, 1948, 62 Stat. 1757, T.I.A.S. No. 1855, art. XXII, para. 1. See H. Steiner & D. Vagts, *Transnational Legal Problems* 697 (1968).

13. Surrey, "Intertax: Intergovernmental Cooperation in Taxation," 7 *Harvard International Law Club Journal* 179 (1966).

14. W. Bishop, *International Law* 443 (1962); *cf.* H. Steiner & D. Vagts, *supra* note 12, at 660–66.

15. *Schooner Exchange v. McFadden*, 11 U.S. (7 Cranch) 116, 136 (1812). As the U.S. District Court for the Southern District of New York has succinctly noted, this case "has been considerably modified in the twentieth century. The sovereign is no longer personalized in the person of a king. Modern governments engage in commercial activity on a scale never dreamed of at the time of Chief Justice Marshall's famous decision. Moreover acts of foreign sovereigns decreed in their own territory in violation of principles of international law may have a direct effect on the property rights and claims of citizens of the United States within the territory of the United States." *Republic of Iraq v. First National City Trust Co.*, 207 F. Supp. 588, 590 (S.D.N.Y. 1962). For a full discussion of the relaxation of this doctrine see Garcia-Mora, "Doctrine of Sovereign Immunity of Foreign States and Its Recent Modifications," 42 *Virginia Law Review* 335 (1956). See also Timberg, "Sovereign Immunity," 56 *Nw. U.L. Rev.* 109 (1962).

16. Early in U.S. antitrust history Justice Holmes prohibited the courts from passing on the legality of acts committed wholly outside the United States. *American Banana Co. v. United Fruit Co.*, 213 U.S. 347 (1909). Two years later, however, the Court generated the "objective territorial" principle by which courts can assume jurisdiction if the acts committed outside the United States set in motion a force which produces an illegal act within the United States. *United States v. American Tobacco Co.*, 221 U.S. 106 (1911). The American Tobacco rule has been limited somewhat since its enunciation. See K. Brewster, *Antitrust and American Business Abroad* 65–74 (1958). Thus the Sherman Act probably applies directly only to arrangements (1) between U.S. companies, or (2) between U.S. companies and foreign firms which have a substantial anticompetitive effect on U.S. foreign commerce. On the other hand, arrangements between foreign firms are illegal only if there was intent to produce an anticompetitive effect on the foreign commerce of the United States and such an effect actually did occur. *Report of the Attorney General's National Committee to Study the Antitrust Laws* 76 (1955).

17. *United States v. Imperial Chemical Industries, Ltd.*, 100 F. Supp. 504 (D.C.N.Y. 1951).

18. *British Nylon Spinners, Ltd. v. Imperial Chemical Industries, Ltd.*, [1953], ch. 19 (C.A.), made permanent, [1955] 1 ch. 37.

19. International Quinine Cartel, 12 *E.C.J.O.* L192, 5 (1969). 2 *CCH Comm. Mkt. Rep.* ¶9313 (1970). See generally Comment, "Developments in Common Market Competition Policy: The Quinine and Dyestuffs Cases," 2 *Law & Pol. International Business* 259, 271–77 (1970).

20. See *N.Y. Times*, Nov. 28, 1969, at 63, col. 2.

21. *The Economist*, Nov. 29, 1969, at 83.

22. See C. Kindleberger, *American Business Abroad* 66 (1969).

23. *Id.* at 35.

24. The Webb-Pomerene Act, 15 U.S.C. §§61–65 (1964). "U.S. exporters may join an association entered into for the sole purpose of engaging in export trade and actually engaged in such export trade . . . provided such association . . . is not in restraint of trade within the United States, and is not in restraint of the export trade of any domestic competitor of such association." *Id.* §62. There is, however, the proviso contained in the act that the associations are valid only as long as they do not enhance or depress prices in the United States. Exporters who enter into such agreements are required to submit specified material to the Federal Trade Commission which is, in conjunction with the courts, responsible for enforcement of the Act.

25. U.S. Department of State, Pub. No. 3117, *Havana Charter for an International Trade Organization*, art. 46 (Commercial Pol. Series 113, 1948).

26. See C. Edwards, *Control of Cartels and Monopolies, an International Comparison* ch. 14 (1967).

27. See U.N. Economic & Social Council, *Restrictive Business Practices—Statement of Views of the United States Government*, U.N. Doc. E/2030 (1951).

28. See U.N. Economic & Social Council, *Report of the Ad Hoc Committee on Restrictive Business Practices*, U.N. Doc. E/2380 (1953).

29. "The revocation of U.S. support was predicated on differences which presently exist in national policies and practices . . . of such magnitude that the proposed international agreement would be neither satisfactory nor effective in accomplishing its purpose. . . . Present emphasis should be given not to international organizational machinery but rather to the more fundamental need of further developing effective national programs to deal with restrictive business practices, and of achieving a greater degree of comparability in the policies and practices of all nations in their approach to the subject." U.N. Economic & Social Council, *Restrictive Business Practices*, U.N. Doc. E/2612/Add. 2 at 4–5 (1955).

30. GATT, Decisions of the Seventeenth Session, Dec. 5, 1960, GATT Doc. L/1397, at 17.

31. See note 26 *supra*, at 238.

32. Message of President Johnson to the Congress, Feb. 10, 1965. 111 *Cong. Rec.* 2488.

33. Beale, "The Australian Business Climate," *Cal. Mgt. Rev.*, Winter, 1966, at 187.

34. In 1968 Australia's plight was partially remedied by its classification as a schedule B country. See note 37 *infra*. This permits a U.S. direct investor to invest up to 65 percent of his 1965–1966 outlays in Australia. Business International Corporation, Australia, *New Business Power in the Pacific* 34–35 (1968). The latest Australian rules are substantially more complex, but do remove the uncertainty that surrounded previous regulations. *Business International*, Sept. 19, 1969, at 299. A "foreign" firm is one with more than 25 percent foreign equity, and a "new firm" is one that is less than 10 years old. Maximum local borrowings are determined by formulas incorporating these two factors. Administration is similar to past arrangements, and early indications are that the Reserve Bank will give a liberal interpretation to the new rules. *Id.*, Jan. 2, 1970, at 38.

35. *Worldwide P & I Planning*, Nov.–Dec. 1967, at 38.

36. See note 67.

37. Exec. Order No. 11,387, 33 Fed. Reg. 47 (1968). These mandatory controls simply turned the voluntary program into law. Three schedules of countries, with differing percentages of permitted outflow and required remittance of foreign earnings, form the foundation of the system. 15 C.F.R. §1000.319 (1970).

a. Schedule A countries are all foreign countries designated as less developed countries in the Executive Order, as from time to time in force, issued under section 4916 of the Internal Revenue Code.

b. Schedule B countries are such other foreign countries as the Secretary may determine to be developed countries in which a high level of capital inflow is essential for the maintenance of economic growth and financial stability, and where those requirements cannot be adequately met from non-U.S. sources. The following countries are hereby determined to fall in this category: Abu Dhabi, Australia, The Bahamas, Bahrain, Bermuda, Canada, Hong Kong, Iran, Iraq, Ireland, Japan, Kuwait-Saudi Arabia Neutral Zone, Libya, New Zealand, Qatar, Saudi Arabia, and the United Kingdom.

c. Schedule C countries are all foreign countries not included as schedule A or B countries.

d. The Secretary may at his discretion, from time to time, transfer any foreign country from any one of the schedules to another.

Id.

38. 15 C.F.R. §1000.802 (1970). The Foreign Direct Investment Appeals Board is composed of three officials of the Commerce Department, appointed by the Secretary of Commerce. Parties who feel that an administrative action or a decision on a petition for reconsideration caused that party an unusual hardship or does not comply with the goals and objectives of Executive Order 11.387 may appeal to the Board for relief. *Id.*

39. See The Chase Manhattan Bank, *Euro-Dollar Financing* (1968).

40. See, e.g., the offering circular of the $70,000,000 issue of Eastman Kodak International Capital Co., Inc., issued May 9, 1968 by Morgan & Cie International S.A. It is interesting to note that even though the debentures were not registered with the SEC (nor were they sold within the United States or to its nationals or residents), the information supplied satisfied prima facie the disclosure requirements of Form S-7 of the Securities Act of 1933, *as amended*, 15 U.S.C. §§77a–77aa (1964). For an account of the registration process from an economist's point of view, see Nevin, "Some Reflections on the New York New Issues Market," 13 *Oxford Econ. Papers* 84 (1961).

41. *Cf.* Ellicott, "Foreign Investment Controls, A First Year Review," *Law Notes*, Jan. 1969.

42. 15 C.F.R. §1000.503 (1970).

43. See, e.g., "Overseas Investment in Australia," Statement to Parliament by Mr. John Gorton, Prime Minister of Australia, in the House of Representatives, Canberra, Australia, Sept. 16, 1969, dealing with the access of foreign-owned subsidiaries to the Australian capital market. Mr. Gorton said, "We do not believe that we can or should seek to legislate in such a complex field. But we reiterate our wishes, and have little doubt that overseas companies of repute will note and respond to those wishes." 15 *Parl. Deb.* 1382.

44. L. Ebb, *Regulation and Protection of International Business* 6 (Supp. 1968).

45. Société Fruehauf v. Massady, [1968] D.S. Jr. 147.

46. *Id.* 1965 J.C.P. II 14.274 bis (Cour d'Appel, Paris), *translated in part in* 5 *International Legal Materials* 476 (1966).

47. "U.S. French Clash over Red China Case Dramatizes the Plight of Multinational Firms," *Business International*, Aug. 6, 1965, at 250.

48. *Report of the Task Force on the Structure of Canadian Industry, Foreign Ownership and the Structure of Canadian Industry* (Privy Council Office, Ottawa, 1968).

49. 50 U.S.C. App. §§1–44 (1964).

50. Rubin, "The International Firm and the National Jurisdiction," in *The International Corporation* 198 (Kindleberger, ed., 1970).

51. Mutual Defense Assistance Control Act of 1951 (Battle Act), *as amended*, 22 U.S.C. §§1611–13d (1964). The United States participates in COCOM under the provisions of Sec. 301 of this act. See Baker & Bohlig, "The Control of Exports—A Comparison of the Laws of the United States, Canada, Japan and the Federal Republic of Germany, 1 *International Law* 163, 187 (1966).

52. Pub. L. 91-184, 83 Stat. 841, *amending* 50 U.S.C. App. §§2401–13 (1964).

53. 31 C.F.R. ch. V (1970).

54. See Baker & Bohlig, *supra* note 51, at 188.

55. Until quite recently, all trading, both direct and indirect, with mainland China was forbidden. There were, however, a few very closely guarded exceptions to this law. One of these was a 1958 agreement between President Eisenhower and Prime Minister Diefenbaker of Canada to permit exports by U.S. subsidiaries to China if a firm order were in hand and no other Canadian company could supply the products. Two instances where the agreement has been exercised have been unofficially reported. See Litvak, Maule & Robinson, *U.S.-Canadian Business Arrangements* (1970).

Now, United States subsidiaries abroad can, by regulation, export non-COCOM goods to China and trade in goods of Chinese origin with third countries, but not with the United States, 31 C.F.R. §500.541 (1970).

56. L. Loss, *Securities Regulation*, ch. 4 §E (1951).

57. See, e.g., *The Financial Post*, March 22, 1969, at 3, regarding the unsuccessful attempts of the SEC to prevent Mr. C. V. Myers, publisher of *Myers Finance Reviews*, from mailing his newsletters from Canada to U.S. subscribers.

58. SEC Rule 6c-1, 17 C.F.R. §270.6c-1 (1970).

59. See text at note 40 *supra*.

60. 405 F.2d 200, 206 (2d Cir. 1968).

61. Securities Acts Amendments of 1964, 78 Stat. 565, *amending* 15 U.S.C. §78l (1964). See Goldman & Magrino, "Foreign Issues and Section 12(g) of the Securities Exchange Act of 1934," 23 *Bus. Law* 135 (1967).

62. 17 C.F.R. §240.12(g)3-2 (1970).

63. *The Economist*, Feb. 12, 1966, at 642.

64. 279 F. Supp. 935 (S.D.N.Y., 1968) *aff'd*, 405 F.2d 421 (2d Cir. 1968), *cert. denied*, 394 U.S. 975 (1969). See Note, "Extra-territorial Application of the Securities Exchange Act of 1934," 69 *Colum. L. Rev.* 94, 103 (1969).

65. [1964–1966 Transfer Binder] *CCH Fed. Sec. L. Rep.* 91,615 at 95,310 (mem. S.D.N.Y. 1965). See Goldman & Magrino, "Some Foreign Aspects of Securities Regulation: Towards a Reevaluation of Section 30(b) of the Securities Exchange Act of 1934," 55 *Va. L. Rev.* 1015, 1030 (1969).

66. Rubin, *supra* note 50, at 179. Perhaps the authors are more cynical than he, but it is our opinion that the point of convergence of the antitrust views of the world's nations is very far off and that previous attempts at agreement have been blatantly unsuccessful. Contemporary jurisdictional rules are very broad; still it is too much to expect any one nation to argue global economies in an antitrust case.

67. M. Debré was quoted as having told Mr. Katzenbach: "The principle of Mr. Johnson's program inspires me with satisfaction." He went on, however, to express several reservations and warnings. These were:

a. The program will meet with difficulty in other countries unless they are accompanied by firmer measures to restrict demand in the U.S.

b. It would be hard to acquiesce in lasting discrimination against developed countries, the implication being that the French would oppose granting Britain an exemption from the spending curb.

c. Since the American subsidiaries are French companies under French law with the same access to the financial markets and government credits, if the new U.S. regulations are imposed on them "it will be impossible not to draw the consequences." Hess, "French Endorse U.S. Dollar Policy," *N.Y. Times*, Jan. 7, 1968, at 32, col. 1.

68. "Hearings on S. Res. 191 Before the Subcomm. on Antitrust and Monopoly of the Senate Comm. on the Judiciary, 89th Cong., 2d Sess., pt. 1, at 494 (1966).

69. Motions for *supoenae duces tecum*, however, are forcefully contested in cases involving foreign jurisdictions. See Sheehan, "Thousands Linked to Swiss Deposits," *N.Y. Times*, Dec. 5, 1969, at 22, col. 1. Usually efforts to quash such motions succeeded only after protracted efforts to remove the documents from the country in which they were situated. See, e.g., *United States v. Watchmakers of Switzerland Information Center*, 1965 Trade Cas. ¶71,352 at 80,492 (S.D.N.Y. 1965), wherein the critical portion of the summons was suppressed only after nine years of litigation.

70. See Ball, "Cosmocorp: The Importance of Being Stateless," *Colum. J. World Bus.*, Nov.–Dec. 1967, at 6.

71. Guido Colonna Di Paliano, "Why Europe Needs Continental Scale Firms," *European Community*, Sept. 1968, at 3.

72. A group of legal experts from the six countries which was empaneled as a commission to prepare a model "European company" statute produced radical proposals for a special intergovernmental convention that would determine the ground rules for European companies, have the force of law throughout the Community, and operate side by side with the various national company law systems covering domestic companies (the supranationalist approach). This commission is now pressing for action along these lines.

A familiar conflict has developed between the supranationalist approach and an intergovernmental one favored by the French whereby all countries add a new section to their company law statutes to allow a new type of company still based in one country or another and under the statutes of that country, but the statute governing it thus being uniform throughout the community.

To complicate matters, the Dutch are now arguing that because a European company convention lies outside the aims of the Treaty of Rome, there is no reason why other European countries wanting to join the EEC, such as Britain, should not be brought into any scheme that emerges. The Dutch also urge that since discussions are technically intergovernmental rather than community, other governments could take part now.

73. See *Havana Charter for an International Trade Organization, supra* note 27. See also "Completion of ITO Charter Hailed as Hope for Troubled World," 18 *Dept. State Bull.* 441 (1948).

74. For a discussion of the background, formation, and a detailed analysis of the Havana Charter for the International Trade Organization, see C. Wilcox, *A Charter for World Trade* (1949).

75. See W. Diebold, *The End of the I.T.O.* (Princeton Essays in International Finance No. 16, 1952).

76. Multilateral agreements on restricted issues have been achieved mainly in the trade area. See generally Shawcross, "Trade and the Tangled Web of Law," *The Sunday Times,* Mar. 5, 1967, at 33. The record is particularly dismal in the antitrust area. Furthermore the antitrust provisions of geographical arrangements have not always been applied impartially. For example, in 1953, steel producers of five European Coal and Steel Community (ECSC) countries formed an export price cartel. When the United States objected, the ECSC high authority asked that the cartel be dissolved. Its request was rejected. Since the governing body of the Community has accepted a fairly restrictive, but probably correct, interpretation of its powers under the ECSC treaty, the high authority does not forbid an export agreement unless it curtails competition within the Common Market or leads to practices that would be illegal under the treaty. It may, however, if it thinks necessary, impose maximum or minimum prices on exports. But the Consultative Committee and the Council of Ministers have both recommended against imposing maximum export prices, and the high authority has therefore never taken a formal step to invoke this power, although it has cautioned the cartel against rising prices, using its inherent powers to set the maximum as a lever to reinforce its "requests." See W. Diebold, *The Schuman Plan* 491–501 (1959).

Nonetheless, these export cartel agreements appear to violate the spirit of the GATT waivers which were intended to ensure equitable prices to Community producers in markets outside the Common Market. When complaints arose that export prices were above internal Community prices, the high authority answered that it did not accept a comparison of domestic and export prices as the proper measure of equitable limits within which prices should be kept; it suggested that comparison with world prices was a much more suitable measure. In that regard the Community fares well as compared to the United States and Great Britain. *Id.*

77. See Hymer & Rowthorn, "Multinational Corporations and International Oligopoly," in Kindleberger, *supra* note 22, at 84.

78. See C. Kindleberger, *Foreign Trade and the National Economy,* ch. 10 (1962).

79. Moreover too many exceptions were built into the charter to make it acceptable to most governments. It failed also because support of the business community was lacking. We strongly suggest that initial goals be kept modest and that the business community from the outset be involved in the process by means of self-regulation.

17

The International Corporation in the Atlantic Community: An Economist's View

In the sweep of history the efficient size of firm has continuously risen as a result of declines in costs of transportation and communication, on the one hand, and of converting inputs into outputs, on the other. The typical enterprise has grown from the single proprietor to the partnership, the local corporation, to the regional, national, and now international corporation. Business management has become a "brain," able to coordinate widely separate operations more efficiently in many cases than decentralized markets. In the literature of international business, moreover, there has been an evolution from the national firm with foreign operations, which has a single national identity though it operates outside its nation's boundaries, the multinational corporation which takes on a national identity wherever it operates, to the international corporation which belongs everywhere and nowhere. Some of you may be familiar with the terminology of Howard Perlmutter of the University of Pennsylvania who calls these stages of evolution: the ethnocentric, the polycentric, and the geocentric, respectively. Some of you moreover may be aware that there is controversy over the classification with many political scientists and a few economists denying that a firm can lose its nationality in a cultural sense when it goes abroad and that the nation-state is threatened by the rise of the international corporation.

In his *The American Economy*, J. K. Galbraith claimed that as the firm rose from local to regional to national reach in the United States, it had to be met by a parallel rise of local to national labor unions and of federal at the expense of state and local government. In the long run it may be anticipated that the rise of the international corporation

Previously published in *Antitrust Law Journal* 11 (1971):852–857.

will be paralleled by the development of international political sovereignty to guide and in some respects to constrain it. In Europe, Central and South America, and to a limited extent in other parts of the world, the merging of sovereignty is taking place fitfully at the regional level. On a wider world basis some harmonization of the environment in which corporations operate is under way, especially perhaps in the field of taxation, but to a limited extent in other types of regulation. Political evolution typically proceeds at a slower pace than economic, and political resistance is perhaps harder to overcome than economic—which can be bought out. The economist of course objects to the allocation of resources based on differences in rules of taxation, definitions of income, benefits available to corporate enterprise, and the like, which distort the pattern of investment from that called for by real economic scarcity. Bit by bit this neutrality of regulation has been achieved at the national level. It has allowed the national corporation to stimulate the equalization of the prices of land, labor, and capital of similar resources in a way that the land, labor, and capital markets have not succeeded in doing by themselves. The economist predicts that the international corporation will make its greatest contribution to efficient world resource allocation when tax, benefit, and regulation neutrality exists worldwide. If not world government, this means at least a large measure of harmonization, and in harmonization there is a considerable loss of national sovereignty since national regulations can be changed only by agreement.

Neutrality of tax, benefits, and regulation are not enough to assure efficiency, however, unless regulations provide for competition and especially freedom for new entry. Laissez faire, which permits one company to buy up its rivals, leading to monopoly, will give too little production and too little consumption as compared with a competitive solution. Thus although there is no merit in the rule once enunciated by Michel Debré that France would permit new investments but not takeovers, on the ground that the plants taken over were French and the new buyer contributed nothing, the rule may make sense from the viewpoint of maintaining competition. Takeover leaves the number of firms in the industry unchanged, if there is a new entrant, or reduces it by one if a foreign firm buys out a domestic, whereas construction of new plant adds to the strength of competition. This is the justification for the Department of Justice clearance of such an operation as the British Petroleum purchase of Sohio. This competitive point aside, the view that there is no contribution when a foreigner buys out an existing plant rests on the fallacy of misplaced concreteness. Typically the foreigner is willing to pay a higher price for the plant and equipment than a domestic buyer because he can earn a higher return on them, through the introduction of superior management, marketing techniques, technology, superior credit, or some other advantage. He typically has to have an advantage since he operates at the disadvantage of being far from his decision center. With no advantage and this disadvantage, he would be unable to outbid the local investor for the assets, unless of course he was being foolish, which events of recent years show some U.S. investments abroad to have been.

The point should be noted that it is possible for takeovers both to heighten the monopoly of the taking-over firm, and to increase competition in the market in which it enters. This result occurs when a large firm outside enters a localized market where monopoly is based not on the fewness of firms but on the sluggish quality of enterprise. The welfare implications from a world point of view are evidently complex.

Distinctions among the national firm with foreign operations, the multinational firm which takes on local coloration wherever it goes, and the international corporation which stays aloof from identification with any nation or nations can be drawn in a variety of dimensions. The three classes of firms behave differently with respect to their rates of growth in separate markets, return on assets in separate markets, readiness to take foreign-exchange risk, financing practices, and the like. My interest today is to discuss their personnel practice insofar as it leads into a discussion of joint ventures. The national firm with foreign operations uses its own nationals; the multinational corporation makes a point of using local citizens in its separate operations; the international corporation is prepared to use a good man anywhere without regard to nationality.

Many host countries insist on the use of its own nationals in management and on boards of directors. In Canada the discussion is of the need for a "Canadian presence" in foreign-owned companies, with the thought that nationals in management will somehow ensure that the foreign investor takes into account Canadian interests which would otherwise be threatened. One particular form of this attention to national representation is the insistence in a number of host countries throughout the world of local participation in ownership through joint ventures or sale to local investors of a portion of the equity in the enterprise. Japan, that honorary member of the Atlantic community, is particularly insistent on no more than 50 percent foreign ownership, and preferably less.

There is a substantial body of opinion that applauds these joint ventures, represented notably by Professor Wolfgang Friedmann of the Columbia Law School who has written extensively on the subject. Businessmen, however, typically resist them. Joint ventures build in conflicts of interest. There is some harmony of interest, to be sure, since all partners want to make as much money as possible, but beyond this there are likely to be differences of horizon within which the separate partners maximize, in capacity to stay the course in investment to overcome early teething problems, of viewpoint on the extent to which the world viewpoint is usefully modified for local conditions, and so forth. Businessmen somewhat irrationally state that they will willingly enter joint ventures where the contribution of the partner is something real, rather than merely money. The irrationality to an economist lies in the view that everything real can be translated into money through pricing it. Some ingredients of successful investment may not be for sale separately in distinct markets, however, which is why the attempt by host countries to buy technology, management, access to market, and the like, separately in place of admitting foreign investors is so seldom successful. Most American investors in Japan probably welcome a local partner on the ground that the culture is so strange that they need someone with parallel interests to mediate between the foreign investor and local employees, markets, the government, and the like. It is reported with uncertain reliability that one strong reason for joint ventures in Latin countries and in Europe is the arbitrary basis for administering the corporate income tax. A major automobile company is said to have been on the verge of buying an Italian company with a notable record in the production of racing cars when it realized that it was uncertain how it would be charged corporate income tax. The local company was a national hero and treated on a generous basis. The foreigner could hardly hope to inherit the status of a national monument and would probably have to pay on the strictest standard of accountability (I have heard a number of American businessmen say that their major problem in Italy was the minimal taxes paid by the competition). A major U.S. investor reputedly went into Spain on a joint-venture basis for five years to establish a basis of taxation after which it would buy out the local interests. This runs exactly in the opposite direction to the prescriptions of Professors Hirschman and Rosenstein-Rodan who propose, in the less developed countries at least, that initial understandings provide for eventual divestment.

The cultural, political, and fiscal-administrative reasons for joint ventures are persuasive. The economic justification is weak. A foreign firm with different local partners in each of several jurisdictions is under reduced incentive to allocate production to the cheapest sources and to sell output in the dearest. It is true that the presence of local owners weakens the incentive of the foreign firm to adjust transfer prices on intersubsidiary sales so as to funnel income into the most advantageous tax jurisdiction. But the national tax commissioner is a silent partner in every jurisdiction, and if he is on his toes, he will frustrate attempts to set transfer prices in an arbitrary way. Moreover harmonization of tax rates and the elimination of jurisdictions which offer tax advantages—which strike me as inevitable if future results of shrinking economic space—eliminate the incentive to divert profits from one jurisdiction to another. To rely on local owners to help the corporation stay within the spirit and the letter of local law is a forlorn policy in many less developed countries where the local partners work rather in the opposite sense, to mitigate the impact of local regulation rather than to strengthen it.

The joint venture makes sense when the two partners complement one another's strengths, as in the Concorde which combines French brilliance at producing airframes with British virtuosity in airplane engines. As a rule of thumb it may have noneconomic justification—though I permit myself to be skeptical—but it lacks economic sense. If the local investors pay what their share of the enterprise is worth, they get no bargain, and the country as a whole has less capital to invest. If the host government intervenes in the pricing process and insists that the local share of the enterprise be sold cheaply, it in effect penalizes the foreign investor and discourages investment. This may be appropriate from a political point of view. But the economic cost should be recognized.

In conclusion let me refer again to the need I see for international machinery to cope with the problems of jurisdiction of the international corporation, especially in taxation, antitrust, trading with the enemy, and the like. The nationalization and compensation questions that arise especially in investment in less developed countries should not be handled this way. They should, in my judgment, be "privatized," if you will forgive the solecism, rather than internationalized. (I should like to see the U.S. government out of investment guarantees and the Hickenlooper amendment, and the task of representing investors in these matters left to such a body as APPI, the Association for the Promotion and Protection of Investment, somewhat beefed up, for the purpose of indicating to countries that they cannot expect to deal arbitrarily with investors on one day and invite in more on the next.) But among the developed countries there is need for international machinery to deal with specific questions. It evidently makes a difference to world welfare whether Honeywell takes over Machines Bull or IBM does. We prefer to be regulated by laws rather than men, but circumstances alter cases. Elsewhere, alone and with Paul Goldberg, I have laid out the case for a General Agreement on the International Corporation, a GATT for international business, and I will not summarize the argument further here. I would hope, however, that you lawyers would get on with the task of assisting evolution in producing the environment in which the international corporation can contribute optimally to world welfare.

18

Statement Submitted to the Sixth Meeting of Members of Congress and of the European Parliament

September 17, 1974

Gentlemen, I am honored to be asked to speak to this distinguished body on the possibilities and prospects for an international general agreement on multinational enterprise, or general agreement on tax and investment, policies which would collect information and make recommendations to national governments on the control of activities of multinational corporations. My interest in this subject goes back some distance. Five years ago in *American Business Abroad* I suggested the need for an international body to monitor the activities of international corporations. In 1970, with a young lawyer, I put forward a proposal for a GATT for investment in *Law and Policy in International Business.* At the same time I recognize the force of the argument set forth by Seymour Rubin in *The International Corporation* which I edited in 1970, that in the final analysis every corporate activity occurs in a national jurisdiction and that, if that jurisdiction is unwilling or unable to control such activity, there is little that can be done by a supranational body.

Today the woods are full of proposals for more information, the constitution of international bodies, and the enunciation of codes of behavior applying to corporations, and in some cases to governments. I applaud this activity, although I am not completely convinced that all of it is convergent. The chamber of commerces at one end of the spectrum want to restrict the rights of sovereign governments to na-

Previously appearing in Committee on Foreign Affairs, *The Multinationals: Their Function and Future*, Report on the Sixth Meeting, Washington 1974 (Washington, D.C.: GPO, 1975), pp. 62–64.

tionalize properties within their jurisdiction without conforming to a high international standard of compensation. The United Nations' "Report of Eminent Persons," at the other end, setting out, not without dissent, a fairly nationalistic and populist view of large-scale business, seems to be interested rather in restricting the activities of corporations. Between are many who are convinced that there is a problem, without being entirely sure what the problem is and who want to collect information.

In these circumstances let me suggest a few principles on which I would hope there would be agreement in this body.

Futility of a Code

First, it seems to me futile to seek to work out a code of conduct either for corporations or for countries in their relations with one another. Circumstances alter cases. Moreover there is no agreement even in principle between developed and developing countries, as the "Report of Eminent Persons" makes clear. The economic case, perhaps not overwhelmingly but presumptively favorable for the multinational corporations, runs into a political and social case that is negative. Governments in developing countries exhibit uncompromising nationalism and economic populism toward international corporations and are resolved to end their dependence on the United States. Developed countries rely on market decision making: developing countries are highly suspicious of the outcomes produced by markets. There is thus little point to be served by attempting to achieve worldwide agreement. I would focus on an agreement among developed countries open to any country that wants to join—much like GATT in the trade field.

Ending Subsidies

Second, I would urge that governments of developed countries withdraw from support and subsidy to the international investment process, and in particular terminate tax subsidies, investment guarantees on the positive side, and legislation like the Hickenlooper amendment on the negative. Developing countries and multinational corporations can decide on the costs and benefits of direct investment in developing countries by themselves without intervention in the process by the governments of developed countries. If the terms offered by developing countries are too stringent, or more likely if their attitude toward foreign investment is too inconsistent and wavering, international firms will stay away. At the same time it seems clear that the days when foreign corporations used means of bribery, corruption, undue influence, duress, misinformation, and failure to disclose are, if not over, rapidly waning. European and American business to some degree has a historical record of which we must be ashamed, but the opportunities for such methods, if not the appetite, have been vastly reduced.

Third, international agreement cannot, in my judgment, substitute for effective national action where actions take place wholly within a national jurisdiction. I have reservations, for example, about a number of items on Herr Lange's list of problems, such as labor-market policy and social policy, which seems to me to lie in the competence of national governments. An international organization may usefully assist the national authorities in such complex issues as determining what an arm's-length transfer price should be, but enforcement must be national, and I see no way to substitute an international body for the national authorities.

Business Confidentiality

Fourth, there is a temptation to substitute information gathering for the careful enunciation of principles and their application in particular cases without much of a clear idea of the purposes to be served by such information. Congressman Gibbons in the paper on the subject presented a year ago, and reproduced in the "Report of the Second Official Visit," lists the request for information set forth by Ralph Nader to be furnished by multinational corporations to the United Nations and published. I do not profess a very high regard for the principle of business confidentiality, but this list with 13 categories of information sought by countries would seem to leave that principle in shreds. In our own Department of Commerce, for example, statistics on direct investment are available to the public only on an aggregated basis which cloaks individual companies in anonymity. More important in principle, I would urge that the compilation and publication of statistics is an expensive operation for companies and governmental bodies alike and should not be undertaken unless the governmental or intergovernmental organization has a fairly clear idea of what the information is needed for. Information is desirable on many points, such as agreements among firms in the same industry, interlocking directorates, and the like, but requests for information should be pinpointed to problems, not omnium-gatherum in character.

Harmonization Needed

I believe that there are problems in the tax, antitrust, balance-of-payment controls, export controls, and security regulations fields where at least two national governments and one corporation are involved, in which there may be need to harmonize or coordinate governmental action, and that an international organization could be helpful in these respects on a case-by-case basis. An international agreement based on very broad principle—since applications are complex—would be needed to get it started. The GAME (General Agreement on Multi-national Enterprise) or whatever it was called would then be open for business for a government to raise a question about a corporation and another government, a corporation to complain that it was being pushed in divergent directions by two governments, or even third parties to raise publicly the damage done to them by two governments and a corporation (as in the farm machinery case where Ontario farmers were not able to buy Massey-Ferguson machinery in Britain for import into Canada, because of restraint of trade, and neither the British nor the Canadian government would take action to correct the situation). The issues necessarily arise case by case: for General Electric or Honeywell to buy Machines Bull is not only tolerable but to be welcomed, if it introduces more competition in the international computer field. IBM should not be allowed to buy it.

In the long run the world has a duty of eliminating tax havens. The prospect is not particularly attractive philosophically, since it involves large countries leaning on small to get them into line. As the optimum economic area grows and grows to encompass the world, it is necessary to ensure that resource allocations are made on the basis of real economic variables—scarcities and demand—and not difference in tax laws, effectiveness of law enforcement, antitrust regulations, and the like.

I see the reduction of the cost of transport and communication working in the world to widen the optimum economic area for efficiency, provided that market prices reflect real scarcities in relation to demand. At the same time the optimum political and social area remains small. This creates tension which makes it unlikely that surveillance of the multinational corporation to ensure its economic effectiveness will be accomplished painlessly.

19

Testimony before Hearings of the Subcommittee on Foreign Economic Policy of the Joint Economic Committee, Congress of the United States, 91st Congress, 2d Session, July 27, 1970, on the Multinational Corporation and International Investment

I am grateful for the opportunity to put forward my views on the need for some machinery to resolve differences of viewpoints between governments, and if possible to harmonize attitudes and action, toward what is variously called the multinational, international, or transnational corporation. The world has machinery for the settlement of questions regarding policy in macroeconomics, money, trade, foreign assistance, lending, and similar issues. Questions involving action by a corporation of one nationality in another jurisdiction are sometimes ignored and sometimes the subject of diverging action by two or more nations. The basic role embodied in U.S. treaties of friendship, commerce, and navigation, that all foreign corporations shall be given national treatment except in some restricted fields such as banking, transport, communication, is frequently violated in practice.

Foreign nations discriminate against U.S. corporations, on the one hand, and the United States itself is unwilling in its turn to leave American corporations to the mercies of the Calvo doctrine which holds that foreign corporations in a national jurisdiction cannot claim the support of their home governments but must be content with local justice.

My conviction that some machinery would be useful rests to some degree on Galbraith's view of countervailing power. You will recall

Previously appeared in Joint Economic Committee, *A Foreign Economic Policy for the 1970s, Part IV, The Multinational Corporation and International Investment*, Hearings, July 27, 1970 (Washington.D.C.: GPO, 1970), pp. 759–762.

that this suggests that as the corporation rose from the locality to regional and national power, it was necessary for trade unions to become national and for the federal government to acquire strength to prevent corporate domination of the economy. I am not suggesting that the international corporation, often but by no means exclusively American in origin, is exploitive or dominant or dangerous. It is simply that there will be some number of instances, perhaps few, when private profit must be subordinate to broader considerations of national purpose in this country and in others. Where two or more purposes clash through the corporation or where, on the contrary, the corporation is able to evade a reasonable national purpose of one country by seeking another jurisdiction, there is need, in my judgment, for machinery to work out a reasonable solution.

Note that the recommendation is for machinery, not rules. This is because in this field, as in most of industrial regulation, circumstances alter cases. To use an illustration that I have given before, it is one thing for General Electric to take over Machines Bull in France, but it would be quite different if IBM were to do so. In the one case world competition in computers is enlarged; in the other it would be reduced.

It is also for some machinery, not a great deal. There is a wide spectrum of opinion in this field. At one extreme Seymour J. Rubin, my former colleague in the Department of State, has argued that there is no problem likely to arise in this area that cannot be settled through the ordinary channels of diplomacy.[1] On the other hand, the distinguished former Undersecretary of State George W. Ball recommends a system of world incorporation which would submit international corporations to a special form of world law.[2]

My suggestion, for what it may be worth, is to steer between these extremes and to focus on a few troubled issues, but only a few in the hope that if progress is made, and further problems arise, the machinery developed can be extended.

A vast number of problems should be excluded, especially those that fall within the national jurisdiction. I am not interested in modified or common law rules on hiring local labor, access to local means of finance, nationalization, and similar questions which involve primarily one government and one firm. The International Bank for Reconstruction and Development is concerned with working out a code of conduct in some of these areas, though with little hope of success, in my judgment. These are matters on which I am content to let competition develop standards. Any country that applies too harsh a rule will find itself unable to get access to foreign management, capital, and technology in direct investment. I would expect that the less developed countries would in the first instance be unwilling to join the organization here proposed though they would be welcome if this guess is wrong. Perhaps as in trade, with GATT and UNCTAD, there is need for a double standard, one for developed countries and one for the less developed countries which they ultimately outgrow.

For the moment the GATT for international corporations that is envisaged might be concerned with five problem areas: taxation, balances of payment, export controls or trading with the enemy, antitrust, and the issuance of securities. In taxation a good deal of the work is done by double-taxation agreements, but these could readily be generalized so as more nearly to harmonize income definitions, if not rates which competition seems to be leading to convergence. Double taxation is one problem in which one can expect to hear from the subject, but zero taxation where a company threads its way between jurisdictions so effectively as to escape both is less likely to be called to notice. A GATT for the international corporation might be an effective organization for bringing pressure on a few jurisdictions such a Luxembourg, the Bahamas, Panama, and some Swiss cantons to attract business by remitting normal levies. The attraction of Delaware and Hoboken, N.J., for national corporations in this country waned as the federal income tax took over.

In a world of mobility, moreover, states must protect themselves against the tax concessions of other states by offering the same terms, thus eroding the tax base. The less developed countries receive much advice suggesting caution in tax bargaining with foreign companies lest they give away too much. Here is an area in which international consultation on a continuous basis may be useful for developed and undeveloped countries alike. And the international corporation that was subject to double taxation could use it as a forum in which to raise the question of relief.

The balance-of-payments issue is one of double jeopardy: one country such as the United States telling a firm to bring home profits, or to invest abroad, but not to take money, whereas the other has rules against profit remittances, let us say, or requires both investment and money from outside. I must confess that the problem is perhaps more theoretical than real. In a given situation it will be clear which country is in the more trying balance-of-payments difficulties, as it was when Under Secretary of State Katzenbach informed then Premier Michel Debré that the United States was about to impose foreign exchange regulations on January 1, 1968. But here may readily be difficulties in overlap between foreign exchange regulations, and there is merit in machinery to resolve them.

The trading with the enemy problem is one that has excited especially Canada, Belgium, and France in the past. This occurs when the United States tries to stop subsidiaries of U.S. corporations abroad from selling to Cuba or China, when those companies come under another jurisdiction which may have a different policy. More generally it is seeking to require foreign subsidiaries of U.S. firms to adhere to the purposes of U.S. foreign policy rather than the policies of the country where the subsidiary is located. An early and famous example was the U.S. requirement that IBM not sell a certain computer to the French atomic program since the government of France was opposed to nonproliferation of atomic weapons. It seems evident that there will be more problems of this sort unless foreign policies converge. It would be useful to have a forum for their resolution.

The most troublesome area is in the field of antitrust. Here the United States has tried to get other countries to adopt its policies in the draft charter of the International Trade Organization of 1948, in a UN effort under Sigmund Timberg, in the Constitution of the Coal and Steel Community, and in the Rome Charter of the European Economic Community. Occasions arise from time to time when U.S. courts seek to subpoena documents in other jurisdictions in connection with antitrust suits here. The Congress of the United States has felt strongly on this issue at many times in recent history.

But the problem does not arise solely from the fact that U.S. policy in the antitrust field has been more positive, or perhaps more negative, than that of other countries. There are real issues for the international corporation as to whether particular takeovers that reduce world competition should be allowed, or whether one country's policies in the antitrust field should reduce competition in another country. Recently a Canadian Royal Commission on Farm Machinery Prices disclosed that British law allows the farm machinery industry to forbid sales of machinery for export to Canada, not only by dealers but also second-hand by individuals who buy from dealers, making it impossible for Ontario farmers to buy combines in England at a saving over Canadian prices of $1,400 after paying for transportation and extra commissions.

One substantial problem that will probably need international attention relates to the tendency in many industries for various companies to feel need to be represented in every market, with the result that a number of small countries find themselves with the same eight or ten companies that compete in the U.S. market, struggling for business in a market one-fiftieth the size, each plant small and each inefficient. In a number of countries and industries steps are being taken by national policy to reduce numbers and achieve more efficient scale, whether by subsidies to one, designation of a chosen instrument, or other device. International decisions on appropriate sorts of solutions may be helpful. It concerns the United States: a recent example of the tendency of various competitors in an oligopolistic industry to want to be represented in every market is the current entry of a new set of European and prospectively Japanese firms into the U.S. market.

In the security field a recent amendment to the Securities Exchange Act requires foreign issuers whose shares are held by 300 or more U.S. persons to register with the Commission if their securities are traded only on the over-the-counter market, the issuer did not seek to have his securities listed and took steps to prevent their being traded. Another question arises where foreign investment trusts operate abroad without selling to U.S. investors in an effort to avoid SEC supervision but may transgress U.S. rules by operating as an insider—with more than 10 percent of the common stock of a single registered corporation. In the long run it may be intolerable to have securities issued in the Eurobond market with this jurisdiction responsible for the protection of investors from the effects of security manipulation. At this early stage in the development of the market, the borrowers are almost entirely large corporations with an international credit rating, borrowing from sophisticated investors. As the market continues to develop, this may no longer be true.

My suggestion, which I have elaborated with a young lawyer, Paul Goldberg, is that the U.S. government take the lead in convening a conference of experts to propose agreement on a few simple principles plus machinery by applying them in particular cases that are put to it by governments or by corporations. The beginnings should be modest, but I would envisage that with time, there could develop a forum for the resolution of problems affecting the international corporation rather similar to GATT in the field of trade. The international corporation is here to stay, I believe, and it will present in the future more rather than fewer problems. I suggest it is utopian to try to answer all the problems it raises at one fell swoop, with an international code, and naive to think that all the issues can be dealt with ad hoc.

Notes

1. See S. J. Rubin, "The International Firm and National Jurisdiction," in C. P. Kindleberger, ed., *The International Corporation*, Cambridge, Mass.: The MIT Press, 1970, pp. 179–204.

2. See G. W. Ball, "Cosmocorp: The Importance of Being Stateless," *Columbia Journal of World Business* (November–December 1967).

20

A GATT for International Direct Investment: Further Reflections

In 1970 I proposed, with Paul Goldberg, a lawyer, an international agreement to create to body a deal with problems of international direct investment. The idea was not new then; it has since been made more familiar by codes of conduct worked out by the Organization for Economic Cooperation and Development, the start on a code by the new UN Commission on the Transnational Corporation, and by many authors—George Ball, C. Fred Bergsten, Thomas Horst, and Theodore H. Moran, Lloyd Cutler et al. I present here less a scholarly survey of the literature than a more or less orderly review of the issues by an economist, without the benefit of the legal point of view. I will nonetheless inescapably touch on legal points.

The traditional bilateral treaty of Friendship, Commerce, and Navigation (FCN) that regulates the commercial dealings between states typically provided "national treatment" by each country for the enterprise of the other, promising to treat foreign firms on the same basis as domestic firms. Apparently not much thought was given to the matter in a period when foreign direct investment was limited. In retrospect it seems anomalous to have accorded national treatment to real and corporate *persons*, when such treaties provided at best only "most favored nation" (MFN) treatment for *goods*—that is, treatment no worse than the most favored nation with which the country dealt, but admittedly discriminatory compared with domestically produced goods. National treatment was modified in FCN treaties of the United States to forbid controlling foreign ownership of companies engaged

Previously published (with commentaries) by the Carnegie Center for Transnational Studies, New York, 1980, pp. 1–16.

in communications within the United States. Banking was excepted, since this was the jurisdiction of the fifty individual states. As it turned out, the capacity of foreign banks to deal separately with states made it possible for them to operate in more than one state, a right denied to domestic banks.

Problems involving disputes between the host country and the foreign investor were handled largely on an individual basis. From time to time the home country was brought in by the investor when it felt it was being discriminated against, or when the host country was considered in violation of international law as laid down by treaty, decisions of international courts or tribunals, custom, and so forth. History offers examples of home nations using military force to safeguard the rights of their citizens in portfolio and direct investment abroad. In the well-known Mexican Eagle case, when Mexico nationalized oil-producing properties of the U.S. Standard Oil Company of New Jersey, the United States asserted the doctrine that, under international law, a host country had the sovereign right to nationalize only if it paid "prompt, adequate, and effective" compensation, meaning immediate cash dollars, for the full value of the property. This doctrine was modified in at least one case after World War II: the United States agreed that Poland, which had nationalized some U.S. properties in nonferrous metals in Silesia, was obliged to pay in dollars for the original investment and for reinvestments that had been made when profits were convertible into dollars, but profits that had been reinvested during a period of exchange control could be paid in blocked currency.

In addition to the application of international law, another device used to dilute the force of domestic law on foreign investors was the provision in original investment agreements for third-party arbitration.

In Latin America the intervention of the home government and the use of arbitration were resented as an affront to the dignity of the host government. An Argentine international lawyer produced the "Calvo doctrine," holding that foreign investors were bound to abide by decisions of local courts and governmental agencies without entitlement of third-party support. Certainly, a foreign investor was unlikely to appeal the judgment of the authorities of the United States, the United Kingdom, France, and so forth. Now the Calvo doctrine sought to make explicit with respect to smaller and less powerful nations what was implicit with the powerful. Some, like Raymond Vernon in his *Sovereignty at Bay*, were attracted to the Calvo doctrine, believing it one that all countries might readily agree to. But the notion that sovereignty must be absolute appears less compelling when one contemplates how it has been used in the past—for example, the view of only a few decades ago that blacks in Mississippi should be subject only to Mississippi law, without recourse to federal intervention. Only when views of equal treatment and justice converge can a responsible government allow its citizens to be subject to other jurisdictions without recourse. The basic divergence of views over the treatment of foreign investment among developed and underdeveloped, north and south, rich and poor countries at once argues for some international mechanism for handling disputes and makes the construction of that machinery difficult.

The divergence has always been acute on the subject of compensation for nationalized property. No home government has denied the right of a sovereign host government to nationalize property; the issue is always over the appropriate level of compensation. In the best of circumstances disagreements are possible between reasonable men as they contemplate different methods of valuation: book value, the capitalized value of the property's earning power at different rates of interest (at a minimum those in the home and host markets), value in forced sale, and so on. Host countries can go further, however, and assess fines and taxes retroactively for alleged historic wrongs, whereby the foreign investor loses his property and still owes the host government damages. Disagreements over compensation for nationalized property run deep.

The first attempts that I know of to produce international codes were made by business groups such as the International Chamber of Commerce and focused primarily on the compensation issue. It was easy to achieve acceptance of principle on the part of developed countries but difficult to obtain effective consent of the countries that were likely to undertake the nationalization. The International Bank for Reconstruction and Development had a certain leverage with countries that were interested in obtaining loans for development, and it managed to negotiate a document on the compensation issue that was adhered to by a number of developed and developing countries alike. For ten years no appeal to the terms of the agreement was made. When the Aluminium Company of Canada first appealed to the code against the nationalization of its bauxite properties in Jamaica, the Jamaican government, a signatory, refused to recognize the applicability of the terms of the code, thus emphasizing the uselessness of agreement on wording without underlying agreement on principles of equity and justice.

The origins of foreign direct investment go back to the middle of the nineteenth century—in finance at least to the eighteenth—but its spread occurred primarily after World War I and especially with the coming of jet aircraft and the transoceanic telephone after World War II. Companies went multinational for a variety of reasons—to circumvent tariff walls, to obtain cheaper raw materials, to stake out a position in a foreign market on the ground before they lost an export market, to prevent a competitor from building a commanding lead, and so on. With the rise of the multinational corporation, fears were expressed that it would undermine the nation-state and that its powers and strengths were such as to overwhelm those of poor states. In Europe there were expressions of fear, especially of the American multinational enterprise (MNE), such as J.-J. Servan Schreiber's in *The American Challenge*. The Dominion of Canada issued a statement that said foreign corporations domiciled in Canada would be expected to conduct themselves in all respects as Canadian citizens, though it did not specify what citizenship for a corporation might mean other than obeying the law. And developing countries increasingly sought to organize in the United Nations—the Assembly, the Economic and Social Council (ECOSOC), the Conference on Trade and Development (UNCTAD), and the regional commissions—to arm themselves against the intrusive MNE. A series of resolutions was passed in the United Nations on such issues as the Permanent Sovereignty of Countries over Their Natural Resources (a sovereignty that no one denied, but the restatement of which implicitly spoke to the issue of compensation after nationalization and came out on the side of minimal compensation) and the Code of Rights and Duties for Host Governments and for Foreign Corporations, in which the emphasis was on the duties of corporations and the rights of governments. The United Nations established a panel of experts on what it chooses to call the Transnational Corporation (TNC), which produced a unanimous report but with an underlying divergence of viewpoints evident in the supplementary statements of individual experts from developed and developing countries. A Commission on the Transnational Corporation was established, as well as a Center on the TNC, to continue studies and to prepare a code of conduct. Meanwhile, in Paris the Organization for Economic Cooperation and Development (OECD) had been working on a code of its own, a voluntary code rather than a binding treaty requiring ratification. This code was in process when the U.S. Securities and Exchange Commission inadvertently turned up evidence of a substantial number of illicit payments by American multinational corporations to foreign countries; the code, like the latest version of the International Chamber of Commerce document, incorporates provisions against such payments.

The interest in agreements, treaties, and codes that regulate the behavior of governments toward firms, but more especially firms toward governments, is thus evident. Most of these have issued from one or the other side of the different interests: from firms seeking protection against governments, and especially expropriation by governments, or governments concerned that their powers were being weakened by the presence of firms owing allegiance elsewhere. The choice seemed to be between a code and bilateral dealings. A number of lawyers and political scientists, including Seymour J. Rubin and Joseph S. Nye, argued that problems that arose could be handled best on a case by case basis, without the need to create international machinery. These voices seemed on the whole to be overwhelmed by those calling for some more formal mechanism. J. Kenneth Galbraith had noted in *American Capitalism* that as the firm rose from the local and then regional to the national level, and the local union to the national level, national government extended its power at the expense of local and state government. The rise of the corporation from the national to the international level has seen no like extension of international government with sovereign power, and international unions, with only one or two exceptions, have been ineffectual and their growth limited. Thus, apart from normal diplomacy for intergovernmental conflicts, there seems to be no evolutionary mechanism for dealing with the wide range of issues in the multinational corporate field.

Strategies of Conflict Resolution

Some of the past and present attempts to produce a code for the behavior of multinational enterprises and home and host governments have been strongly partisan, from the side of business or from host governments, especially those of developing countries. The difficulties of producing an overarching general code of behavior acceptable to the several interests strike me as so overwhelming that it seems futile to try. Experience under both the International Trade Organization and the UN Declaration on Human Rights demonstrates that an attempt to write a general code capable of wide acceptance inevitably attracts a host of exceptions to the statements of general principles. So numerous and encompassing do exceptions become that one is in danger of drowning the general principles altogether and enthroning the exceptions as rules of behavior. Consequently it seems superior technique to begin with a smaller group, one capable of acceding to a strong statement of principle, and to leave out such issues as nationalization and its compensation, on which disagreement divides the various constituencies, and concentrate on (1) areas of agreement and (2) machinery for evolving effective procedures for resolution of differences. This agreement should be open to adherence by additional countries willing to subscribe to the general principles and to work toward standard procedures. Countries should be invited to join, but without application of pressure.

This proposal for a "GATT for the multinational enterprise" should not be taken to imply a conclusion that the UN code for the Transnational Corporation will not be acceptable to the developed or host countries. A year ago I would have said this was the likelihood. The odds are probably still against striving at an arrangement embodying a few principles and an evolutionary approach of the sort I have described. It appears that the work of the last year or so has moved away from an aggressive lesser developed country (LDC) attitude and toward a more pragmatic approach. But as a university economist, not in close touch with events either in the UN or the OECD, I offer reflections on principles, rather than practical judgment on whether either the UN or OECD approaches, or both, are workable or unworkable.

One aspect of the GATT approach in trade that is not appealing is found in its practice of providing for retaliation by the aggrieved party in cases of violations. If one country is forced by circumstances to renege on a concession in trade, its trading partner is entitled to withdraw another trading privilege (i.e., to punish the first one). Punishment in these cases hardly fits the crime. Tit for tat is a widespread notion in diplomacy but has a certain childish quality. The qualities of GATT that are appealing if an attempt is made to extend it from trade to the multinational enterprise are the frank exchange of information, the discussion of principles and standards of behavior, and their concretization into a set of rules. The attempt to enforce these rules by sanctions other than public opinion, however, is something that should be looked into with care and without ready adoption of the GATT principle of retaliation.

Issues

The issues with which a GATT for multinational enterprises would deal are those involving two governments, the one government using a MNE to intrude its policy into the jurisdiction of the other. These issues include government-to-corporation problems, wherein a corporation is pushed in different directions by the two governments and wants relief, or manages to escape the normal obligations of corporate citizenship by evading the reach of any and all governments, and a few cases in which the actions of a corporation approved by two governments are deemed nonetheless abhorrent to the world interest and evoke concern in the international body.

Governmental Issues

The two main types of governmental issues can be loosely characterized as trading with the enemy and antitrust. The trading with the enemy case arises when a foreign subsidiary of a MNE undertakes trade, or more generally an action, that is legal in the host country and illegal in the home country, and the latter in turn orders the head office of the MNE to make its subsidiary abroad conform to the home country policy. Most cases have arisen because of the American rules on trading with the Soviet Union, China, and Cuba and the U.S. government's attempts to enforce compliance with its rules upon foreign subsidiaries of U.S. corporations—to the dismay of such countries as France (in the Fruehauf case), Canada (on trade with China), and Argentina (on sales by the Buenos Aires subsidiary of General Motors to Cuba). The issue of course is largely one of international law, and most lawyers believe it best adjudicated in case by case diplomatic negotiations. To an economist the best approach is the one that attempts to reach harmonization or agreement on basic policies. Failing such agreement, one understands the desire of the home country to extend its reach to those of its citizens who deliberately go abroad to carry out actions illegal in their home country. To order them to stop is in the nature of "hot pursuit," and those of us old enough to have lived through Prohibition remember this sort of thing in the case of the "I'm Alone" rum-runner being chased by the U.S. Coast Guard into Canadian territorial waters. But surely, if a country cannot persuade other countries of the correctness of its policies, the attempt to enforce them in foreign jurisdictions through the MNE head office and instructions to MNE branches constitutes an invasion of the foreign jurisdiction.

The antitrust issue conforms fairly closely to the trading with the enemy model. Optimal for the world would be a harmonized antitrust policy, but one that reflects the best policies rather than one that conforms to the most lax standard. Like the United States, most countries at the moment adopt a double standard—that is, one policy for domestic trade and another for foreign. In the United States the Sherman and Clayton Antitrust Acts live side by side with the Webb-Pomerene Act, which permits (encourages?) the association of firms in the same trade for the purpose of export trade. The argument for this exception of course is the existence of cartels in foreign markets; for American firms to enter such markets singly and unprotected would be to expose them to harm. A decision of the European Coal and Steel Community Court of Justice in the early days of ECSC held that combinations in restraint of export trade lay beyond the jurisdiction of the ECSC, whereas those within the Community were prohibited — the same distinction between the domestic and foreign markets. Canadian, German, and other foreign jurisdictions have been outraged by U.S. courts that order U.S. firms to produce documents in the possession of their foreign subsidiaries (i.e., in foreign jurisdictions). The doctrine of "hot pursuit" may apply here. Principally, however, the issue seems to be that in antitrust cases U.S. courts assert jurisdiction over actions taken abroad that restrain trade in the United States.

The difference between the case by case and the GATT for MNE approaches seems to rest on the fact that the former may resolve individual cases — and even establish machinery for bilateral resolution of cases, as has been accomplished between Canada and the United States — but the GATT approach is more likely to produce an evolutionary movement toward harmonization of national standards.

The evolution of standards is needed in other areas in which practices differ. One is bribery. The Securities and Exchange Commission in the United States stumbled on the widespread offering of bribes abroad by American corporations by asking an open-ended question about corporation practices abroad that would be illegal in the United States. It is often possible to affect what happens abroad by questions raised in a home country. But rather than making the arrogant implicit assumption that the rest of the world has to be brought up to the ethical level of a particular home country, it would be better to make the effort to agree on what a proper world standard might be. Legal distinctions between bribes, commissions, and payments for one or another kind of service are often subtle and run the risk of misunderstanding. An evolutionary bargaining approach that evolves a set of agreed-upon rules (with emphasis, again, on the highest possible standard) has strong political advantages over a national or bilateral approach. Nothing in this, however, should be taken to condone actions that are illegal and unacceptable in the host country but legal or acceptable in the home country.

Equally illicit with bribery is the use of the MNE as a cover for clandestine intelligence or other operations undertaken by one government on the territory or against the citizens or government of another. Here again the main remedy lies in the hands of the host country to uphold its own laws.

In chapter 16 Goldberg and I paid considerable attention to the question of differences in international laws governing financial disclosure, and it is unnecessary to repeat that discussion here. Suffice it to say that the rise of the multinational enterprise and the ownership by citizens of one country of a major or dominant share of a corporation in another may make those citizens subject to the laws of another jurisdiction. In the long run, again, harmonization is the answer for limiting the capacities of the Cornfelds and the Vescos to operate legally in one or another jurisdiction. But the question is complex. The Chicago solution of laissez faire and *caveat emptor* is tempting as a means of escaping the convolutions and interactions of intricate sets of rules. Yet there is need for some fundamental code that requires minimal disclosure and penalizes misstatements. Canada and Australia have both moved away from treating as private companies, not subject to disclosure requirements, foreign investors who hold a vast majority of the stock of a locally organized company. I suspect that I have a difference here with George W. Ball, who wants to provide for world registration of multinational enterprises, with world rules for publications of statements and standards for accounting. Nonetheless, a means of evolving toward such a position would be to elaborate appropriate standards in a GATT for the multinational enterprise.

Subsidies to MNEs

A tricky area of current conflict and possibly greater political conflict between countries is the enticement of firms through remission of taxes. This takes many forms: participation or nonparticipation in tax-sparing agreements; tax remission for MNEs contingent on certain export performance that may be regarded abroad as a subsidy to exporting rather than a subsidy to investment, thus subjected to countervailing duties (the Michelin Nova Scotia case); agreements among potential host countries to limit subsidies; and Article 24 of the Andes agreement that discriminates among MNEs, depending on whether or not local investors own a majority of the stock. None of these issues is so clearly international that it cannot be handled bilaterally. Nonetheless, there may be virtue in formulating international rather than purely bilateral solutions to questions as they arise, to gain the benefit of earlier experience of other countries and to achieve a measure of worldwide uniformity where desirable.

The United States takes a position opposed to tax sparing—that is, sparing the profit on a foreign income that arises from a tax concession made abroad to attract a foreign investment. If Israel, for example, grants freedom from income tax to foreign corporations for ten years, the concession will not apply to U.S. corporations in the United States, which taxes that income fully. The U.S. attitude, it may be said, is based on the fear that competitive tax concessions by a large number of countries anxious to attract foreign investment would erode the tax bases of such LDCs, much as competition among the fifty states for new businesses and industry has done in the United States. In partial equilibrium, where one country alone offers a concession, investment behavior is altered; if all countries in "general equilibrium" retaliate by making similar concessions, no concession has any effect beyond diverting income from the LDC to the MNE (if the tax is spared). In such a case refusal to spare the tax prevents ineffective and inequitable concessions. Whether the United States is correct in believing that tax concessions belong to a class of general and not partial equilibrium problems is just one issue. If some countries join tax sparing and others do not, the national pattern of foreign direct investment is distorted. A full investigation of the effects of tax concessions would be a valuable long-run benefit from a GATT for MNEs.

Where a country attracts foreign investment through a tax concession and the MNE exports to yet another country, there is evidently room for disagreement between the host country and the third (importing) country as to whether the subsidy went to employment or to exporting. If proved to be the latter, the third country might have a basis for objection under its antidumping rules or under the GATT rules affecting subsidies to exports. In Ireland, I understand, the Industrial Development Authority grants long exemptions from income tax for foreign firms engaged in exporting, though no one seems to have characterized this as an export subsidy. I have no interest in finding make-work for a potential GATT for MNEs, but the Michelin case in Nova Scotia and the Irish policy lead me to think that there may be a problem here. Perhaps there is not.

The countries engaged in the Andes Pact have sought to prevent the erosion of their tax bases by agreeing among themselves not to compete in offering tax concessions to foreign MNEs. The motive of course is the same as that of the United States in refusing to enter tax-sparing agreements. This is surely their right. There may be difficulties of enforcement and policing. That too is their concern. But there may be merit in having a GATT for MNEs monitor such agreements so as to be in position to offer LDCs its advice about whether to go forward with or draw back from agreements among host countries to limit tax concessions.

The Fallacy of Composition

Before we proceed to the problem corporations have with governments and governments with corporations, in contrast to the problems governments have with each other through corporations, it is well to address a fundamental dilemma. To work smoothly, a system needs a few loopholes. When the loopholes become large, the system breaks down. What is good for the system when it helps the occasional individual may destroy the system when it is taken over by the mass. This applies to the opportunity for migration that enables persecuted individuals to escape their tormentors, but which, when it develops into a mass phenomenon, tends to overwhelm both the countries it leaves and those to which the migration flows. Secret bank accounts in Switzerland are good if they hold the savings of persecuted Jews but bad if they belong to the Mafia and to myriad tax evaders and lead to massive derogation of foreign tax laws. (As I write, I note the circulation of a study by Murray L. Weidenbaum called "The Case for Tax Loopholes." Without having read the paper, I can imagine that the case he builds is a strong one as it affects the individual, but considerably weaker in the aggregate.)

Taxation

The international-trade economist usually espouses a principle of tax neutrality. The allocation of investment and the flow of trade should be directed by relative scarcities and abundance, not by differences in taxation. The difficulty with tax neutrality as a slogan, however, is that it is ambiguous in particular cases. The U.S. Internal Revenue Service argues that taxes on foreign-earned income should be neutral in the sense that they favor neither foreign nor domestic (home) investment. The multinational enterprise, on the other hand, thinks of neutrality as running between the foreign and domestic investor in the host country. When host taxes are lower than those at home, anything that favors foreign investment—such as deferral until earnings are remitted—is neutral in the host market, nonneutral in the home jurisdiction. (This same distinction, it may be noticed, applies to such issues as bribery or apartheid. To apply home standards abroad when foreign standards differ is nonneutral abroad, but to adopt host country standards abroad is nonneutral as between home and foreign investment under the same circumstances.)

Neutrality is thus an unattainable standard until such time as countries all over the world adopt the same rates of taxation and the same definitions of what constitutes income. Although neutrality is a distant goal, there is much to be done to eliminate gross inequities. I would hope that a GATT for the multinational enterprise would improve individual taxation, for example, by negotiating agreements for the elimination of bearer bonds—a prime source of tax evasion. It is recognized that there would be costs to such elimination insofar as interest rates for borrowers would rise, but the inequity of organized tax evasion by bondholders in Europe is a blight on the international system and calls for suppression. Similarly, I would hope that a GATT for the MNE would seek to eliminate tax evasion and tax havens, along the lines suggested in the OECD recommendations prepared by the Working Party on Tax Avoidance and Evasion, created in 1977 by the Committee on Fiscal Affairs (see the OECD *Observer* for November 1977). These recommendations call for strengthening domestic powers of investigation, exchanging information between tax authorities, and extending the network of conventions and other arrangements bilaterally or multilaterally among national administrations, "with due regard to the provision of adequate safeguards for taxpayers." Special attention is called to the experience of Belgium, Canada, France, Germany, and the United States in undertaking domestic measures to counteract the diversion of taxable income to tax havens. This appears to involve such devices as limiting the foreign tax credit to jurisdictions in which at least 30 percent of value added is realized in production (as in the U.S. Revenue Act of 1962) and inclusion of questions about ownership of foreign assets in individual income tax returns under penalty of perjury for false answer. The Working Party report raises questions of shipping profits and international entertainers and athletes who pay their earnings into companies in tax-haven countries. Such cases may seem *de minimis* and not worth pursuing. Tax havens would be tolerable if only a handful took advantage of them and there was no exemplary effect. But as with migration, what is salutary in relieving the hardship of a few is antisocial when it is elevated to the rule for the many. Respect for the sovereignty of small countries is an important value. It is impossible to take action against tax evasion solely in the major countries, however, and if the practice grows as mobility increases, some forceful steps at harmonization of tax laws may have to be undertaken jointly.

One issue is tax evasion; another is double taxation. In the initial period after World War II the U.S. Treasury appears to have taken a fairly relaxed attitude toward the statements of U.S. corporations as to where they earned their profits. United States policy was to encourage foreign direct investment as an aid to reconstruction in Europe and to development in the Third World. As the U.S. balance of payments worsened and labor expressed concern for U.S. jobs being lost to foreign countries, this attitude shifted. The Revenue Act of 1962 limited tax havens, as indicated earlier, and the Treasury sought unsuccessfully to eliminate deferral of corporate income tax on foreign profits until remittance. Section 482 of the Internal Revenue Code later put a stop to arbitrary transfer prices that had been used in some instances to reallocates profits among tax jurisdictions. Most recently, the Internal Revenue Service has been reexamining the definition of income earned in a given jurisdiction by questioning multinational enterprises on their allocations of overhead costs, especially management overhead, and such expenses as research and development. Foreign operations, it is held, should bear an appropriate proportion of such joint costs, thus raising the proportion of total income taxable in the United States and lowering that abroad. Of course where two jurisdictions differ on the definition of income earned in a tax jurisdiction, the taxpayer may pay double taxes on the same income.

The OECD has drawn up a model convention for bilateral agreements on taxation of corporations and individuals, first in 1963 and later, on a revised basis as international operations took on more and more complex forms, in 1973. Moreover the United Nations has had an Expert Group on Tax Treaties between Developed and Developing Countries. The question is whether, as the world shrinks, these matters can continue to be handled bilaterally or multilaterally in separate compartments among the developed countries in OECD and between developed and developing countries in the United Nations. In view of the progress that has been made—with 179 bilateral treaties among the 17 OECD countries out of the possible 276, and 30 more under negotiation—it is clear that there is no emergency here. In the long run, however, harmonization of rates and definitions of incomes seem called for, perhaps with the kind of rule-of-thumb resolution of the knotty question of where a given corporation's world income is earned that is practiced among the states of the United States. As I understand this practice, the proportion of total income earned in a particular state with a corporate income tax is calculated by an unweighted average of three percentages: those of the company's sales, employees, and capital assets in the state as a proportion of the national totals.

This of course is very rough justice within the United States, but it sidesteps the impossible problem of allocating joint costs. Moreover it is far more rapidly done in the United States with its fairly uniform standards of accounting by states than internationally, which demands the unique determination of a company's sales, employees, and, especially, capital assets country by country.

Transfer Prices

Section 482 of the Internal Revenue Code deals with the problems of American corporations with transfer prices in trade with foreign subsidiaries on sales to and from the United States. This section allows the IRS to "construct" a profit when it can establish that the prices used in intercompany transactions diverge from those that would have obtained in an arm's-length, market transaction, and to levy its tax on what it states the U.S. profit to be, rather than on the company's calculation. Tax authorities all over the world have been made sensitive to the problem by Australian proceedings against oil refiners who charged posted prices for oil sold to a wholly owned subsidiary from Middle East production, rather than the lower offtakers' prices, and by the revelations of Constantine Vaitsos of the Harvard Development Advisory Service that multinational pharmaceutical companies in Colombia had been charging high transfer prices for intermediate products sold to subsidiaries in Colombia. Section 482 of course will not affect transfer prices from one foreign subsidiary of an American multinational to another, as in the case of the pharmaceutical sales to Colombia from a Panama tax haven, nor the alleged (by a former disgruntled employee) wash sales of foreign exchange by an American bank between England and France, on the one hand, and a Bahamas tax haven, on the other.

I see little role for a GATT for the multinational enterprise in policing or patrolling transfer prices in international intracompany dealings. This is evidently a matter for the national tax authorities. The OECD 1973 Model Double Taxation Agreement provides that when a firm's profits are adjusted by the tax authorities of one country and taxed at a higher level, the other country that is taxing them on the initial basis should make an appropriate adjustment to eliminate what it calls "economic [as against legal] double taxation." This of course would not apply where one of the countries is a tax haven. Nonetheless, though the GATT for MNEs might have no direct role in checking transfer prices, its tax experts might be made available in cases where a country's tax machinery was not sufficiently developed to detect evasion by this means, as the Harvard Development Advisory Service did more or less accidentally in Colombia.

One provision of the Andes Pact to which MNE objection has been taken is Article 24, which says that subsidiaries in the Pact countries owned by MNEs cannot avail themselves of the benefits of customs remission unless they embark on a course of acquiring local majority ownership within a stipulated period. Corporate objection seems to be that the rule sets up a double standard for corporations within the Andes countries. The matter has been studied from an economic point of view in a doctoral thesis at MIT by Ernesto Tironi, who concludes that the Andes countries would be loath to form a customs union in the first place if substantial share of the benefits were to accrue to outside firms. There may be legal objection to this sort of discrimination, but to economists there is merit in making sure that steps taken to benefit local enterprise redound to it and not to foreigners. (By the same token it has seemed a defeat for national policies if a country imposes infant-industry tariffs in order to stimulate local enterprise, only to have the opportunities thereby created grabbed by foreign entrepreneurs. To the extent that the infant-industry argument for a tariff is justified on "second-best" grounds, a parallel argument can be made for limiting foreign investment.)

Restrictive Business Practices

The draft of the abortive International Trade Organization charter contained provisions for the organization to concern itself with business practices in restraint of international trade. When the charter failed to be ratified, and the General Agreement for Tariffs and Trade was substituted, the provisions of the ITO charter dealing with business practices were dropped, presumably because of their controversial nature. In 1954 I suggested to the secretary-general of GATT, Mr. Wyndham White, that GATT gradually move into the restrictive business practice field, especially to make rules for firms on the subject of price discrimination. The suggestion was ignored, partly, perhaps, for good and sufficient reasons having to do with the difficulty of choosing between the rules of profit maximization and price nondiscrimination on a netback basis, the difficulties of enforcement, and, doubtless most important, the lack of fundamental agreement among countries on the appropriate standard to apply.

In the last several years the UN Conference on Trade and Development (UNCTD) has compiled a list of LDC grievances against the MNE under the heading of "restrictive business practices." Most have to do with the normal practice of MNEs in instructing their subsidiaries not to export to new foreign markets without the concurrence of the head office. Objection to the rule is that it restricts the subsidiaries' markets and presumably hurts the balance of payments of the LDC. But this assumes that the subsidiary is the cheapest source for the market in question and that the MNE is not maximizing profit in sourcing at the cheapest-cost location (in the case of the MNE with an equal interest in each of two or more subsidiaries). It may be of course that the TNC would prefer to export from a higher-cost source in which it has 100 percent interest than from a cheaper one in which its share of the profits is smaller. Business observers by and large take the view that what the head office wants to avoid is surprises (i.e., competition among its subsidiaries that erodes profit margins or exports from a high-cost subsidiary with government help given for mercantilistic reasons).

It may also be noted that if the firm in the LDC is indigenous but uses foreign technology under a patent, it is likely to be limited to the domestic market by the conditions of the license and expressly forbidden to sell in any market for which it is not expressly licensed. Irritations of LDCs over MNE restrictions on exporting have thus escalated into a full-scale attack on the international patent system — which may or may not be merited but lies somewhat outside the bounds of this discussion. One could pursue the LDC dissatisfaction with technological transfers from the developed countries into the question of the appropriateness of the technology transferred by MNEs to LDCs, and whether or not there may be a moral commitment to develop new technology for the LDCs appropriate to their factor proportions. There are forums available for discussion of these issues: the OECD, ECOSOC, even the UN Industrial Development Organization (UNIDO). But there may be merit in agreement on a few principles in this area in the abstract and in working out in practice a resolution of real issues. The "take it or leave it" solution of the market appeals to economists in Western economies but strikes representatives of the LDCs as callous and cynical. It is hard to see how a GATT for the MNE can do better than to air grievances and push in the direction of competitive solutions. There is not much mileage here, but there may be some.

Subsidies to Foreign Investment

I would like to see a reduction in the subsidies to foreign investment by developed countries, as well as reduction or elimination of competitive subsidization on the part of LDCs. I have in mind the type of insurance for foreign direct investment (FDI) embodied in the U.S. Overseas Private Investment Corporation (OPIC) and similar organs in other countries. As with tax concessions in host countries, and the competitive matching of easy credit to exports of the Export-Import Bank (U.S.), the Export Credit Guarantees Department (U.K.), Compagnie Française d'Assurance pour le Commerce Extérieur (France), and so forth, each country, in seeking to protect its own position, assures the hurt of all. OPIC finds itself increasingly facing the "moral risk" that is involved in insurance: Once covered, an insured party is less inclined to take the same precautions as when he was bearing the entire risk. Moreover governmental insurance converts private business disputes into diplomatic issues. Congress has recently mandated that OPIC be converted from a public to a private company. This will help, though it is unlikely that the risks covered lend themselves to actuarial calculation, and often semiprivate organizations, like the Councils of Foreign Bondholders in the United States and Britain in earlier times, have close ties with official arms of government.

To the extent that an international GATT for MNEs served to intermediate between corporations and host government and also between home and host government, it should be possible to weaken the ties between MNE and home government that George Ball seeks to sever with his proposal for registration of global corporations on an international basis. Just as the Berne Agreement of 1936 was intended to monitor and reduce Western democratic credits to the Soviet bloc by pooling information on them, so a GATT for MNEs might help to limit national subsidies for foreign investment, in one or another form, and move the activity to a more nearly competitive market exercise.

Market Failure

There will be times, to be sure, when market solutions will not work because the conditions for a competitive solution have not been met. The most obvious of these are in the antitrust field. International mergers that reduced competition at the world level might be agreeable to the two home governments concerned but should be opposed in the world interest. At one stage shortly after World War II, the U.S. government gave permission to Singer Sewing Machine Company to buy what was during the 1930s the second largest world company in the field, Pfaff, at a time when the German authorities were probably unable to resist the move. Happily, the directors of Pfaff themselves refused to sell. Or consider the difference today had IBM sought to buy up Machines Bull instead of General Electric and later Honeywell. There are national interests concerned in these antitrust questions, but there is also a world interest; a market solution approved by national governments may still not always be acceptable worldwide. It is clear of course that in a world of sovereign states an agency like a GATT for MNEs could do little more than point with alarm. It would nonetheless be useful to have its view of the world interest forcefully stated.

Market failure occurs within countries—not normally or continuously, but occasionally. At such times a country is justified in not permitting the market to work. I have in mind an occasion some years ago when Brazil undertook to deflate on the advice of the IMF and precipitated a stock-market fall, in the course of which some Brazilian shares were bought up abroad at low prices. Brazil thought it was being plotted against. In such circumstances a country should temporarily forbid foreign investment and gain the sympathetic hearing by informing a GATT for MNEs of the reasons for its actions. However, a more devious policy, such as that followed by Japan of continually proclaiming adherence to liberal principles while actually inhibiting foreign investment, would be beyond the scope of a GATT for MNEs, given the residual strength of national sovereignty. To give another example, Italy could justify limiting foreign takeovers of national firms in trouble when the weakness of the Italian capital market prevented them from borrowing to correct deficiencies of liquidity. Public opinion cannot do much, but it ought to have an outlet should there be another takeover of properties under chaotic market conditions such as the United States permitted in Cuba after 1898 but prevented in Germany from 1945 until monetary reform in 1948.

OPEC of course is another example of market failure. For the most part the necessity is to protect the LDCs against monopolies or potential monopolies of developed MNEs, but it should be recognized that most countries, including LDCs, are not so much interested in dissolving monopolies and cartels as in taking them over and appropriating their rents. A GATT for MNEs can probably do little to affect these attitudes, but it should have an educational role in the long run that might move us in the correct direction.

Summary

It is suggested that the 17 governments of the OECD funnel off the work on MNEs, tax evasion, and double taxation into a separate international General Agreement on Multinational Enterprise (GAME) open to all countries, that it seek to find a basis for agreement on behavior with the UN Center on the Transnational Corporation (leaving aside altogether the question of expropriation and the disputes it engenders) on issues of trading with the enemy, antitrust, bribery, the use of business cover for intelligence activity, standards of financial disclosure, subsidies to MNEs, taxation (including the definition of income and tax havens), transfer pricing, restrictive business practices, subsidies to DFI, and when interference with market processes is justified on second-best grounds. Any subject in which the distance between the OECD group and the UN is substantial should be dropped and returned separately to the two bodies. Agreement on principles should be minimal; the main effort should be directed at forming an organization for case by case settlement of complaints by corporations against one or more governments regarding action taken beyond their jurisdiction, and by one government about the activity of another taken through an MNE. There should be no sanctions other than public opinion, and certainly no retaliatory action. Many issues would have to be returned to national or bilateral diplomatic action. The hope is that in due course a corpus of common international law would be built up that would serve to reduce the scope for conflict in the functioning of the MNE.

Appendix: Summaries of Three Discussions of a GATT for MNEs

Eugene V. Rostow, Joseph S. Nye, and George W. Ball in chapter 10 of George W. Ball, ed., *Global Companies, The Political Economy of World Business* (Englewood Cliffs, N.J.: Prentice-Hall [for the American Assembly], 1975).

Rostow refers to the UNCTAD resolution of 1968 and the UN Report of Eminent Persons of 1974, notes that Nye opposes a treaty and would prefer to rely on individual bargaining and negotiation, case by case. He cites the arguments of Ball, Goldberg, and Kindleberger and emerges with a plea for a treaty, saying that the world cannot afford to delay a decade or two.

Nye analyzes opinion on the issue in terms of optimists who expect the MNE to erode the sovereignty of the nation-state and the ideological cleavage between East and West, and pessimists who see economic interdependence as inevitably leading to inequality and conflict and to the wreckage of the nation-state that makes possible internal order and community disaster. His synthesis is that the MNE–nation-state relationship will proceed uneasily, alternating between complementarity and conflict as efforts are now made to enlarge the pie and divide the existing one. In principle, policies and procedures could be made to establish codes and devise international institutions in the arena. In practice it is not simple either between LDCs and DCs or among DCs. LDCs may not be economically important, but they are politically important.

Ball wants to denationalize MNEs in order to limit interference with them by host governments, and to do so by giving them world charters.

Lloyd N. Cutler, *Global Interdependence and the Multi-National Firm* (New York: Foreign Policy Association Headline Series 239, April 1978).

In chapter 5, "Toward a Regime for Transnational Investment," Cutler states that the time may be ripe for the leading industrial democracies to develop binding rules and create an administration to regulate tax allocations and incentives, financial reporting and investment markets, restrictions on entry and nationalization of firms, antitrust policy, illicit payments, and environmental restraints. He approves the Treaty of Rome provisions, faults the OECD code for being only voluntary, and considers that Ball's authority to grant charters to international firms is unlikely to gain a consensus. Stating that the United States should take the initiative, he believes the UN is not the place, considers GATT too unwieldy, and recommends an OECD agreement open to all countries that would be submitted to the Committee of 77.

C. Fred Bergsten, Thomas Horst, and Theodore H. Moran, *American Multinationals and American Interests* (Washington, D.C.: The Brookings Institution, 1978).

The first part of chapter 13, "Proposals for a New Policy," makes a series of proposals for changes in the United States, including retaining the foreign tax credit but eliminating deferral, repealing DISC but allowing FCI to qualify for investment tax credit and accelerated depreciation, and supporting tax sparing for the Fourth World (non-oil Third World). Also proposed are an escape clause by which the United States can forbid any foreign investment that hurts the national interest; adjustment assistance for special groups that are hurt by a foreign investment; antitrust policy that considers spinoffs of foreign subsidiaries of U.S. corporations as a measure to increase competition in the United States; changes to reduce and redirect OPIC, rescind privatization, and to make it responsible under a special presidential representative for foreign direct investment policy; plus repealing the Hickenlooper and Gonzales amendments. The second part outlines a new international regime that consists of two parts. One, for home countries alone, proposes harmonization of taxation of foreign income, joint action to limit subsidies and to coordinate investment insurance, agreement on a convention on "hot products" sold in Third World countries by an expropriated firm judged in default, and coordination of restraints on investments in Socialist countries. The other proposes cooperation between home and host countries together, with provision for a safeguard mechanism to bar FDI where there are adverse effects, extension of antitrust, settlement of expropriation disputes, limitation of tax incentives in both host and home countries, and methods to allocate income for tax purposes.

Index